Think and Grow Fit

Jose Silva's guide
to
Mental Training
for
Fitness and Sports
by
Jose Silva
with
Ed Bernd Jr.

First edition copyright 1996 by Jose Silva with Ed Bernd Jr.

CreateSpace edition © Copyright 2014

Printed in North America

ISBN-13: 978-1496165169

ISBN-10: 1496165160

Cover background image courtesy of Photos8.com

All rights reserved under the Pan-American and International Copyright Conventions. This book may not be reproduced, in whole or in part, in any form or by any meals electronic or mechanical, including photocopying, recording, or by any information storage or retrieval system now known or hereafter invented, without written permission from the author.

For information please contact:

Avlis Productions
P.O. Box 691809
Houston, TX 77260 USA

help@avlispub.com

www.SilvaCourses.com

Acknowledgments

The authors extend their grateful appreciation to several people who helped with this project:

Bob Hicks and Sherry Dircks for proofreading the manuscript and checking it for accuracy.

Vera Christensen for checking the accuracy of the information in Chapter 4 regarding different body types and the appropriate training for each of them.

Al and Vera Christensen for introducing Ed Bernd Jr. to the Silva Method 20 years ago. They promised that it would be the best thing he could do to help his weightlifting. It has been that and much, much more.

Dr. Malco Patterson from Texas A&M University for contributing his knowledge of philosophy and sportswriter Salo Otero for his special editorial help.

Dr. John M. La Tourrette for his support and encouragement.

And a special "thank-you" to all of the Silva graduates who bared their souls and told their stories for inclusion in this book. They are among the most successful at using the Silva techniques for fitness and sports, and they have generously allowed us a glimpse of how they train and what they have been able to achieve.

And thanks to you, the reader, who will use the Silva techniques to correct problems, to achieve your goals, to serve as a role model for others, and to help make the world a better place to live.

Jose Silva
with Ed Bernd Jr.

Contents

Introduction: How to use this book 7

Section 1 The fundamentals
1. The power of alpha thinking 19
2. Developing a championship attitude 35
3. Inside the mind of a superstar 55
4. Know yourself 75
5. Relax, it's good for you 89

Section 2 Program yourself for success
6. The mental imagery of the superstars 101
7. Advanced techniques 115
8. Triggers and other ways to get "in the groove" 123
9. Developing anticipation 131

Section 3 Specific training routines
10. Training for fitness 143
11. Program yourself to win 155
12. Using mental techniques during competition 175
13. Post-competition programming 191

Section 4 General self-improvement techniques
14. Develop success habits 201
15. Self-management techniques 209
16. Rest and recovery 217
17. Nutrition and weight control 229
18. The healing power of your mind 241

Section 5 Additional topics
19. Training under special circumstances 255
20. Biofeedback equipment 263
21. The student athlete 269
22. Your responsibilities as an athlete 283
23. A note to parents and coaches 303
24. Persistence 319

Introduction
by Ed Bernd Jr.

Olympic athletes, the pros, athletes at the highest levels - you've watched them do it: play the mental game. They all have different explanations for just how they do it:

The professional level. On television, the coach of a world champion basketball team talks about his "Zen approach" and how he uses meditation, visualization and mental rehearsal. You watch his players standing at the foul line, their bodies mimicking the shot before they even touch the ball, as they visualize what they are about to do.

Elite Olympic athletes. Members of the Olympic bobsled team, before making their run, stand together, their eyes closed, their bodies swaying from side to side as they mentally run the course. Olympic athletes of the Eastern European countries have played the mental game for years, using everything from hypnosis to meditation.

College and beyond. The CBS television program *48 Hours* reports that the United States Military Academy at West Point teaches future army officers to meditate and visualize - to win football games and much more. They call it "performance enhancement."

"We want to be able to eventually provide this kind of training for all our cadets so that it's a part of their leadership development," a West Point instructor tells CBS, "because this is no different really than the ability of a leader to think, problem-solve, react, eliminate distractions in combat.

"On the battlefield - tremendous chaos," he continues. "The ability to maintain focus, to maintain a calm state and to make critical decisions is paramount to our profession."

Why don't these methods work for everybody?

If you're like me, you've probably wondered just what it was these athletes were doing and whether it actually helped them.

You listened closely to their explanations of what they did, and you searched for techniques that could help you to get into shape and perform better.

And often all you found were ideas that other people might have gotten to work for themselves, but which did nothing for you.

A long search finally produces results

Back in 1975, while I was training hard to enter an Amateur Athletic Union (AAU) Olympic Weightlifting contest, I began investigating the role of the mind in physical performance.

First I tried "concentrating" as hard as I could.

It didn't help.

Then I had a professional hypnotist come and hypnotize me.

That didn't help, either.

I read several books about something called "alpha rhythm," but I never even understood what they were talking about, much less if and how I could apply it to sports.

Then late in 1975, my friends Al and Vera Christensen gave me the answer. They had operated a fitness and health club where I used to train.

I went to see them. They were all excited about a course called Silva Mind Control.

"You've got to take this course," Al kept telling me. "It's the best thing you can do to help your weightlifting."

It turned out that he was right.

Where it all began

For 22 years, Jose Silva had labored anonymously in the small town of Laredo, Texas, on the Mexican border, conducting research into the mind and its relation to human potential.

During this time he developed a system of mental training to help his children overcome their problems in school and achieve their goals. His neighbors were interested, so he taught them his system, too. Word eventually spread, and by 1966 people outside of Laredo began inviting Jose to come teach them his method. Nine years later, Al and Vera Christensen insisted that I take the course.

It sounded too good to be true, but there was a money-back guarantee: If I wasn't satisfied, I'd get a refund. So I signed up.

It turned out that this was one program that worked. It even satisfied me, a skeptical newspaper reporter. It not only helped my athletic performance, it helped me in every aspect of my life. It was the best-kept "success secret" in the world!

Going straight to the source

Once I discovered that Silva Mind Control worked for me, I became totally involved. I even became a Silva Method lecturer. Later, when I was offered an opportunity to join the Silva staff at its world headquarters in Laredo, Texas, I jumped at it. What could be better for a reporter than to go right to the source?

I learned a lot. I learned that Jose Silva had been a pretty good athlete when he was young.

He had taken boxing lessons so that he could defend himself. He was good enough to fight in clubs throughout south Texas.

His brother Juan told me about a time when Jose was sparring with a Mexican national champion, who was getting ready to defend his title. Jose did some flashy moves, Juan recalled, and knocked the champion to the canvas. While the champion composed himself, Juan got Jose out of there. They weren't sure what the champ might do now that they'd made him angry.

Mental training for fitness and sports

Even though Jose Silva had never offered any special training for athletes, I discovered that many of our graduates were using the Silva techniques to help them get into shape and to improve their performance. I sought advice from Jose and Juan Silva on specific ways to use the basic Silva techniques to improve physical performance, and they obliged.

They drew on their athletic experience and showed me new techniques I could incorporate into my own fitness training. Jose showed me how to create a mental duplicate of my best coach and use this "mental coach" to encourage me and spur me on when I was tired and discouraged. You will learn this same technique in Chapter 7.

They continued to help me as I recorded a series of audiocassettes to help athletes practice mentally at the right state of mind, the alpha level, which you will learn about in Chapter 1.

In addition, they helped me design a workshop for athletes to be presented by coaches who were Silva graduates. I began to work with coaches and athletes here in Laredo and eventually all around the U.S. and overseas. In Chapter 23, you can read about basketball coach who used the workshop to help his players make it to a championship.

The athletes with whom we worked - as well as some who learned on their own - will tell their stories in the pages of this book. They will tell you what they accomplished with the Silva techniques and how. The numerous success stories in this book - told by athletes at all levels from a wide variety of sports, as well as average people who keep themselves in better-than-average condition - will demonstrate exactly how to apply the Silva techniques to your own situation.

And I will share with you what Jose and Juan Silva taught me. Best of all, you'll learn firsthand from Jose Silva how to use more of your mind and how to use his techniques to get in shape, build the kind of body you want and improve your physical performance.

Jose Silva describes in detail the correct mental state for effective mental rehearsal: the alpha brain wave level.

He reveals how to build desire and get your feelings involved, without getting so worked up that you bring yourself out of alpha. He also explains:

- How to visualize in order to maximize your training and performance, whether you're training for world-class competition or simply for your health and appearance.

- How to get more nutritional value from the food you eat.

- How to speed recovery from injuries and maintain superior health.

- How to eliminate bad habits and develop good ones that make it easier for you to reach your goals.

- How to use your imagination to train your muscles without straining your muscles, and multiply the benefits of your physical exercise many times over.

- How to attain - and maintain - the weight you desire.

Step-by-step guidance will help you learn to enter the alpha state whenever you desire and program yourself for success. It's not complicated. There are no esoteric philosophies to learn, just a simple scientific method that has proven effective for millions of people in more than 100 countries around the world.

What you must do to learn Jose Silva's System

If you are willing to invest a few minutes a day in the specific mental training routines outlined in this book - in addition to the physical training that you already do - then you will learn to function mentally like the top athletes. You can obtain the one extra advantage of every great athlete: the power to play the mental game. This will help you move into the winner's circle and receive the recognition and rewards that you desire.

Not everyone can be a crowned champion, of course. Genetics play a part; so does natural, God-given talent. But a person who invests the most in training, practice and study has a definite advantage.

Specific guidance for athletes, coaches, parents

This step-by-step manual gives specific training routines and guidance for athletes at all levels for a wide variety of team and individual sports, as well as fitness routines for those who simply want superior conditioning. Specific chapters are devoted to:

• Fitness, health, nutrition, stress reduction, weight control and appearance.

• Guidelines for coaches and parents who want to help young athletes develop a winning attitude and the ability to excel in sports and in the game of life.

• Everything from developing and maintaining a positive mental attitude for motivation to sportsmanship and how it can help you win more often.

• Developing your intuition so that you will have better "anticipation" the ability to predict upcoming events in order to know what you have to do, an ability that distinguishes superstar athletes from average ones and is the key to achieving superstar status in every human endeavor.

How this book is organized

Section 1 covers the fundamentals. You will learn step-by-step how to enter the alpha brain wave level with conscious awareness. After completing Section 1, you can go on to any topic in any section of the book and use the mental techniques immediately.

Section 2 covers the most powerful mental rehearsal techniques of the Silva Method and teaches you advanced techniques you can use during training and competition to help you improve your performance.

Section 3 deals with specific training routines first for fitness, then for both individual and team sports. Learn what "mental toughness" really is and how to develop it.

Section 4 covers general self-improvement techniques. Learn how to develop self-mastery to relieve tension and migraine headaches, overcome insomnia, stop bad habits and develop good ones, control your weight, gain more nutritional value from the food you eat, use your mind to speed injury recovery and keep your body healthy, and program yourself for success.

Section 5 includes several additional topics relating to fitness and athletics. Learn how to determine training routines for young people, older people and people with disabilities. A special chapter addresses parents and coaches. A list of resources tells you where to go for additional help and guidance in mastering the mental game.

People who used this System and succeeded

You will read exciting stories about the following people who got great results by using Jose Silva's mind training system:

Freddie Benavides. Professional scouts said he might be able to carve out a career with a second-tier baseball team, but he didn't have the talent to play for any of the top teams. He used his secret weapon, the Silva Method, and eventually became a member of the world champion Montreal Expos.

Bucky Dent. He learned Silva Mind Control back in 1975 near the beginning of his baseball career and went on to become the Most Valuable Player in the 1978 World Series. More than a decade later, while serving as manager of the New York Yankees, he said that he recommended the Silva Method to his younger players.

Natalie Lacuesta. Natalie took the Silva course along with her mother when she was 11 years old. She used the techniques to help her gain the number-one ranking in rhythmic gymnastics, beating out older, more experienced athletes.

Giuseppina Del Vicario. The former Italian Martial Arts National Champion, known to her fans as Vidheya, thinks the Silva Method is the most pragmatic mind training program available. She explains exactly how she used the Silva Method techniques to help her beat both men and women to become the national champion.

You will also learn how a wide receiver with the Los Angeles Rams professional football team mentally "programmed" himself to play a great game and later used the exact same technique in his career as a sportscaster.

You will read about how the young members of a hockey team surprised the experts by making it all the way to the finals in a tournament even though they were short of players.

You will read the story of a bowler from the Philippines who credits the Silva techniques with giving him the edge he needed to win the World Cup in his sport.

You'll read about one change that basketball coach Hector Chacon made in his halftime talk that changed his team from losers to winners.

And you'll hear the story of a junior high school field hockey team that combined visualization at the alpha level with physical practice. Everybody expected them to improve, but nobody expected the tremendous gains that they made by using the Silva Method techniques.

"The techniques in the Silva Method were the single most important factor in changing me from a 'choker' to a winner," said tennis professional Jim McWalters from the United States Professional Tennis Registry (USPTR), a national association for tennis instructors. "I emphasize these techniques to all my students, as I feel they are crucial to success in competition."

Groundbreaking research

Can you actually learn to change your inherent characteristics? Yes, according to exciting research on the Silva Method from Haifa University in Israel, reported in Chapter 5. Read about it, and then imagine what it can mean to you... to be able to actually change your personality characteristics.

In addition, in Chapter 21 you'll read about a research report that was published in The Journal of the Society for Accelerative Learning and Teaching (SALT) about how students in Australia were taught just one Silva Method technique and improved their scores during the next school term an average of one letter grade! They did this without even taking the complete Silva Method. Find out which Silva Method technique their professor taught them that enabled them to boost their scores so quickly and so dramatically.

A step-by-step mental training program for you

You are beginning this book at the perfect time: today. This is the only day you can ever do anything; if you wait until tomorrow, tomorrow becomes today. So start today.

In the next few weeks, you can learn to relax and to visualize your goals in a manner that will make the things that you visualize come true. These techniques give you benefits far beyond your athletic career. The skills you learn can help you to improve your business life and your personal life.

Get started right now. The first chapter contains your first alpha exercise. Your complete training routine is detailed in Chapters 2 through 5. Forms at the end of each chapter will help you keep a detailed training record to track your progress, and information about how to obtain additional help is included in the back of the book.

Program yourself for success

When the hand is raised in victory, will it be your hand? Or will the glory go to someone else, someone who is no better than you but who has learned how to awaken the mental power within?

If you learn to do the same, the next person to stand in the winner's circle and be crowned champion could be you.

How to use this book

This book is designed to be a comprehensive teaching tool and a reference work for everyone interested in fitness and sports.

The fundamentals

In order to use Jose Silva's mental techniques, you must know how to function at the alpha brain wave level. There are 2 ways you can achieve this:

- Practice the 40-day program of countdowns to learn it on your own.

- Better and faster – used the guided instructions at our Free Introductory Lessons for the Silva UltraMind ESP System at www.SilvaNow.com

Section 1 includes a 40-day program you can use to learn to function at the alpha level.

If you have already learned the Silva Centering Exercise for entering the alpha level through a home study course or a Silva seminar, you can skip this 40-day program, but can still benefit from reading Section 1.

Section 2 covers basic "programming" techniques, including visualization, imagination and mental rehearsal. These are the foundations for the programming you will do to help you excel in fitness and sports activities.

Choose what you need

The remaining three sections include information about and techniques for a wide range of fitness- and sports-related topics. Use them as you need them. As you improve, and as your interests change, you can come back to these sections and use different parts of them.

Section 3 covers various athletic activities, from fitness for improving health and appearance to athletic competition at all levels.

Section 4 covers many of Jose Silva's self-improvement techniques, techniques to control weight and unhealthy habits, to relieve tension and migraine headaches, to overcome insomnia, to help you wake up when you desire, to relieve pain from injuries, even reduce or stop bleeding and hemorrhaging, and to speed healing.

Section 5 covers additional topics of interest, including physical training for children, older people and people with disabilities, using biofeedback equipment, special techniques to help student athletes improve their grades, advice for parents and coaches about helping athletes use mental techniques more effectively, and the responsibilities of an athlete.

Section 1: The fundamentals

The five chapters in this section will teach you the basic skills you need to successfully use the mental techniques described in the remainder of the book.

Each of these first five chapters consists of two parts:

1. Information and examples to help you understand how your brain and mind work and why you will be practicing the mental exercises; some basic information about training for fitness and sports and how you can benefit from using the alpha level in these areas.

2. Step-by-step instructions from Jose Silva on how to enter the alpha level, in which you will use the mental techniques.

It is not necessary for you to read every example before you begin practicing the techniques. When you are ready, you can go directly to Jose Silva's instructions at the end of the chapter. On the other hand, if you wish, you can read ahead even while you are practicing your mind exercises for the first 40 days.

If you are a graduate of a Silva seminar, or if you have used a Silva Home Study Course or a recording of the Silva Centering Exercise (the Long Relaxation Exercise), then you have already learned how to enter your level, and you can begin using the mental techniques in the other sections of the book immediately.

You can also learn with the Free Silva UltraMind ESP System Introductory Lessons at www.SilvaNow.com

If you are just starting, please be patient and learn to enter your level, either with the Countdowns or with recordings, and then it will be easy for you to learn to use all of the mental techniques in this book.

Chapter 1

The power of alpha thinking

Can your mind affect your physical performance?

Sure it can. To see how your thoughts can influence your body, do the following exercise. (You will need a friend to help you.)

1. Hold one arm out straight to your side, parallel to the floor, hand open, thumb pointing down. Have your friend test your strength by pushing your arm down while you resist.

If you are too strong for your friend, then test your strength by forming a circle with the thumb and first finger of either of your hands, holding them tightly together and seeing if your friend can pull them apart.

2. Now relax for a moment. When you are ready, hold your arm out again in the same position but this time think about a time when you lost, when you were defeated and humiliated, when you felt terrible about your loss.

While holding this thought, have your friend test your strength again. This time your friend will find it much easier to push your arm down.

3. Relax again. Then think about your most recent victory, a very satisfying success, one that you are proud of. Once again have your friend test your strength. You will be much stronger when thinking about success.

Have your friend test your strength as you think about different opponents, different coaches and trainers and your performance at various times. You will find that when you are confident, you are strong; when you have doubts, you are weak. Your mind definitely controls your body by directing and regulating the neurotransmitters in your brain.

Science discovers how your mind works

As impressive as that demonstration is, it actually raises more questions than it answers. You might be saying to yourself, "But I am a positive thinker. I think about winning. I imagine myself performing perfectly. I do all the things the superstars say they do. But I still don't perform like the superstars, and I still get beaten. Why? Somebody please tell me why!"

What one piece of knowledge are you still lacking even after you've learned everything that the champions can teach you? What one advantage separates the great athletes from the good ones? Many researchers have tried to find the answer.

They have studied training methods, rest and recovery time, nutrition and drugs, biomechanics, psychology, psychiatry, morphology and a whole lot more. They have found many things that help, but the real difference between the good athlete and the great athlete has eluded them for thousands of years.

The difference is actually quite simple: The superstars use more of their minds, and use them in a special manner. You can also learn to use the untapped power of your mind the way the superstars do to improve your fitness, enhance your athletic performance and win more often. But what does that mean: use more of your mind?

That's what Jose Silva wondered. And he found the answer.

Jose Silva's story

Even though he was born to poor parents in Laredo, Texas, on the Mexican border, Jose Silva was always successful. In many ways, his story is a true American success story.

As a 4-year-old boy, Jose Silva actually watched his father, who had been fatally injured in a terrorist attack during the Mexican revolution, collapse in front of him just before passing away.

As the eldest male in his family, Jose, when he was just 6 years old, began to support his family by selling newspapers on the streets of Laredo, shining shoes and cleaning offices.

Because he was working instead of going to school, Jose learned to read and write on his own - in both English and Spanish.

By the time Jose was a teenager, he was hiring other youngsters to work with him, going door to door to sell merchandise he purchased in San Antonio. The youngsters were earning as much money after school as their parents earned working full-time. And young Jose was earning as much every day as the typical adult in Laredo earned in a week.

Jose became an outstanding athlete, too. That came after he got into a fight when he was a teenager. Jose was losing the fight when somebody broke it up. The next day, he went to a local gym and signed up for boxing lessons.

He became good enough that he fought professionally in clubs around south Texas.

One day, while Jose was reading the magazines in his barber's shop (as he sometimes did to improve his reading), he came across some instruction books for an electronics correspondence course. Jose, who was 14 at the time, wanted to study the materials, so he struck a deal with his barber: The barber agreed to "rent" the course materials to Jose for $1 per lesson, provided that Jose answered the test questions at the end of each lesson and sent them in under the barber's name.

When Jose earned the diploma, it was in the name of the barber, who then displayed "his" achievement proudly on the wall for all his customers to see.

Jose, in turn, used his newfound knowledge of electronics to begin selling and repairing radios. He eventually built one of the largest electronics repair businesses in south Texas. (Today, many people in Laredo remember Jose as the TV repairman and find it hard to accept him as a scientific researcher whose course is taught all over the world!)

Jose earned the respect of the people in his community.

These accomplishments were pretty impressive for a youngster who had to educate himself and support his family since age 6. But after he got married and started his own family, there was one area where Jose's hard work and street smarts weren't paying off:

Why weren't his own children like him?

Even though Jose had experienced success in many areas, his children were not following in his footsteps. Some bad report cards convinced him that he had to find the answer.

The answer seemed to lie in the way that super successful people like himself used their minds.

Jose Silva had grown up using both his logic and his imagination/intuition (the alpha level, which you will learn about later). He had used his imagination, which all children do naturally, to come up with ideas to fill needs and earn money. And he had used his intellect, too, to keep track of business. But most people, as they mature, leave their imaginations behind and think only in terms of logic and the physical world.

Jose made good decisions, but his children sometimes failed to do the correct thing. He could concentrate on a task and complete it, but his children didn't seem to have that same ability. He was never ill; in fact, he had never even been examined by a doctor until he got his physical for his induction into the U.S. Army in 1944! But his children got all the usual childhood diseases.

Jose was usually in the right place at the right time, and this had led to much of his success. But his children, like so many people who never see their dreams come true, sometimes seemed to wind up at the worst possible place at the worst possible time.

These differences between his children and himself raised several questions in his mind:

- Why could some people learn more easily than others? Jose learned without ever attending school, while his children were bringing home some F's on their report cards.

- Why were some people so much better at earning a living than others?

- Why did some athletes become superstars, while others remained average and ordinary?

He felt that the answer was in the mind. But how could he explore the mind?

Studying the mind

Jose decided to study psychology on his own by reading books on the subject. One of the things he learned is that the brain operates on a small amount of electrical energy and that this electric current vibrates or pulsates at different rates.

Sometimes the brain's electrical energy vibrates rapidly, 20 times every second, or 20 cycles per second (20 cps). Sometimes it vibrates slower, at 10 cps or 5 cps. Jose wondered why this was so. Then he drew on his experience in radio repair and realized that some radios sound better than others. What makes the difference between a good electrical circuit and a bad one? he wondered.

Jose knew that in electronics, the most desirable circuit to use is the one with the least impedance - the least total opposition to current flow - because that circuit provides the greatest power. The same principle applies to athletics: If the opposing team is weak in one area, that's the area in which you aim to defeat them.

Since the brain operates on a small amount of electrical energy, Jose concluded, the same principle should hold true: Find the operating mode where the brain has the least impedance - the least opposition to the flow of the brain's electrical energy through its neural pathways - and you've found the best mode for mental activity.

The mind did not reveal its secrets to Jose Silva so easily. He persisted, investing his own time and money, continuing even though critics scorned him. After investing 22 years and half a million dollars, he had uncovered the secret and harnessed it so that his children - and anyone else - could use it.

Today, Jose Silva is recognized as a leading researcher in the field of the mind and human potential. Now we will teach you how to use his system for sports and anything else you need.

How your brain works

Your brain operates on a small amount of electricity, just like a computer. It can process and store information, retrieve that information and use that information to make decisions and solve problems.

Unlike a computer, however, the brain generates and functions with electricity that does not remain at a fixed frequency. Sometimes the brain's electric current vibrates rapidly - 20 times per second or more. Other times it vibrates very slowly, one time per second or less. Scientists call these vibrations "cycles," or "Hertz," and have divided the brain frequency spectrum into four different segments, based on the number of cycles per second (cps):

1. Beta, more than 14 cps (typically 20 cps), occurs when your body and mind are active and you focus your eyes.

2. Alpha, 7 to 14 cps, is associated with light sleep and dreaming.

3. Theta, from 4 to 7 cps, is associated with deeper sleep and with the use of hypnosis for such things as painless surgery.

4. Delta, below 4 cps, is associated with deepest sleep.

Jose Silva reasoned that the best range to use for mental activity would be the range with the least impedance and the most energy.

Alpha is the strongest and most rhythmic frequency. That's why it was discovered first by scientists in the 1920s with a primitive sensing device called an "electroencephalograph," which measures electrical energy in the brain. Scientists named it "alpha," the first letter in the Greek alphabet.

A map of the mind

This chart is a map of your body (left side), brain (center), and mind (right side).

As you can see, the Alpha brain frequencies are in the center of the normal operating range - the strongest part of the brain.

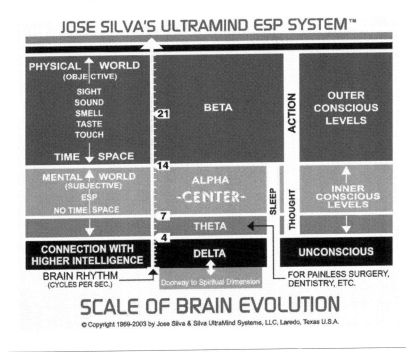

How people use their minds

If it actually was possible to actively use one's mind to analyze problems and come up with solutions while in the alpha state, it seemed logical to Jose Silva that this state would be the ideal one in which to think. Why would the alpha level be ideal?

- It would allow one to think more clearly because of its extra energy.

- It would enable one to maintain concentration better.

- Alpha is in the absolute center of the brain's normal operating range, so it would allow access to more information more easily.

But there was a catch. Research revealed that most people do their thinking at the beta frequency! Jose's research led him to discover that only 10 percent of the population are natural alpha thinkers. It turned out that he himself was one of them.

Most people are using the weakest, least stable frequency to do their thinking: the beta level. Most people, when their brain frequency slows to alpha, enter the subconscious state, then fall asleep. But the superstars stay awake at the alpha level, and do their thinking at alpha.

Improving athletic performance

How can this information be used to improve fitness and athletic performance?

Your brain is under the direction of your mind, and every movement of your body is controlled by your brain. When you decide to pick up a glass of water and drink it, your mind sends a mental picture to your brain, your brain carries out the instructions to your body and your thirst is quenched.

How does this work? The brain sends tiny electrical signals down nerve pathways to your muscles, causing muscles to contract. When the signal is turned off, muscles relax.

Again, brain neurons send signals down neural pathways to the appropriate muscle fibers, and they contract while others relax. Practice mentally - and at the correct level, the alpha level - and your brain will learn to send the signals more quickly, with less effort. That is why so many athletes find mental rehearsal such a valuable tool to help them improve their performance. Just as you train your body, you can also train your brain, by training your mind, which controls your brain.

But you must do it at the correct level - the alpha level.

Functioning at alpha... successfully

To function at alpha successfully, you must learn to do two things:

- To produce alpha brain waves with conscious awareness - that is, reach the alpha level without falling asleep.
- To become mentally active - that is, to analyze problems - and come up with solutions - while remaining at the alpha level.

Everybody can daydream. When people just sit back, relax and daydream, they may very well lower their brain frequency to the alpha level, especially if they are not focusing their eyes on anything.

When they focus their eyes, however, they go immediately to beta. Beta is required for focusing the eyes. People can daydream and remain at alpha with their eyes open as long as they are not focused on anything specific. But once they start thinking about and analyzing a problem and searching for a solution, their brains usually go back to beta.

With training, you can learn how to become mentally active - to think about and analyze problems and devise solutions - while remaining at alpha. That's what we teach you to do in the Silva courses.

Later in this chapter, and in the chapters that follow, Jose Silva will teach you a specific, step-by-step mind training routine that you can use to function at the alpha level with conscious awareness, so that you can program yourself for even greater success in your athletic career.

But first, here's some additional information about the alpha level, why it is so powerful and exactly how it can help you.

Double your pleasure

Besides being the most efficient operating level in terms of low impedance and high power output, the alpha level has another very important advantage: At the alpha level, you can use both brain hemispheres to think instead of just one.

At beta, you think with the left half of your brain - your left brain hemisphere. It is highly specialized for certain tasks: talking, reasoning, using logic, examining details. At alpha, you can think with either your left brain hemisphere or your right brain hemisphere. The right brain hemisphere is more creative and intuitive. It deals with form and shape, with movement and rhythm. Instead of operating in a sequential fashion - one step follows another - it operates in a spatial mode, a random access fashion. You could say that the left hemisphere counts the trees, while the right hemisphere admires the forest. Your left brain hemisphere is great for tallying up your golf score, for computing batting averages and for figuring out whether you try for a two-point conversion after a touchdown. Your right brain hemisphere coordinates the body for a perfect swing to get a great drive, to hit a home run or to make the perfect cutback to score the two-point conversion.

Will you double your ability when you learn to think with both brain hemispheres? You will do much more than that. To illustrate, imagine that you are playing a sport, and your teammates and your opponents all have one of their legs in a cast, while you have full use of both legs. Even if it's a sport you do not play very well, you will still look like a superstar compared to the people who can only use one leg. Learning to use both brain hemispheres has the same outcome: You will get into shape faster and perform better in everything that you do.

Research demonstrates success

Cecelia Prediger of Nyack Junior High School in New York wanted to test the Silva System on a group of students who had gone out for field hockey. She called our office in Laredo and told us about the project she had set up. She had originally designed the project so that instructors would read the exact same instructions that we use in Silva classes to a group of players, guiding them completely through visualization for the first three or four sessions. For the final few sessions, the instructors would get the students started and tell them to continue to imagine that they were performing.

We suggested that she allow the students to do as much of the mental rehearsal on their own as possible. Greater benefits result from doing things on your own. For instance, working out using a machine to move your body around does not give you as many results as does performing the exercises on your own.

She divided the team into three groups. She set up simulated hockey goals by placing sets of cones at a certain distance from each other. Each group practiced a specific shooting skill for five minutes. But they practiced in entirely different ways. One group of 40 student athletes practiced shooting towards the simulated goal for five minutes each day for seven practice sessions. Another group of 40 sat in the bleachers, entered the alpha level with the Silva techniques and, for five minutes, imagined shooting at the goal. The third group of 40 students entered alpha and, for two-and-a-half minutes, imagined shooting, then went onto the practice field and actually shot at the goals for two-and-a-half minutes.

The results produced one big surprise:

The group that performed the physical practice went from 13 hits at the start of the project to 22 hits after the seven practice sessions, an improvement of 70 percent. That was no surprise. The group that entered the alpha level and imagined shooting at the goal for the seven practice sessions improved from 12 hits to 20 hits, an improvement of 68 percent. Again, this was not a big surprise but confirmed previous research projects.

It was the third group that produced the big surprise. No one had ever published a report about what would happen if you combined both mental and physical practice. Would the practice time be so short as to depress the overall results? Would the results be similar to the other two groups?

Cecelia had done some research and found that researchers in the field of sports psychology had speculated that improvement would be even greater with physical practice and mental practice than with either of the two alone. But how much better?

The group that divided their practice time between mental and physical practice started with virtually the same number of hits on target as the other two groups. But when tested again after seven practice sessions, they scored a total of 31 hits, an

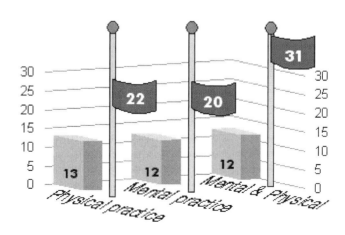

improvement of 160 percent - more than double the improvement of either of the other two groups!

The evidence is clear: When you combine effective mental rehearsal - as Jose Silva will teach you to do in this book - with appropriate physical practice - as your coach or trainer will instruct you - you will be a superstar compared to athletes who use either physical practice or mental practice alone. In Section 2 you will learn to use visualization and imagination at the alpha level, the way the field hockey players did.

But first, you need to learn how to enter the alpha level. Will you invest 15 minutes a day to learn to enter the alpha level with conscious awareness? If so, you will learn how to apply the techniques of the Silva Method to succeed. We'll provide step-by-step guidance, so you will know exactly what to do.

It is easier to do it than to explain it, so let's get right on to the first mental training exercise - also known as a conditioning cycle - from Jose Silva.

Your first mental training exercise

In the 2-day Silva UltraMind ESP System seminar, attendees learn how to function consciously at alpha in just a few hours because they have the help of a trained lecturer who guides them step-by-step and answers all of their questions.

If you have not yet attended a live Silva seminar, then you can learn how to enter the alpha level in just a few days with the guided instruction in the Silva UltraMind ESP System Complete Home Seminar, or with the Silva UltraMind ESP System Free Introductory Lessons at www.SilvaNow.com

If you prefer to learn by reading this book, it will take you approximately 40 days.

Training your mind requires you to relax and lower your brain frequency to the alpha level. It does not require a forced effort. You use force in your physical training. In mental training, you relax and practice using imagination and visualization.

You will begin learning the Silva System for improved athletic performance by following positive mental instructions while in a relaxed state. Jose Silva will give you a simple way to relax, and you will become better and better at it as you practice. He will also give you a simple statement to affirm to yourself.

The mental exercise you are about to learn from Jose Silva will help you learn to lower your brain frequency while maintaining conscious awareness. In other words, you are going to learn how to consciously think with both brain hemispheres.

If you have already learned how to function at the alpha level by attending a Silva Method seminar or by listening to the recordings in a Silva home study course and practicing and directed, then you do not need to do the 40 days of countdown exercises that Jose Silva is going to explain to you in just a few minutes. However, if you have not yet learned how to use the Silva Method, then you must do the countdowns.

The choice is yours

Do you want to perform better? To be more in charge of your life? Your desire, belief and expectation are the "green lights" to go ahead and start improving your athletic performance and changing your life for the better. On the other hand, if you are saying to yourself, "Well, I'll do the exercise, but I don't really think it is going to do any good," then you won't get very good results. If you find yourself feeling this way, just acknowledge that it is okay to feel that way. Then relax, do the exercise confidently and it will work.

Since you cannot read this book and relax simultaneously, it is necessary to first read the instructions. Then you can put the book down, close your eyes and complete the exercise. Let's begin.

Your First Alpha Exercise

1. Sit comfortably in a chair and close your eyes. Any position in which you're comfortable is a good position.

2. Take a deep breath. As you exhale, relax your body.

3. Count backward slowly from 50 to 1.

4. Daydream about some peaceful place you know.

5. Say to yourself mentally, "Every day, in every way, I am getting better, better and better."

6. Bring yourself out by mentally telling yourself that when you open your eyes at the count of 5, you will feel wide awake and better than before. When you reach the count of 3, repeat this, and when you open your eyes, confirm it again: "I am wide awake, feeling better than before."

You may already know steps 1 and 2; you may be in the habit of doing them daily when you come home in the evening. When you add a countdown and a peaceful scene, you enter deeper levels of mind (and lower brain frequencies). To come back out, you count up from 1 to 5; we refer to this as a "bring out." When you add your affirmation to help you become better and better, you are ready for this final bring out.

Read the instructions above once more. Then put the book down and do the exercise.

The magic of thinking at alpha

What you have just experienced, through Jose Silva's instruction, is called "programming." Your ability to program gets better with practice. With practice, you relax more quickly and reach deeper, healthier levels of mind; you visualize more realistically; your levels of expectation and belief heighten, yielding bigger and better results.

Programming at the alpha level produces far better results than programming at beta. You can repeat affirmations a thousand times at the outer level (beta) and not have as much effect as with just one repetition at alpha.

Jose Silva found in his research that only about one out of every 10 people naturally thinks at the alpha brain wave level and acts at the beta level. That is why some people are able to visualize their goals and then reach them, while most people get very little result. Remember, the only way to get superior results is to learn how to function at the alpha level with conscious awareness, the way the 1-in-10 natural alpha thinkers do.

When you practiced the simple relaxation exercise a few minutes ago, you took the first step in learning to think and function mentally like a superstar. And as you continue with the mental exercises in this book, you are sure to strengthen your mind and achieve greater success than ever before.

Chapter 2

Developing a championship attitude

Swimming coach Wade A. Shore was walking down the beach one morning when he spotted a bottle washed up by the waves. As he was brushing the sand off of it, a big, powerful-looking genie popped out.

"Thank you for freeing me," the genie said gratefully. "You have saved me. In return, I will grant you any wishes that you want."

"Really?" Wade said. "Anything that I want?" The genie assured him that all he had to do was say the word. "Then give me a new sports car," Wade said.

"As you wish," the genie said, pointing to a bright red sports car just beyond the dunes. Wade went up to look at it and found the keys and the registration in his name.

"Wow! Can you give me a new house, too?" Wade asked.

"Just say the word," the genie answered, and a beautiful new house appeared, overlooking the beach.

"Do you know what I'd really like more than anything else in the world?" Wade asked solemnly.

"Just say the word, and it is yours," the genie answered.

"I'd like for you to make me the greatest athlete in the world. But," he continued, "I know that even you could never do that!"

"Okay," the genie said, "your wish is my command: I can never do that!"

Be careful what you wish for

As the old saying goes, you need to be careful about what you wish...because you just might get it.

You need to be sure that you know exactly what it means to

have a positive mental attitude. Positive thinking is thinking about what you want - not what you do not want. Remove all doubt, and eliminate all thoughts about the things that you do not want.

Everybody knows the importance of the "mental game" in athletics - of believing in yourself and how good you are. But not everybody understands exactly what constitutes a positive mental attitude. Some people give you bad advice about staying positive, while others serve as good models of positive thinking. Here's what some sports stars have to say on the subject:

The great golfer Arnold Palmer was quoted by George Plimpton in *The Bogey Man*, a book about Plimpton's experiences participating as an amateur golfer with a Professional Golfers Association (PGA) tour - stated: "When I'm working well, I just don't think I'm going to miss a shot or a putt, and when I do, I'm as surprised as hell. I can't believe it. A golfer must think that way. He must say to the ball, 'Go to that spot.' The best players who ever played must have thought that way - willing the ball there, you see. I don't mean to suggest that it's easy. In fact, the hardest thing for a great many people is to win. They get scared. And they doubt, which gets them into trouble."

Former Dallas Cowboys football coach Tom Landry said that one of the things that helped make Randy White a great defensive lineman was his attitude. He didn't go into the game with the attitude that he would do his best - he told himself that he was going to be the best. "Randy White plays everyone the same, whether they are good or bad," coach Landry said. "When you have that, you have a player who dominates."

Young tennis champion Andre Agassi said in a television interview during the 1991 Wimbledon tournament that if he had to choose between having the best athletic skills or the best mental attitude, he'd prefer to have the right mental attitude.

Here's a curious thing: While everybody knows how

important a positive mental attitude is to success, most people cannot explain how to develop one. In fact, most people cannot even accurately define the term "positive mental attitude."

So, what exactly is a positive mental attitude? First, let's discuss what it is not. It is not a matter of bragging about how good you are, as some people think. Nor is it a matter of concentrating on avoiding mistakes.

Jose Silva's research into how the human brain and mind function has given us a very precise definition of "positive thinking." More importantly, Jose has devised specific techniques that you can use to develop a positive mental attitude and maintain it even when things are going wrong for you.

Defining a positive mental attitude

Simply stated, a positive mental attitude is thinking about what you want, rather than what you don't want. A negative mental attitude is thinking about what you don't want. Here are some examples of how both attitudes can affect performance:

• When the amateur tees up on the golf course and takes a furtive look at the water hazard to the left, then the wooded rough to the right, he has just programmed himself for a poorly aimed drive. The professional, by seeing only the flag at the hole, programs herself for the straight drive.

• The couch potato considers exercising and thinks about how much work it is. The positive thinker focuses on the end result: the healthy, fit, attractive body that results from a few minutes of exercise three or four times a week.

• The bush league player concentrates on correcting the problems in his swing, while the major league baseball player forgets about being in a slump and concentrates on hitting the ball. By doing this, he gets out of the slump.

• The aspiring gymnast faces the balance beam and repeats

to herself that she won't lose her footing while mounting the beam, which is one of the trouble spots in her routine. The veteran gymnast recalls the times she was "in the groove" and performed flawlessly. Her mind creates the correct mental picture, her brain sends the correct signals and she scores high marks for her performance, as she expected.

- The football coach cautions his players (and especially his young quarterback): "We can win if we don't turn it over." They turn the ball over four times. The coach who understands what positive thinking is really all about tells his team that they can win if they protect the ball. They hold onto the ball, and they win the game.

In each example, the first person focused on what he or she didn't want, while the second focused on what he or she did want.

Bad advice: easy to give

Even people who should know better often don't.

Sportscaster Pat Summerall and analyst John Madden were the commentators during a telecast of a National Football League game. The two men had an interesting discussion as they watched the teams bungle through the game. The home team's rookie quarterback was having another in a series of bad games.

"I don't understand it," commented Madden, the former coach of the Oakland Raiders. "You practice all week, do everything you are supposed to do. You keep saying, 'Don't make mistakes don't fumble, don't jump offside, don't drop passes, don't miss blocks' you do that all week, and then come out on Sunday and do all those things you've been told not to do!"

Without realizing it, Madden gave a perfect definition of

negative thinking. He wanted to express a positive thought, but he used all negative mental pictures. All of the words he used produced negative pictures - pictures of what not to do.

By contrast, Jimmy Johnson, who coached the Dallas Cowboys to two consecutive Super Bowl victories, would tell his players, just before they left the locker room to compete in a championship game, to "protect the ball and make the plays." Johnson's words produced positive pictures - pictures of what to do.

Always remember this: Positive pictures produce desirable effects; negative pictures produce undesirable effects. Let's look at some real-life examples of positive and negative mental attitudes.

How a diver used positive thinking to win gold

When Olympic diving champion Greg Louganis smashed his head into the high board during the finals of the 1988 Olympic Games, with a worldwide television audience watching, he could have easily filled his mind with negative thoughts.

He could have reviewed videotapes of the dive to see what he did wrong, so he could correct it. He could have asked his coach to analyze it for him and make suggestions. He could have tried to forget the incident, to force it out of his consciousness.

All of those options involved negative thinking. Why? Because they focused on the problem on what he did not want.

What did he actually do? After he got back on the board and went on to win the gold medal, Louganis told a television interviewer exactly what he did to prevent the incident from affecting his performance. First, said Louganis, he refused to watch a tape of the dive. He did not want to make any further impressions of that error on his brain. Then he recalled the thousands of times he had made that dive successfully.

But wasn't he scared when he climbed onto the board the next time? Sure he was. He admitted it. But he used his powerful concentration to recall the thousands of times he had done that dive successfully. He thought about what he wanted, rather than what he didn't want. Positive thoughts, positive mental pictures.

Beating out an injury - and the world champ

To overcome her injury and win, tennis player Zena Garrison took an approach to positive thinking similar to the one taken by Greg Louganis.

Garrison was playing Monica Seles at Wimbledon in 1990. The following year, Seles would be ranked the number-one woman's professional tennis player in the world. Even under the best of conditions, this would be a difficult match for Garrison.

In the midst of the competition, Garrison fell while going after a shot. She got up carefully and checked her bloody knee to see how much damage she had done to her body. Then she checked the scoreboard: It was match point for Seles. If Seles won this point, Garrison would be eliminated from the tournament!

But Garrison won the point. And she came back to win the match.

As she walked off the court a winner, sportscaster Bud Collins interviewed her for a worldwide television audience. He asked her what she was thinking about after the fall.

"Even in my junior days," Garrison answered, "when I'd fall, I'd come back and win the match. I kept that in mind today."

Zena Garrison could have thought about a thousand other things that day. But she thought about what she wanted coming back to win the match, as she had done many times before.

The body follows mental pictures

Remember that great Denver Broncos football team that went to Super Bowl XXII to play the Washington Redskins? There was a subtle, but very significant, difference in the two teams' attitudes and expectations about the game.

Washington quarterback Doug Williams talked about how the Redskins set out to play their game to do what they could and to do the best they could. They knew that Denver had a fabulous team and one of the greatest quarterbacks of all time. They decided to just go out and do the best they could and see what happened. Some people would say that they did not have a very positive attitude.

The Denver players, on the other hand, had a very strong motivator. They had been to the Super Bowl the year before - and lost. It was a terrible feeling, especially when they returned home and had to face their fans. They were determined to win. To remind themselves of how much they wanted to win, the Broncos said, over and over, that they didn't want to go home losers again. They kept reminding themselves - and a worldwide audience - of how unpleasant that had been.

Have you figured out which team had the more positive attitude?

Here's a hint: What kind of mental pictures did the Washington players create by talking and thinking about playing the best they could? What kind of mental pictures did the Denver players create by talking and thinking about (not) going home losers again?

One team was thinking about playing their best. The other team was thinking about going home losers. Can you guess who won that game?

It was the biggest blowout in Super Bowl history. Washington won. Denver lost.

The players who thought about doing their best played their best game of the year. The players who thought about going home losers went home losers. Sure, they kept saying they didn't want to go home losers, but saying that doesn't create a picture of going home winners. The only mental picture that results from those words is... going home losers. And what the Denver Broncos mentally pictured came to pass.

So often, the difference between winning and losing is a matter of attitude. If the Broncos had simply thought and talked about going home winners, who knows what might have happened?

Tennis star Chris Evert, who was named the "Greatest Woman Athlete of the Last Twenty-five Years" by the Women's Sports Foundation in 1985, once told late-night television host David Letterman that she doesn't consider herself a great athlete. She said she considers herself good, but many athletes are better. Then she pointed to her head and said, "I have it here."

How mental pictures affect you

Jose Silva's research has revealed some basic truths:

• Your mind guides your brain, and your brain guides your body.

• You tend to move in the direction of your dominant thoughts.

• The most effective way to program your brain is with mental pictures. When you picture something in your mind, your brain will instruct your body to act out what you have pictured. That's one of the reasons athletes find watching films of their past performances so valuable. It is helpful to watch game films to analyze the mistakes you've made, but before you go out and perform once more, make sure the last film you watch is of successes. You want your mental images to be positive - to show you performing correctly.

Your wonderful biocomputer

Your brain functions much like a computer. It operates on electrical energy. It can store information, which you can retrieve later. It can use the information that is available to it to solve problems. It has certain modes that are designed especially for performing specific tasks, such as thinking, acting and sleeping.

In order to use this wonderful "biocomputer" (your brain) most effectively, you need to first be in the correct mode - the alpha brain wave level - and then do the correct things, which you can do by using the formula-type techniques in this book.

In Section 2, we will teach you how to use visualization and imagination at the alpha level to rehearse mentally before performing and to improve your performance. Right now we want to help you develop and strengthen a winning attitude and believe in yourself and your ability.

What you will learn now will be excellent practice for what you will learn later. It is similar to learning the fundamentals in your sport.

Consider a positive mental attitude to be one of the fundamentals.

Entering the alpha level with conscious awareness is another.

First, let's cover the specific steps for developing a positive mental attitude.

Mental Housecleaning

With the Silva Mental Housecleaning technique, you practice canceling negative thoughts and replacing them with positive ones.

Human thought is naturally drawn to problems. This often helps protect us from danger and can even be important to our survival. In athletics, if you do not solve problems, you will not win and many times will not even get to compete.

You can use Mental Housecleaning any time there is a problem or an undesirable situation - when you make an error, you do not succeed at something you attempt, your opponent beats you or you miss a training session. Whatever the situation, you can use this technique.

Here's how it works: Since your brain operates much like a computer, when you want to "delete" a negative thought from your brain, you will do something similar to hitting the "cancel" button on a computer. You will say "cancel-cancel" to get rid of the negative thought - the thought you do not desire. Then you will immediately replace it with a positive thought.

Those are the two steps involved in Mental Housecleaning, and it is important to do both. After an undesirable situation, immediately:

1. Say "cancel-cancel" to cancel the negative thought. Then...

2. Replace it with a positive thought.

Here are some examples of when and how you can use Mental Housecleaning:

- You swing and miss. Say "cancel-cancel" and imagine hitting the next ball, and it will go where you want it to go.

- You begin to dread your exercise routine. Immediately say "cancel-cancel" and think of the end result: the healthy, fit, attractive body that you want.

- Your opponent blocks you. Say "cancel-cancel" and imagine getting through the next time.

- The weight is too heavy, you can't lift it and it falls back to the lifting platform. Say "cancel-cancel" and imagine lifting it.

- Your shot goes out of bounds. Say "cancel-cancel" and imagine making a perfect shot next time.

- Your opponent beats you to the finish line. Say "cancel-cancel" and imagine getting there first.

- You drop the ball and your opponent scores. Say "cancel-cancel" and imagine catching the ball next time.

Help yourself forget. Say "cancel-cancel" and immediately start thinking about what you want.

Hank Stram, former coach of the Kansas City Chiefs football team, told a national television audience why he thought former Chiefs quarterback Jim Plunkett was so good. "The great thing about Jim Plunkett is that he has the ability to forget; he doesn't let bad thoughts linger."

Practice makes perfect

Now you have an important assignment:

As soon as possible, go practice what you just learned. Toss a ball. Lift some weights. Do some exercises. Make some shots. Whatever activity you're trying to perfect, go do it. When you miss, say "cancel-cancel" and immediately imagine doing it right. Then do it again.

You already know that whenever you learn a new technique, it is important for you to practice it. That's how your coach trains you. Your coach explains the technique, demonstrates it and then tells you to practice it.

You have to practice this new technique before you get into competition because you are too busy during competition to start learning something new. Learn it first so that when you are competing, the technique is automatic for you. So practice Mental Housecleaning right away.

Again, when you don't accomplish what you wanted, say

"cancel-cancel" and immediately imagine yourself succeeding. Recall a time when you succeeded when you were "perfect." With this thought in mind, try again.

Create a positive environment

By now, you may be getting the idea that everything you say and think has an effect on you.

This is true.

Your thoughts direct your energy. In addition, everything that you hear affects you.

As former PGA Champion Dave Marr said in George Plimpton's book *The Bogey Man*, "The best thing you can do to improve your game is to play with professionals, the best professionals. That's the one piece of advice I've never forgotten.

"Jackie Burke told me," Marr continued. "He said never stick with the losers on the golf course. Stay away from rabbits, if you can. No matter how nice they are as golfing companions, if they are perpetually rabbits, they've got a streak in them that's no good for you to be around too much. Always play with the winners."

Vince Lombardi took the same approach when he took over as head coach of the Green Bay Packers professional football team. He got rid of the players who didn't have the right attitude, according to former Packer lineman Jerry Kramer in his book *Instant Replay*.

You will benefit from hanging out with other positive thinkers - with winners. By the same token, always think positively around everyone with whom you come into contact.

Bobby Bowden, legendary football coach at Florida State University, was in bed for a year with rheumatic fever when he was 13 years old. His doctor said he would never play football again. "That's why we changed doctors," Bowden said.

Do unto others

Negativity can easily creep into your thinking even when you have the best of intentions. For example, it is fun to kid around with your teammates, but sometimes a little joke can backfire and hurt the team - and hurt you. "After a date, Pat can't hit the ball even if it were standing still!" may sound like an innocent joke, but think about what kind of mental picture it creates. What impression does it make in the memory banks of Pat's biocomputer?

If anyone makes a joke like that about you, you know what to do. Immediately "cancel-cancel" it, and replace it with a positive thought - a mental picture of you hitting the ball.

Praise your teammates. Talk about them doing the things that you want them to do. Encourage them. And support your coaches. When you criticize your coaches, you undermine your own belief in their ability to help you.

Make yourself healthy

You can even make people - including yourself - feel sick or healthy just by what you say to them.

Have you ever played that game in which everybody approaches one person and tells that person that he or she doesn't look too good today - that he or she looks sick? When enough people ask that person if he or she is sick, the person often starts feeling sick.

Even when you feel bad, use Mental Housecleaning. When you think of how bad you feel, immediately say "cancel-cancel" and imagine feeling fine and in perfect health.

Your thoughts direct your energy; your mind tells your body what to do. Doctors recognize this when they say that as much as 80 percent of an illness is psychosomatic in nature. The mind (the psyche) influences the body (the soma). You can actually use your mind to help heal your body. You will learn more about this in Section 4. (One word of caution: Whenever you are working on your health, always work under a doctor's supervision.)

How to psych out opponents

What is the best way to use your mind to beat your opponents? Should you imagine them making mistakes, losing?

To answer this question, recall our earlier discussion of the kind of images you should store in the memory banks of your biocomputer. Remember, whatever you deposit into your memory banks is going to affect you. When it is time to make a decision, you will draw on the information and images that you have stored there. In competition, this happens very quickly. So do you want images of winning - or of mistakes?

Basketball coach Hector Chacon puts it this way: "I don't want to beat a bad team. I want to beat a good team. That's why I hope that my opponents will play very well... and that we play a little bit better."

You have heard the golden rule: Do unto others what you would have them do unto you. Apply this teaching to the way you think about your opponents.

Never think about an opponent playing poorly. When you do, the negative images you conjure up - of mistakes, of failures - can backfire on you and make you lose.

Remember, you tend to move in the direction of your dominant thoughts. It is only to your benefit to wish that your opponents play the best game possible.

Serious business

Here is a tragic example that may illustrate the connection between mental images and performance.

During a telecast of a sprint car race, announcers centered their discussion on a team that was racing a Ford automobile. Ford's biggest competitor has traditionally been Chevrolet, whose motto at the time was "The Heartbeat of America."

The team racing the Ford had mechanical problems and dropped out of the race. As the team finished loading the car onto their truck, the broadcasters talked about how this team had been having trouble ever since their long-time crew chief had been laid up after triple bypass heart surgery.

Then the television camera followed the truck as it drove out of the pits. The motto on the back of the truck read, in large print: "The team that stopped the heartbeat."

The right environment

Every time you suit up for competition, you have a choice. You can say one of two things to yourself:

"Please don't let me make a mistake."

"Let me do great today."

If you are thinking about the mistakes, then change your attitude. Use the Mental Housecleaning technique, and do it right away, because the inner images that you create - consciously or unconsciously - are more powerful than all the willpower and determination of a company of marines.

Positive thinking is the first step in learning to use more of your mind to improve your athletic performance. It will create the right environment for you to win more often. The real results will come when you learn to enter the alpha level and use that level for your positive thinking and mental rehearsal to improve your performance.

To get to that point, let's begin with the following instructions from Jose Silva on how to function at alpha.

Learning to use the alpha level consciously

When you attend a Silva seminar you learn to enter and function within the alpha level with just one day of training. You can learn to enter the alpha level with just a few hours of practice with a recording.

However, learning on your own takes longer. To be sure that you learn to reach the alpha level on your own, you need to invest 40 days. After that, you will be ready to program yourself to improve your athletic performance and anything else you desire.

When you enter sleep, you enter alpha. But you quickly go right through alpha to the deeper levels of theta and delta. Throughout the night, your brain moves back and forth through alpha, theta and delta, like the ebb and flow of the tide. These cycles last about 90 minutes. In the morning, as you exit sleep, you come out through alpha and go back into the faster beta frequencies that are associated with the outer conscious levels.

Some authors advise that as you go to sleep at night, you think about your goals. That way, you get a little bit of alpha time for programming. The only trouble is, you have a tendency to fall asleep if you do this.

For now, just practice a simple exercise that will help you learn to enter and stay at the alpha level. Then, after 40 days, you will be ready to begin your programming. In the meantime, you will learn some additional tasks to perform at the beta level that will help you to be able to program more effectively at the alpha level after the completion of the 40 days.

You will practice the following alpha exercise in the morning when you first wake up. Since your brain is starting to shift from alpha to beta when you first wake up, you will not have a tendency to fall asleep when you enter alpha.

However, if you have already learned to enter the alpha level in a Silva seminar or by listening to and practicing the instructions in a Silva home study course, then you can skip this next part, there is no need for you to do the 40 days of countdowns if you have already learned to enter your level with our System.

An Exercise to Enter and Stay at Alpha

1. When you awake tomorrow morning, go to the bathroom if you have to, then go back to bed. Set your alarm clock to ring in 15 minutes, just in case you do fall asleep again. Sit in a comfortable position.

2. Close your eyes and turn them slightly upward toward your eyebrows (about 20 degrees). Research shows that this produces more alpha.

3. Count backward slowly (in your mind, not aloud) from 100 to 1. Wait about one second between numbers.

4. When you reach the count of 1, focus on a mental picture of yourself as a success. An easy way to do this is to recall the most recent time when you considered yourself 100 percent successful. Recall the setting, where you were, what the scene looked like, what you did and what you felt like.

5. Repeat mentally, "Every day in every way, I am getting better, better and better."

6. Then say to yourself, "I am going to count from 1 to 5. When I reach the count of 5, I will open my eyes, feeling fine and in perfect health, feeling better than before."

7. Begin to count. When you reach 3, repeat, "When I reach the count of 5, I will open my eyes, feeling fine and in perfect health, feeling better than before."

8. Continue your count to 4 and 5. At the count of 5, open your eyes and affirm mentally, "I am wide awake, feeling fine and in perfect health, feeling better than before. And this is so."

Why each of these steps is crucial

Keep going over each of these eight steps so that you understand their purpose while becoming more familiar with their sequence. For a better understanding of the reasoning behind each of the steps, read on.

Step 1. The mind cannot deeply relax if the body is not relaxed. It is better to go to the bathroom and permit your body to enjoy full comfort. Also, when you first awake, you may not be fully awake. Going to the bathroom ensures your being fully awake. But in case you are still not awake enough to stay awake, set your alarm clock to ring in about 15 minutes so you do not risk being late on your daily schedule.

Step 2. Research has shown that when a person turns the eyes up about 20 degrees, it triggers more alpha rhythm in the brain and also causes more right brain activity. Later, you will do your mental picturing with your eyes turned upward at this angle. Meanwhile, it is a simple way to encourage alpha. You might want to think of the way you look up at the screen in a movie theater a comfortable upward angle.

Step 3. Counting backward is relaxing. Counting forward is activating. Saying "1, 2, 3" is like saying, "Ready, set, go!" But saying "3, 2, 1" is pacifying; you are going nowhere except deeper within yourself.

Step 4. Imagining yourself the way you want to be - while relaxed - creates the ideal picture. People who relax and imagine themselves making mistakes and losing frequently create a mental picture that brings about failure. You will do the opposite. Your mental picture is one of success, and it will create what you desire: success.

Step 5. Words repeated mentally - while relaxed - result in the feelings they are talking about. Pictures and words program the mind to actually create the state of being they represent.

Steps 6, 7 and 8. These last three steps simply consist of counting to 5 to end your session. Counting up activates you. But it is still a good idea to give yourself "orders" to become activated at the count of 5. Do this before you begin to count, do it again along the way and do it once again as you open your eyes at the count of 5.

8 steps that are really only 3

Once you wake up tomorrow morning and complete this exercise, you will realize it all works down to just three steps:

1. Count backwards from 100 to 1.

2. Mentally picture yourself successful and affirm your continuing success.

3. Count yourself out of alpha by counting from 1 to 5, affirming good health and alertness.

40 days that can change your life... for the better

You know what to do tomorrow morning, but what about after that? Well, here is your 40-day training program:

- For the first 10 mornings, follow the eight steps, counting backward from 100 to 1.

- For the next 10 mornings, follow the steps, counting backward from 50 to 1.

- For the next 10 mornings, count backward from 25 to 1.

- For the last 10 mornings, count backward from 10 to 1.

After these 40 mornings of countdown relaxation practice, count backward from only 5 to 1 and begin to use your alpha level.

People have a tendency to be impatient, to want to move faster. Please resist this temptation and follow the instructions as written. You must develop and acquire the ability to function consciously at alpha before Jose Silva's mental techniques will work properly for you. You must master the fundamentals first. We've been researching this field since 1944, longer than anyone else, and the techniques we have developed have helped millions of people worldwide enjoy greater success and happiness, so please follow these simple instructions.

A reminder

In addition to the exercise just described, remember to practice positive thinking - thinking about what you want.

Whenever you think of something you don't want, immediately say "cancel-cancel" and replace it with a positive thought - a thought about something you do want.

Whenever something that you did not desire happens - you make a mistake, or someone outperforms you immediately say "cancel-cancel" and imagine it happening the way you wanted. Recall a time when you performed correctly, and imagine doing that again.

Chapter 3

Inside the mind of a superstar

A young swimmer named Don asked a former swimming champion to teach him the secret of becoming a world champion swimmer.

"Are you sure that you are ready to learn the secret?" the veteran swimmer asked. The old pro knew that Don had some talent, but he was not sure if Don had the right attitude.

"Oh, I'd give anything to be a champion," Don answered.

With that, the former champion grabbed Don's head abruptly and forced it under water.

At first Don resisted, but then he thought, "Maybe he wants to make sure that I am not afraid of the water." So Don stopped struggling.

But as his neck and back began to ache from the unrelenting pressure of the master's hand and his lungs began to ache and burn, he became alarmed. He began to struggle again to free himself and get a breath of air. Now his eyes and his throat hurt, and his lungs felt ready to explode. He wanted to scream out to the former champion to let him up before he died, but he didn't dare open his mouth while he was still under water.

"If this is what it takes to become a champion," Don thought, "maybe I'll change my mind!"

When he felt he couldn't last any longer, he gave a furious kick. The champion yanked on Don's hair and pulled him up out of the water.

Don gulped in air for a few moments as he watched the veteran swimmer and tried to figure out what it all meant. Finally, the older swimmer spoke.

"What did you desire when I first pushed your head under the water?" he asked.

"To be a swimming champion," Don answered between gasps.

"And just before I pulled you out of the water, what was your greatest desire?"

"A breath of air!"

"When you desire to be a world champion as much as you desired that breath of air," the former champion said, "then you will be willing to work hard enough to become a champion.

"And now you know the secret to my success," he added.

Burning desire: foundation for great achievement

Desire is not something that can be given to you. It comes from within.

"Champions are persistent and dedicated," Jose Silva says. "They are able to control and direct their physical and mental energies. And when they make decisions, they are more often right than wrong."

You can't depend on your coach or trainer - or anyone else - to motivate you. In fact, many of the great coaches interviewed in an ESPN television special called "The Great Motivators" use a low-key approach to motivation.

On that program, Mike Ditka, who within four years coached the Chicago Bears - a football team that had not made the playoffs in years - to a Super Bowl victory, said, "I don't believe in motivation."

Coach Ditka pointed out that millions of dollars' worth of books on motivation have been sold but have made little difference.

"Motivation is a personal thing," he told ESPN. "It's what a person has within himself. That's why they're superstars. They don't need Mike Ditka to motivate them."

Superstars are natural alpha thinkers. As you practice your daily countdown exercises, you are learning how to go within yourself.

You are learning to do your thinking at alpha - at the inner dimension - so you can reach the same inner depths that the superstars can.

In this chapter you will learn how to fan the flames of your desire while at these deep inner levels, which will give you the extra energy you need to achieve greatness.

You will also learn how to motivate yourself, build confidence, avoid burnout, listen to your body and make correct training decisions.

Faith

Jose Silva teaches that faith is essential to any success. "Everybody talks about faith," Jose says, "but they don't tell you what it is, or how to get it."

Faith is composed of three parts:

1. Desire.

2. Belief.

3. Expectation.

Desire is the motivating force that pushes you forward.

Belief is the confidence that you can achieve your goal. It sustains you as you move towards the goal.

Expectation is the image of the goal itself.

Desire pushes you forward. Belief sustains you along the way. Expectation attracts you.

1. Desire

Motivation without agitation

Whether you are simply doing calisthenics to get into shape or competing for a world title, motivation is extremely important to you. A lot of self-styled experts seem to be pretty confused about the whole issue of motivation as part of the mental game.

Let's take a moment right now to straighten it out.

On the one hand, sports psychologists have begun to recognize that athletes need to use a deeper level of consciousness when preparing mentally and doing mental rehearsal. While they do not know exactly how to teach a person to enter the alpha state, they do realize that relaxation plays an important part.

They try to get their athletes to a deeper state of mind through meditation, hypnosis or just plain relaxation, none of which assures reaching and staying at alpha.

Then after they get the athletes relaxed, they tell them to think about playing and to be enthusiastic, to get excited about it. But you don't remain at alpha when you get excited - if you become agitated and too mentally active, you return to beta!

Since that doesn't work, sports psychologists try to motivate athletes by getting them all excited about playing well and winning. They show them exciting game films to the beat of the latest rock music.

That can get the athletes "pumped up," which will probably do them some good as it gets their adrenaline pumping. But it certainly is not conducive to entering the alpha state, especially if they have not practiced and developed reliable ways of entering and functioning at alpha.

The good news is: There is a way to motivate yourself while remaining relaxed at the alpha level.

We'll show you how in this chapter.

In chapters to come, we'll also teach you techniques that you can use to function in alpha during the heat of competition, just as the natural alpha thinkers - the world champions - do.

For now, while you contine to practice your countdowns as you learn to enter the alpha level with conscious awareness (or continue to practice the Silva Centering Exercise at least once a week if you have taken a Silva course or home study course), let's see where motivation comes from and how you can motivate yourself, so that you will have the desire that you need to become a champion.

Measuring desire

Near the end of the 1993 football season, Dallas Cowboy superstar running back Emmitt Smith suffered a terrible, excruciatingly painful injury to his shoulder during a must-win game against the New York Giants. Although suffering the worst pain in his life, Smith stayed in the game. Without Smith's contributions after the injury, the Cowboys wouldn't have won.

Later, Smith talked about that experience. And he talked about the people who had told him in the past that he wasn't big enough to play professional football. "I won't name them on television," he said. "They know who they are."

He had a message for all those people who would tell a young athlete that he or she cannot make his or her dream come true:

"I say to them, 'They can measure size and weight and speed and all that. But they can't measure the size of a person's heart'."

Call it heart, desire, courage, will or guts - it is one of those intangible factors that you can measure only by the results that are attained. Jose Silva calls these "spiritual factors."

You cannot strengthen spiritual factors by using resistance and putting stress on them the way you do to strengthen a muscle.

But you can accumulate spiritual energy that will strengthen the spiritual factors of desire, belief, hope and confidence.

"Confidence is easy to talk about," sportscaster John Madden said to his broadcast partner Pat Summerall during the telecast of a game in late 1993. "But you don't get it by talking about it. It comes from within."

Madden has demonstrated that he understands the subject. Before he was a sportscaster, he was head coach of the Oakland Raiders professional football team. He was the first coach to win 100 games in his first 10 years in the National Football League.

Building desire

So how do you accumulate spiritual energy?

Jose Silva says that to build your desire for something, you should enter your level - the alpha level - and think about it.

- Imagine yourself competing and winning.
- Imagine how it feels.
- Recall a previous success and that special feeling that comes with success.
- Recall all the details about it.

Juan Silva, Jose Silva's brother and business associate for many years, was a scratch golfer when he was younger. He recommends the following technique for motivation.

At your level, think of the reasons you have for wanting to succeed. How will it make you feel? Why do you want to win? If you can think of five reasons, he says, then you have a certain amount of desire. If you can think of five more reasons - a total of 10 reasons to succeed - then you will have twice as much desire.

You could have many reasons for wanting to win:

- You might want to succeed because it will boost your ego, make you popular, get your name in the newspaper. Maybe it will even help your social life.

- Depending on your age or circumstance, it could help you financially. Perhaps you could get a college scholarship, a better job or a promotion. And being in a better financial position could benefit your family, and maybe your friends, too.

- People who have supported you would feel good to see you win.

- People who don't even know you personally will enjoy watching you achieve your objectives. They will relate your efforts to their own efforts to succeed and perhaps become more motivated as a result.

To motivate yourself to get into shape, think of a list of reasons like the ones above. Think of all the reasons: good health, attractive appearance and so forth.

2. Belief

Building confidence

There is a special feeling that comes with success, Jose Silva says. The only way to get that special feeling is to have a success, which builds confidence. So how can you believe that you can do something if you have never done it before?

"We used to be told," Jose says, "to build our ladder to success from the failures that we had. We were told to learn from our failures.

"Now we know that there is a better way. Now we know that the best way to have new successes in the future is to build our ladder out of our previous successes."

When you stop and think about it for a minute, that is exactly what we were talking about in Chapter 2 when we talked about positive thinking.

Fill your mind with thoughts of what you desire. This will build your belief - your confidence - as well as your desire.

Your coach is a great help to you in this. Your coach will give you drills and tasks that you can accomplish, and these small successes will be used to help you achieve a greater success.

An interesting thing happens when you recall a success while at the alpha level: You accumulate spiritual energy, almost the same as if you actually just had the success.

Every time you enter your level and vividly recall and relive a success, especially when you recall the feelings associated with that success, you are making impressions on your brain that are very similar to the impressions you made when you actually had the success.

Remember the experiment you did in Chapter 1 to test your physical strength while thinking positive and negative thoughts? You found that a change took place in your body when you thought certain thoughts.

When you thought about successes that you had, your body, as well as your brain and mind, became prepared to expect success. To expect success is to be confident.

A word of caution here: Mental practice never takes the place of physical practice. You need to do both.

Golf great Lee Trevino told interviewer Dick Cavett, "If you practice enough, you have confidence."

Trevino suggested that instead of sitting in a chair and

watching television, get up, get a wedge and chip balls into the chair.

Notre Dame football coach Lou Holtz shares Trevino's viewpoint on the importance of physical practice. "The way to handle pressure is hard work," he says.

And former Italian national martial arts champion Giuseppina Del Vicario - known to her fans as Vidheya - points out that the best way to build confidence is to gain as much experience as possible.

"In the beginning you have to have hope," Vidheya explained. "With experience, you just need desire, because experience has shown you that it is possible."

Invest the time both physically and mentally, and be a champion.

3. Expectation

Expect the best

The third part of the formula, expectation, will be covered in more detail in Section 3, in which we discuss visualization and mental rehearsal. The main thing we want you to do now is get a clear idea of what you want to achieve.

For example, do you want to shoot scratch golf? Do you want to be on the Olympic team? Do you desire an athletic scholarship to college? Do you want to have a more attractive body? Do you want to get into condition so you do not run out of breath so quickly?

Keep an image in your mind of what you desire. It will attract you and draw you towards that success. There's an old saying that a ship without a rudder is unlikely to end up in any useful port. Your goal is like a rudder. It keeps you on course and keeps your expectation high.

You can't win unless you try

Former major league baseball great Duke Snyder, conducting a baseball camp for youngsters, told an interviewer, "I always tell them to swing hard, because they might throw the ball where you're swinging."

Approach anything in which you'd like to succeed as if it were baseball: When you swing the bat, maybe you'll strike out, or maybe the pitcher will hit your bat with the ball, but one thing is sure if you don't swing, you definitely won't get a hit.

Babe Ruth knew that. The "Home Run King" swatted 714 balls out of the park during his great career. Do you know how many times he struck out? More than 1,300 times! He is 24th on the all-time strikeout list, but nobody ever called him the "strikeout king." Do you know who the all-time strikeout leader is? The great Reggie Jackson.

Winners are people who aren't afraid to take a chance. Losers sit around and wait for the odds to improve. "Excuses are the crutches of the untalented," golfer Ken Venturi said. "Danny's great because he isn't afraid to lose," longtime Dallas Cowboys head coach Tom Landry said of quarterback Danny White.

Go ahead and swing. The pitcher just might hit your bat with the ball.

Refusing to lose

Some athletes use the bad feeling that comes with losing as a motivator. If you do this, just remember to keep positive mental images of what you want to accomplish.

"When I lose," world tennis champion Boris Becker said on the CBS Television program *60 Minutes*, "nobody can talk to me. They leave me alone."

His coach, Ion Tiriac, said, "His determination made me

choose him." Tiriac added, "The reason I selected Boris [to coach] is the look in his eyes, the fact that he wants it so much that's what makes him different from the others."

Tennis player Pat Cash, following his semifinal match against Jimmy Connors at Wimbledon, said, "I started winning when I started hating to lose."

Cash added that he got that attitude from Connors, who expresses it this way: "I hate to lose more than I like to win."

In a television interview during the 1985 U.S. Open, Connors said, "You get to a point in a match where you'll do anything to prolong it. In a match, I turn into an animal. I like that attitude."

Great race car drivers are never satisfied if there is another car ahead of them. A story about legendary stock car racing pioneer Curtis Turner illustrates this.

Try as he might, the story goes, Turner couldn't get around the lead car in a race one Sunday. He ran down into the infield but couldn't get by. He threw his car into the turn so hard that he hit the wall and still couldn't pass.

Finally, coming out of the fourth turn on the final lap, he used his bumper - he bumped the lead car so it spun out, and he got to the finish line first.

When Turner got back around the track to the start/finish line again, he stopped, jumped out of his car and immediately disqualified himself before anyone else could say anything.

Another sports figure, Jim McMahon, quarterback of the world champion Chicago Bears, described himself in one word for a CBS television interviewer:

"Competitive."

He continued, "I'm a poor loser. I've never been able to live with a loss." But he added, "I've learned to control it. I don't throw my helmet around anymore."

"Losing is worse than dying," legendary football coach George Allen said, "because you have to get up in the morning."

The only moment that matters

Champions also have the ability to play in the here and now.

Golf legend Bobby Jones, perhaps the greatest golfer who ever played, is reported to have said that the shot he had to make right now was always the most important shot of his life.

This shot, to Jones, was more important than any shot in the final round of the U.S. Open, the Masters or any other past tournament.

Why? "Because this is the only shot that I can do anything about," he said.

Great coaches encourage this kind of thinking in their players. "Our goal is not to win," Duke basketball coach Mike Krzyzewski said in the ESPN Television special *The Great Motivators*. "Our goal is to play together as hard as we possibly can. Winning takes care of itself if you do that."

And speaking of the great Bear Bryant, football coach at the University of Alabama, someone once said: "He didn't care as much about what plays you ran as how hard you ran the plays."

In other words, once a play began, Bryant wanted his players to only think about playing as hard as they possibly could at that moment not about strategy, momentum or anything else.

According to Jose Silva, "You can achieve any kind of goal you set for yourself if you make it the most important thing in your life and sacrifice everything else for it." But he doesn't necessarily think of that as success.

"To achieve success," he says, "you not only reach your goal but you are also able to take advantage of the benefits that come along with your accomplishments."

You'll show them!

Never let anybody take your dream away from you. You wouldn't believe how many outstanding athletes were doubted along their way to the top, but they wouldn't let others' opinions stand in their way. You can draw your inspiration from stories like these:

Joe Montana, Mark Rypien and Joe Theismann were all selected in the third round of the National Football League draft. All three were passed over more than 50 times before finally being drafted, but went on to quarterback their teams to Super Bowl victories.

Tom Brady was rejected almost 200 times before the New England Patriots drafted him 199th (when there wasn't anybody left that they wanted). Brady told them it was the best decision they had ever made. Now many people consider it the best draft pick of all time.

Orel Hershiser, whose pitching performances helped the Los Angeles Dodgers win the 1988 World Series and were an inspiration to everyone, seemed to have little chance when he was young.

He was small and slight of build. He didn't even make varsity until his junior year in high school.

At college (Bowling Green), he was cut from the team his freshman and sophomore years. "I dreamed of playing major league ball," he said. "I just kept trying."

Boxer Freddie Pendleton lost five of his first six amateur fights. He turned pro at 18 years of age - because he needed the money. After his first 25 fights, he had 12 wins, 12 losses and one draw. In 1991 he was world champion, with a record of 30 wins, 17 losses and three draws.

Walter Payton was one of the greatest running backs in the history of the National Football League. He recalls that in his first game, he carried the ball eight times for zero yards!

Freddie Benavides was told by pro scouts that he might have enough talent to play for a while with a second-tier baseball team. Benavides, who works to stay in shape year round and uses the Silva techniques, was a backup shortstop with the Cincinnati Reds during his first year.

Then he went to the new Colorado Rockies expansion team where he was a starter.

Then he moved to the world champion Toronto Expos. (You'll read his story in more detail in Chapter 6.)

Warren Moon could not find a college that would take him as a quarterback. He sent films to a junior college and got to play there. After college, the National Football League teams didn't think Moon could throw the ball at the professional level. So he went to Canada to play in the Canadian Football League and prove himself... again. He then joined the Houston Oilers as a free agent. Even though Moon started his NFL career much later than other quarterbacks, he remains one of the most successful quarterbacks in the history of the league.

Paul Anderson looked really strange to other weightlifters. He wasn't tall and muscular like other heavyweights. He was short and as wide as he was tall. At five foot ten inches in height, he weighed nearly 400 pounds.

When Paul went to Russia with the American team, the Russian fans laughed at him. They thought he was a mascot, brought along only because the American heavyweight was injured and couldn't lift.

At the first meet in Russia, the Russian heavyweight pressed 335 pounds, a new world record. Paul came out and shattered the record with an amazing press of 402 pounds! Nobody thought he was a mascot after that.

Jerry Rice, San Francisco '49ers wide receiver, told Dick Schapp in an interview televised in December of 1992: "I had to wait my turn. Then I dropped many balls." Rice said it was hard for him to concentrate. "The play book was so large. There was so much to learn."

Schapp asked Rice if he had ever thought about giving the sport up had ever thought that he just wouldn't make it. "Oh, many times," Rice answered. "My teammates helped, told me to hang in there, keep trying."

In answer to a question from a young viewer who called in, Rice said, "I don't think of myself as special, just somebody who practices a lot." Many people do think that Jerry Rice is special. He has scored more touchdowns than anyone else in history and is considered by many to be the best receiver of all time.

Again, never let anybody destroy your dream! "Cancel-cancel" them if they tell you that you can't do it, and imagine yourself doing it. Remember those who have done what people doubted they could do. Remember those like Jerry Rice who even doubted their own ability but hung in there and kept trying. You don't have to say "cancel-cancel" out loud (you don't want to frighten the person who's doubting you), but you must think "cancel-cancel" whenever anyone stomps on your dreams - or whenever you have moments of self-doubt.

Use your inner voice for effective training

As the Greek philosopher Plato said more than 3,000 years ago, it is important to know yourself. Know your body, what motivates you, what you like and dislike and what it takes to get you to make the effort necessary to become a champion.

Learn to listen to your body, but not at the beta level. At beta we push, push, push. We use effort at beta, our logic being: The more effort we use, the greater the results will be. And this is true, up to a point.

Your body knows what it needs, but you don't listen to your body with your ears or your emotions. You listen with your mind. And you observe the results you get when you do what your "inner voice" tells you to do.

Learn to enter your level and analyze your training routine. You will get a sense of what to do. Then do it, and observe the results.

At your level, you may get the feeling that you should practice a certain exercise in order to increase your strength, coordination or timing.

Then practice that exercise, and observe the results.

Did it help in the way that you imagined?

If so, you now have a "point of reference" for future exercise. If not, keep trying.

Remember that learning to play the mental game is much like learning a physical skill; you need to practice and develop your ability.

The first time you tried to hit a ball, throw a block or make a certain movement, you probably had some trouble doing it right. But as you practiced, you got better at it.

When you missed, you learned what not to do.

When you succeeded, you learned what to do.

It is the same with your mental training:

When you don't get the results you desire, then you know what doesn't work.

When you get the results you are after, then enter your level and review your success.

Create a point of reference for exactly what you did and how it felt.

Getting started

One of the most difficult parts of training for many people is getting started. Ed Bernd Jr. can attest to this. Many days, he says, he starts home in the evening thinking about how great it will be to work out with weights.

But by the time he arrives home, it is a different story. Ed no longer wants to put his body through all that work. How does he cope with that?

He recalls his reasons for working out: how good he'll feel, how he'll look and what he'll be able to accomplish. Sometimes he'll enter his level and motivate himself in this manner. But he has to be careful about just talking himself into remaining at level instead of working out.

If he still doesn't feel like working out, he just decides to get into his workout clothes and do a few simple stretching exercises.

After that, he tells himself, he'll stop. But a funny thing happens. The stretching feels pretty good, so he decides he'll take one more step and warm up with light weights.

"Just the warm-up weights, remember," he tells himself. "I'm not going to do any heavy lifting tonight."

Then another funny thing happens. He starts feeling so good that he decides to put a little more weight on the bar. Pretty soon he's in the middle of a heavy workout - and feeling great.

"Some of my best workouts have come on days like that when I was convinced that I was not going to work out," Ed says.

Sensible training

Your body has a great ability to adapt to what you ask it to do. If you pick up a heavy weight, more than you are accustomed to lifting, you will fatigue some of your muscle tissues. You will "break down" muscle fibers.

Your body makes note of this, and when it rebuilds those muscle fibers, it makes them a little bit stronger than before. Your body provides you with a little reserve of strength, a little more than is necessary to lift that weight. So, next time, you are able to lift even more weight.

Your body continues to provide you with a little extra strength in reserve each time. In order for your body to do this, though, it needs time. It needs a certain period of time when you are not stressing the muscles to their limit.

So, you need to rest in order to allow your body to repair and rebuild itself.

This rest period varies for different people.

Paul Anderson, who set Olympic records and made it into *The Guinness Book of World Records* as the world's strongest man, had such a rapid metabolism that he could train with thousands of pounds of weights all day long and into the night, and his body would recover overnight, so he could do it again the following day.

The average person, however, needs a full day's rest to recover from a heavy training program.

Bodybuilder Arnold Schwarzenegger said that when he was a teenager and wanted to become as big and strong as possible, he trained three or four times a week. As an adult competitive bodybuilder, he trained six days a week but trained each muscle group only twice a week. "I rested on Sundays," he said.

But even training three times a week can be overdone, Schwarzenegger cautioned in a column on training advice in *USA Weekend*.

"Some people can get into this schedule so hard that they

end up doing multiple sets on the days that they do work out. And that can lead to fatigue that reduces the quality of the training."

Most people over train. For some, this slows their progress, even causes them to lose rather than gain. For many others who can survive extremely heavy training routines, much of their effort is simply wasted.

Even now, Schwarzenegger admits, he has to remind himself not to over train. "Sometimes I get too ambitious and try to do too many things," he said in his column. "Many times, I've trained two or three times a day: weights in the morning, cardiovascular training at noon and then, in the evening, tennis for an hour and a half, two hours. You do that for a week or so, and you get totally wiped out, and it's difficult to recuperate."

It's a good idea to take periodic "vacations" from your training. Many weightlifters find it beneficial to take a week off every six weeks.

You do not need to train with the same intensity all the time. Weightlifters often train in "cycles." Some will gradually increase the load from week to week for six weeks, then take a week off. When they come back, they start with a lighter routine than before. Others will use light weights and high repetitions to work on their form and technique for a couple of weeks, then use the heaviest weight they can in one workout. Then they drop back and work on technique again.

Please do not use this advice as an excuse for laziness. Occasionally push yourself a little harder than normal and observe the results.

Enter your level and determine what is best for you. Then try it out and observe what kind of results you get. Eventually you will learn to hear what your body says to you. This is what the champions do.

Your Next Assignment

If you are learning to enter the alpha level on your own instead of in a live Silva seminar or with the free lessons at www.SilvaNow.com, then continue with your daily countdowns.

After completing your first 10 days of practice, you are ready for your next assignment.

Continue to practice your previous mental exercise, but shorten the countdown to 50 to 1.

When you have practiced for 10 days, you are ready to proceed to the next phase.

After you have practiced Mental Housecleaning for 10 days, and are satisfied with your results, you can add a new practice to your daily routine. (Of course, continue to practice Mental Housecleaning from now on.)

Now here is your new assignment:

1. Make a list of the reasons you have for wanting to succeed. You can add to your list at any time, as you think of more reasons. This will increase your desire.

2. Make a list of your successes. Recall how you felt when you were performing and how you felt when you succeeded. This will help you to have even more success in the future. It will also help you when you are feeling down because of a loss or a bad workout.

3. Write out what you want to accomplish in the future. Make sure it is something that you can picture in your mind. That is, instead of saying that you want to be a better athlete, specify the specific skills that you want to have.

Chapter 4

Know yourself

A blind golfer challenged club pro Juan Wood to a match. He explained that his caddie would position the club head on the ball for him and, once on the green, would stand over the hole and ring a little bell.

"How many strokes shall I spot you?" Juan asked.

"None," the blind golfer replied. "Just let me select the tee time."

The pro readily agreed. "What time shall we tee off?" Juan asked.

"Ten-thirty tonight," the blind golfer answered.

Work with what you've got

The better you know yourself and what you can expect of yourself, the greater your chances of becoming a champion. While it receives only a brief mention in some psychology books today, a little-known field of science known as morphology can be of tremendous help to you in determining the best training program for your specific body type.

Morphology was developed in the 1930s by William H. Sheldon, Ph.D., M.D., when he was investigating the relationship between people's physical sizes and shapes and their tendency to behave in certain ways. While people no longer put much stock in that aspect of Dr. Sheldon's research, his study of different body types has proven to be valuable to a number of athletes.

All you need to do is look around you to see that some people are big, some are small and others fall somewhere in between. We all inherit certain physical characteristics, and training and hard work have little chance of changing that fact - at least not with any techniques that we know of at the present time. These inherited characteristics include bone thickness, muscle quality (the natural thickness of muscle fibers), internal organs and even the outer skin.

"Everybody has different bone structure," according to Vera Christensen, a pioneer in women's physique training. She has operated health clubs and trained thousands of women and men since the early 1960s and was the women's editor for *Strength and Health* magazine for more than 30 years.

"Any good instructor can look at you and know what kind of training you need," she said.

How can you determine for yourself what your training needs are?

"Most people know what kind of bodies they have," Vera said.

"Women almost always know. When they buy clothes, they can tell. If the top part of their body is too small and the bottom part too big for the clothes, then they know what kind of body they have."

Classifying body types

Dr. Sheldon used a scientific approach to evaluating and classifying body types. He referred to it as somatotyping. He carefully photographed more than 4,000 men without their clothes on and documented the measurements of specific body parts, such as their wrist sizes.

With tons of measurements on which to base his comparisons, Sheldon was able to identify three basic body types. Additional research assured him that these types apply to women as well as men. They are:

- Endomorphs. These are the "big people." Examples would be a sumo wrestler, a big offensive lineman or a super heavyweight powerlifter. They have a "predominance of soft roundness throughout the various regions of the body," Dr. Sheldon wrote in his book *Varieties of Human Physique*. "The digestive viscera are massive and tend relatively to dominate the bodily economy," he stated.

• Mesomorphs. These are the people with the great athletic builds. You see them in every sport. Mesomorphs have a "predominance of muscle, bone and connective tissue," Dr. Sheldon wrote. "The mesomorphic physique is normally heavy, hard and rectangular in outline. Bone and muscle are predominant and the skin is made thick by a heavy underlying connective tissue."

• Ectomorphs. These are thin people with little or no muscularity - the classic "97-pound weakling." Dr. Sheldon notes that, "In proportion to his mass, the ectomorph has the greatest surface area and hence relative the greatest sensory exposure to the outside world. Relative to his mass he also has the largest brain and central nervous system."

Evaluating your potential

It is relatively easy to determine your body type. Take your clothes off and look in a mirror.

Vera Christensen has people send her photographs of their bodies, both front and side views, so that she can evaluate them and prescribe specific training routines for them.

You might want to have someone photograph you in the nude, or in your underwear if you are shy, and evaluate the photos.

Somehow we are often able to see what we want to see and block out what we are not comfortable with when looking in a mirror; with photos we see what's actually there.

Dr. Sheldon took all of his thousands of measurements from photographs, and reported that this was easier and more accurate than measuring the actual bodies. Compare your photos with pictures of various types of athletes. First find examples of endomorphs, mesomorphs and ectomorphs, then compare your pictures to theirs.

You can also go to a good trainer or coach and ask for a complete evaluation.

Dr. Sheldon noted that any coach who cannot quickly spot relatively small variations in physique will not be a successful coach because different training methods are required for different physiques.

Some common physiques

Wrist size is a good indicator of whether you have a light, medium, or heavy skeletal frame.

When you put on a watchband, which hole do you use? How does this compare with the hole your friends would use?

Compare your wrist size and ankle size to those of other people, and you will find out what type of skeletal frame you have.

For example, Ed Bernd Jr.'s wrist and ankle measurements are 6.3 inches and 9 inches, respectively, while Jose Silva's are 7.5 inches and 10 inches, even though he is a couple of inches shorter than Ed.

Vera Christensen has not established specific measurements for women, but notes that the following body types are the most common among women:

1. Small top, big bottom. These women usually need calf work.

2. Big top and middle (waist) and small bottom. Both hips and legs are small and need more development.

2a. Same body type except with rugged, muscular legs.

These women are usually shorter, but not always. While they can be excellent athletes, they are not good candidates for beauty contests.

3. Long legs and big upper hip area. The top portion of their body is usually quite well-proportioned. They often have flat feet, which tends to cause them to slump and leads to back problems.

Men have similar body types, Christensen said. Some of the most common male physiques are:

1. Broad shoulders, slim hips and legs.

2. Narrow shoulders, broader hips and waist, medium to thin legs.

3. Stocky all over and large-boned, like Jose Silva.

"I don't see too many really symmetrical women," Vera said. "There is a slightly higher percentage of symmetrical men than women."

While Dr. Sheldon used the same criteria to somatotype women as he did men, he observed some significant differences.

He noted, "Women are so much more endomorphic than men that at all ages they are heavier in proportion to stature."

In his book *Atlas of Men*, he also noted that in each of the three categories, women "are more closely massed about the center" of each classification and "are rarer at the extreme edges."

Training for your specific body type

In our physical education classes, we all went out and did our calisthenics together. Everybody did the same thing. And when we were tested, we were all expected to achieve the same goals: 10 pull-ups, 50 sit-ups and five laps. And whoever came in last had to do some extra push-ups.

But people are obviously different.

The 250-pound endomorph might be able to lift huge weights but is no match for the 110-pound ectomorph in a 1-mile race. We each need our own individual training routine.

Here are some guidelines for determining what kind of training routine you need:

1. If you have a large, strong body - if you're an athletic endomorph or a mesomorph - you can train for long periods several times a week. Like a body builder, you can use a six-day-a-week, twice-a-day training routine and probably still grow bigger and stronger.

2. If you have a smaller frame and your goal is to gain size and strength, then train for brief periods, using exercises that work the big muscles, and include at least one full day's rest between each workout.

3. You might need a combination of the two. If you have a small top and a big bottom, as Vera Christensen mentioned earlier, then use only a few heavy exercises for your upper body and a lot of repetitions of lighter weights for your lower body.

Enter alpha and listen to your body

Keeping in mind the guidelines above, along with other information from this chapter and recommendations of your coach or trainer, you can determine the best routine for you while in your alpha level.

While you are at alpha, you have access to much more information about yourself and your body than you have at beta. This is because you have conscious access to information that is stored in your subconscious mind.

By teaching people how to enter the alpha level with conscious awareness, Jose Silva found a way to convert the subconscious into an accessible inner conscious level.

Your inner-conscious mind knows what it takes to make your body strong and healthy.

When you convert the subconscious to an inner conscious level, you will make better decisions because you will have access to more information.

Using the information that you learn in this book, information from your coach or trainer and your mind's innate knowledge of your body and its needs, you will make much better decisions than you can by analyzing information and making decisions at beta.

After you analyze and make your decisions (while at the alpha level) about the type of training you need, you still need to verify that you have made the correct decisions. You do this by putting your decisions to the test physically and observing the results you get.

For example, if you feel at your level that you are not training as hard as you should, train harder and observe the results you get. If you make progress, you were correct. If not, enter your level and incorporate your experiences with your new training routine and analyze the situation again. Then you will again physically try out whatever decisions you make.

Whether you are right or wrong at your level, you can use this information to establish "points of reference."

In other words, you learn what works and what doesn't. You do the same thing in athletics. When something works, you know to keep practicing and get better at it.

If it doesn't work - if you grip the golf club a different way and all of your shots slice off into the woods then you know to avoid that grip.

Continue to use this kind of trial-and-error method at your level, and you will soon learn how to be a superstar at the mental game.

The basics

If you really want to be in good condition and experience athletic success, you need seven basic components in your training routine:

1. Stretching. This will provide flexibility and agility. Flexibility is associated with youth; stiffness with old age.

2. Aerobics. These are exercises that cause you to breathe heavier than usual for at least 20 minutes.

3. Strength. Exercise against resistance to give you a reserve of strength.

4. Coordination. Develop your timing and coordination with athletic activities, such as playing racquetball.

5. Nutrition. The development of your muscles and tissues and the proper functioning of your nerves and brain depend upon the food you put into your body.

6. Relaxation. Allow yourself sufficient relaxation and sleep to recuperate and grow stronger.

7. Mental. You need motivation, positive thinking, mental rehearsal and programming to help you achieve the success you desire.

Weight training guidelines for specific body types

1. Ectomorphs

If you are small-boned, have a light skeletal frame and small muscles and are a "hard gainer," then do not try to work your body for too long. Avoid long exercise sessions. One hour is usually enough. You do not have enough muscle tissue at this time to be able to tolerate longer workouts. You do not have the same amount of stored energy as the endomorph for recovering from drawn-out, exhausting workouts.

Work the big muscle groups - legs, back, shoulders, chest. Use heavy weights and low repetitions. Three sets of six are plenty for you. Do no more than 10 different exercises.

If you want to gain size and strength, three different exercises may be enough - squats for your legs, deadlifts for your back and presses for your shoulders.

Work hard and fast, then stop.

Avoid "shaping" exercises with light weights. Do only big, "quality" exercises.

Get plenty of rest. Take at least one full day off after your workout. If you are not making progress as quickly as you would like, try taking more time off to allow your body time to recover and rebuild.

If you are a hard gainer and want to gain muscular body weight, train no more than three times a week for no more than one hour each session.

Work fast, avoiding high repetitions except for "breathing squats."

To perform breathing squats, load the barbell with a weight you can handle for 10 repetitions - no more than about 10 to 15 pounds heavier than your body weight. Then do 20 repetitions with it.

After the first few repetitions, you will need to pause to take two or three deep breaths before performing the next squat. This one exercise will stimulate your entire body and cause you to gain muscle overall.

Besides the squats, exercise other large muscles with presses, deadlifts, power cleans, etc. exercises we discuss in detail in Chapter 17.

2. Mesomorphs

If you have a medium skeletal frame and good muscle size, then you can train harder. After a warm-up set, do a set of 10 repetitions, then add weight to each set until you can do only two or three repetitions. Do not take too much time between sets or between exercises.

You can do high repetitions for your abdominals and your calves. These muscles respond well to high rep work, and you should have sufficient energy reserves to handle this.

Do not start off by working out six days a week. Work your way up to that.

Monitor your progress closely, and remember that even though you may have a natural athletic build, your body still needs adequate rest.

3. Endomorphs

There is room on your large skeletal frame for a lot of muscle, even though it will not be as well-defined as on a mesomorph. You have a lot of body tissue, which gives you a lot of reserve energy.

You can do a lot of repetitions and a lot of sets in order to reach all of those muscle fibers in your big body. You can use virtually any exercise you desire. Vary your exercises to reach different muscle fibers.

You are a rapid gainer, and lifting very heavy weights can quickly pack the pounds onto you. In order to keep from gaining too much weight, you can use long exercise sessions - two or even three hours. But a word of caution:

Make sure you use most of that time for exercise, not for socializing, daydreaming, procrastinating, resting, thinking about your date for tonight - well, you get the point.

4. Mixed body type

If you are a female who has a common female body type - small top and large middle and bottom - you will need to use certain elements of each of the training routines just described.

For your upper body, use heavy weights and medium repetitions to increase your chest thickness, your back muscles and your shoulder size. Exercise your upper body two or three times a week, and give it time to grow.

For your waist, use high repetitions. You might want to do sit-ups five or six times a week.

To shape up your legs, use medium repetitions of appropriate exercises.

If you are a man with this body type, you may need to build up your arms, shoulders, back and chest, reduce your waist, build strong muscular abdominals and build strong, powerful leg and hip muscles. Power comes from your legs and hips.

Some advice for everyone, regardless of body type:

Study your physique.

Listen to your coach or trainer.

Analyze everything at your level, decide what to do, then monitor your results and make adjustments as necessary.

Your body knows what it needs. Learn to listen to it.

Learn to like yourself

Human beings seem to be born with a need to achieve and a desire to be the best. This accounts for the great progress we've made since we've been on this planet.

But this same drive can cause problems, too. We often want to be what we are not. For example, the big endomorph wants a lean body that will attract the opposite sex. The little ectomorph wants to be bigger than the bully; millions of "Charles Atlas" home study courses have been sold on this desire since the 1930s.

Even the naturally athletic mesomorphs are seldom satisfied. Some are willing to endanger their health with drugs - or other ways of enhancing their performance - to achieve that elusive thing called perfection. And people who strive for the unrealistic spend millions on diets to achieve that often unhealthy ideal of looking like a model or a movie star.

With so many people wanting to be what we are, why can't we just be happy with ourselves?

Unfortunately, many people want to be something they just can't be. Remember that your body has certain inherent characteristics. Alter it too much - with drugs, with diets, even with exercise - and you will pay the price.

A case in point: Jose Silva is not very tall - he stands five foot seven inches tall - but he has very thick bones. This makes for a stocky, muscular build. Even now, at 80 years old, he has biceps (the flexor muscle at the front of the upper arm) still measuring more than 15 inches.

Even though Ed Bernd Jr. is a couple of inches taller than Jose, he has a much smaller skeletal structure. His wrists are more than an inch smaller in circumference than Jose's. In fact, Jose's wrists are almost as big as Ed's ankles! Moreover, 15-inch biceps on Ed's ectomorphic body would be the equivalent of 18-inch biceps on an athlete with a large frame.

People who don't know any better ask why Ed doesn't look like a large bodybuilder, since he has been lifting weights regularly since he was a teenager in the 1950s.

His bones simply are not large enough to support that much muscle.

An ectomorph can have a well-defined muscular physique, but it just won't be as large as that of an endomorph.

When people look at Jose Silva's endomorphic body and ask him why he doesn't use his own Weight and Habit Control Technique to trim down, he says that might be the wrong thing to do.

Jose notes that the great tenor Mario Lanza would go on diets time and again to lose weight, only to regain it.

While there is no way to know for sure, Jose suspects that the stress produced on Lanza's body by this constant up-and-down weight situation might have contributed to his early death. (Why is Jose Silva so familiar with Lanza's life? Because Jose is also a talented singer and was once offered a scholarship to study opera in Milan, Italy. But that's another story.)

Plato was right when he advised, "Know yourself."

Use your level to get to know your body, then do what's best for it.

Learn to love who you are.

When you take advantage of your natural potential, you have the greatest chance of success and happiness.

Now here are your assignments for the next 10 days.

Assignments

1. Study your body. Look at it in the mirror. Study photographs of yourself that show your body in a swimsuit, for example.

How does your body compare with others' bodies?

Do you resemble a National Football League lineman with a very large abdominal area that contains a large digestive system, like a typical endomorph?

Do you have a slender build or have trouble gaining weight or muscle tissue, like an ectomorph?

Do you have a natural athletic build, like a well-trained athlete? Perhaps you have aspects of two, or even all three, of these body types.

Review the detailed descriptions in this chapter and analyze your body at your level.

2. Work with your trainer or coach to develop specific training routines for the areas of your body that need work.

3. If you are learning to enter your level by practicing the countdown exercises, then practice entering your level by counting from 25 to 1 every morning, and imagine yourself developing the body you desire.

Chapter 5

Relax, it's good for you

Just before reaching the top of the mountain he was climbing, a mountain climber named Cliff Hanger slipped and began to fall. He managed to reach out and grab onto a shrub that was growing out of the side of the mountain. He couldn't find a toehold and saw that the roots of the shrub were pulling out of the cliffside. Fearing that he had only a few moments before falling 1,000 feet to his death, he looked up for help. Seeing no one, he cried out, "Is there anybody up there who can help me?"

A voice from the heavens answered, "Yes. I am your guardian angel. I can help you. What do you need?"

"Get me back up on top," Cliff pleaded as the roots began to give way.

"Okay," the angel said. "I will get beneath you. Then let go, and I will catch you and place you back on top."

"Let go?" Cliff thought. After a few moments of silence he called out, "Is there anybody else up there who can help me?"

Loosen up!

When playing the mental game, you sometimes have to let go and relax if you want to get to the top.

At beta, in the physical world of the body, you can push yourself and use effort to reach your goals. At alpha, in the mental world of the mind, it is just the opposite: You must relax and attract what you desire.

We need a certain amount of stress, but not too much. You need a certain amount of tension in your muscles in order to use them. But too much tension will cause you to freeze up and not be able to function as you desire. When you become very tense and nervous - when stress becomes distress - that's when the problems begin.

If you can direct that tension into your performance, then you will reach new heights, set personal records and win.

That is what happened with Olympic champion Florence Griffith Joyner. She said that learning to relax helped her improve her times in the 200-meter race.

"For years my coach had told me to relax when I ran, but I didn't understand," she wrote in an advice column in USA Weekend. Then, two weeks before the national championships, she strained her hamstring. "I wanted to make the World Championship team," she recalled, "so I had to run fast but not too hard." She did and finished second, with the second fastest time in the world and her fastest time ever.

"When you try too hard, your body tenses up, which works against you," she explained. "So let your mind and body run free. Soon, your times will get better."

You have to practice relaxing? Yes!

You are going to learn Silva Method techniques that will help you relax. But just like any other skill, you have to practice relaxing if you want to get so good at it that you can relax even during a major competition.

The relaxation exercise developed by Jose Silva will teach you to relax whenever you need to, no matter what the circumstances.

But there's a catch:

You need to practice it - even when you don't need to relax, when you are not nervous or tense.

Why use it when you don't need it? For the same reason that you practice the other skills that you need in order to win: To get so good at it that you can do it without thinking about it.

Basketball coach Hector Chacon explained it this way:

"My players are very good at shooting free throws. But I make them practice them every day.

I don't make them shoot free throws so that they will get better.

I make them do it so that when they are in a tense situation - when the game is on the line - they won't have to think about what they are doing. It will be automatic.

"When a player is at the free throw line, we are two points behind and he has two shots, I don't want him thinking about whether he is going to make those shots or not," Coach Chacon continued. "I want him to be thinking about how he and his teammates can get the ball back and score again in those last two seconds so we don't have to go into overtime."

Relaxation plus alpha equals results

Jose selected a technique that uses only the mind to relax the body. Once you've learned to use your mind to relax your body, it becomes easier to use your mind for other things, such as improving your physical performance, healing your body or getting good grades so that you remain eligible for your school's athletic program.

Using your imagination at the alpha level is what makes it all possible. That's why it is important that you practice your countdown exercises every morning and learn to reach the alpha level quickly, whenever you desire.

Relaxation without entering the alpha level is also beneficial, but it won't give you the outstanding results you are seeking. Relaxing at the alpha level can make fundamental changes that will benefit you in many ways.

Anxiety: mind over matter

Scientists identify two different kinds of anxiety:

1. State anxiety: stress reaction caused by outside circumstances that threaten, anger or worry a person.

2. Trait anxiety: a person's predisposition to experiencing state anxiety when faced with a situation perceived as menacing.

We've all heard the saying that we cannot always control what happens, but we can control our reaction to it. The pass may be intercepted and run back for a touchdown. An athlete may fall and lose points, or lose a race.

These events can, and do, happen. Personality traits determine how an athlete responds to events like these.

Does the athlete regain his or her composure, or does the mistake worry the athlete so much that he or she cannot perform well after that?

Over the years, people develop ways of reacting to situations. In addition, some personality types are just more prone to worry than others.

Until now, "experts" have said that the only way to modify these behaviors is through long, drawn-out treatment.

You certainly could not expect a 40-hour program, presented over two weekends, to reverse years of behaving a certain way, the "experts" claimed.

But it works.

Defying the experts

Research conducted in 1984 under the direction of Dr. Moshe Almagor of the psychology department at Haifa University in Israel concluded that trait anxiety was "significantly lower" at the completion of the 40-hour Silva Method Basic Lecture Series when compared to levels of anxiety before the program. The researchers concluded that Silva Method graduates were not only able to act more relaxed (manage state anxiety), but actually were more relaxed (decreased trait anxiety) according to the research.

The subjects of the study were 70 pupils attending a religious state school. The subjects were divided into experimental and control groups.

Pupils in the experimental group were taught and practiced the Silva techniques, while the control group was given a course in computer games.

Both groups completed questionnaires, which would determine their anxiety level, before their courses, at the completion of their courses and then 10 weeks later.

What is so impressive about this study is not just that people were less anxious and more relaxed after the Silva training, but that they continued to become even more relaxed after the training. The average level of trait anxiety six months later was "significantly lower" again.

As you might expect, there was greater improvement for those who practiced regularly than for those who did not.

"These facts illustrate the importance of daily practice in reducing the level of trait anxiety," the report notes, "although the trait anxiety level of those who did not practice daily also improved considerably."

According to the researchers, the results of the study contradicted the theory that relatively short methods will not reduce the level of trait anxiety, only the level of state anxiety.

"The course provides efficient means for reduction of the level of trait anxiety," the research report states. "There are indications that, in spite of the influence of modifying variables, the method exerts significant influence on trait anxiety."

What makes the Silva System work? The researchers concluded that the secret was the ability of the individual to gain direct access to lower brain frequencies.

"The specific feature of the Silva Method is to teach the subject to think in a state of relaxation, and while he is in this state, to utilize proper programming techniques to accomplish fixed goals," the research report observes.

"The Silva Method is not hypnosis, because the subject is conscious and is completely in control of himself while practicing the techniques; he remains mentally active during the exercise, depending on no external agent.

"As opposed to biofeedback, [the Silva Method] provides techniques of the solution of specific problems, and it requires no apparatus."

Anything applied from the outside only treats symptoms. When you do it yourself, you treat the cause.

Strategies to relieve stress

What do you do to relieve stress, to dissipate the energies that build up when stress strikes?

- Many people take the "use it and lose it" approach. They use physical activity to get rid of all the energy that is stored in the body as the result of stress. A hard exercise session is great for dissipating unwanted stress, and at the same time it helps to get your body in shape.
- Other people say that music helps them unwind.
- For some a whirlpool is great, or a sauna.
- Some people use hobbies or other distractions.

Sometimes, in an attempt to get rid of stress that has become so uncomfortable that it is really distress, people resort to things that create other problems: They eat, drink or get into trouble.

- One thing that everybody can do to relieve stress is meditate. Enter your level and spend 15 minutes relaxing your body and mind. This will drain away excess stress, and you will come out refreshed and ready to go.

Instant stress reducers

Here are two strategies you can use to short-circuit stress and cut it off any time it strikes:

1. Take a deep breath, and as you exhale, relax. This is something that coaches frequently tell athletes to do. It's an easy way to relax.

2. Use the "solution technique" instead of what most people use the "worry technique." Instead of worrying about what has already happened, stop, take a deep breath and relax as you exhale, then think about the solution.

Remember the Mental Housecleaning technique that we taught you in Chapter 2? Whenever you begin to think of a mistake or a problem, pause, take a deep breath and as you exhale, relax and think of your goal. Imagine yourself performing perfectly. Recall a time when you performed perfectly, when you were "in the groove."

Stress for success

You can make up your mind to use stress constructively to help you win. The first step is to be able to tell when you are experiencing stress.

How do you know when you are under stress?

Do you feel a knot in your stomach?

Do your muscles tense up?

Does your performance suffer?

If there were a way that you could use that energy to help you perform better - to come out on top - you would probably like to know more about that, wouldn't you? You are about to learn two Silva techniques, progressive relaxation and the Three Fingers Technique, that can help you control stress and perform better - immediately.

We recommend that you practice these exercises at least once a week.

Progressive Relaxation

You have already practiced counting backward for 30 days. For the next 10 days, shorten your ritual and count backward from just 10 to 1. When you have completed the 40 days, you should be able to reach the alpha brain wave level by the time you get to the count of one. (The alpha brain wave level, defined earlier, has between seven and 14 pulsations, or cycles, per second.)

To help ensure that you are reaching this level, you can practice the following additional exercise, called "progressive relaxation" to accelerate the relaxation process.

Progressive relaxation is the process of being aware of different muscle groups in your body, concentrating on them and relaxing them specifically. It is usually done starting at the top of the head and going all the way down to your feet.

As you hold this book in front of you, eyes open, reading the instructions, actually perform progressive relaxation. Then, tomorrow morning, you will be able to do it without the book.

First, turn your attention to your scalp. Be aware of your scalp - feel it, know it is there. Feel it in the form of a tingling sensation or of warmth caused by the blood circulating within it. If you relax your scalp, it will circulate even better. Relax your scalp.

Next do the same with your forehead. Be aware of your forehead. Let your imagination help you feel the tingling sensation, the feeling of warmth caused by circulation. Relax your forehead.

Relax your eyes and the tissues surrounding your eyes. Feel the tingling sensation and the feeling of warmth, then relax your eyes and the tissues surrounding your eyes.

Now concentrate your sense of awareness on your throat and on the skin that covers your throat. Sense the tingling sensation and the feeling of warmth caused by circulation, then relax your throat.

Continue relaxing your body one part at a time. Be aware of your shoulders, your chest, your abdomen. Notice your clothing in contact with each part of your body, and the tingling sensation and feeling of warmth. Then relax that part of your body and move on to the next part.

Continue in the same manner to become aware of the rest of your body, part by part, relaxing each in turn: Your thighs, your knees, your calves and your feet - your toes, soles and heels.

Even though you are still reading, still mentally active, you should be able to feel the physical relaxation that you have just induced. You will know what to do tomorrow morning in order to enjoy this same deep physical relaxation. You will use progressive relaxation just before you begin your countdown.

And remember to continue to practice this progressive relaxation at least once a week after the 10 days are completed. It will help you to maintain your ideal level of mind.

3- Fingers Technique

While at your level, you can program yourself to be more relaxed in stressful situations. You will use a technique called the Three Fingers Technique. In the Silva Method Basic Lecture

Series, we use the Three Fingers Technique for stronger self-programming and to help produce a better memory. You will learn how to use it to stay calm and manage your energies in stressful situations.

First, enter your level as you have been taught to do.

Once at your level, you can program yourself for relaxation. The first step is to bring together the tips of the thumb and first two fingers of either hand or both hands. Bring them together, forming a circle with them.

A lot of energy radiates out of your body through your fingertips. This technique re-circulates some of that energy so that you can use it for stronger self-programming.

At the same time, this technique serves as a physical trigger mechanism. Every time you bring together the tips of your thumb and first two fingers, whatever you programmed will happen.

After bringing together the thumb and first two fingers of either hand, or both hands, tell yourself mentally, "Anytime I am tense and want to relax, all I need to do is bring together the tips of the thumb and first two fingers of either hand, or both hands, as I am doing now, take a deep breath and, as I exhale, relax physically and mentally. And this is so."

Reinforce this at level from time to time.

Then, when you need to relax, all you need to do is bring together the tips of your thumb and first two fingers, take a deep breath and relax as you exhale.

Section 2: Program yourself for success

This section contains basic visualization and mental rehearsal techniques that you can use at your level to help you perform better.

Advanced techniques to use when you are actually performing to help you improve your performance are also included.

We recommend that you select one of the mental imagery techniques in Chapter 6 and practice it until you are satisfied with your results, then select other techniques from this section or any other section of the book, as you need them.

Always expect perfect results; however, remember that any progress is good.

Any time that you have a success, do these two things:

1. At your first opportunity, enter your level and review the success at your level. Recall how you programmed, how you felt when you programmed, how you felt when you performed and how you felt when you succeeded.

2. When you are ready to program again, first recall your most recent success. Recall how you programmed, how you performed and how you felt. This will help you to enter the same state of mind again and to be just as successful again or even more successful than you were before.

Chapter 6

The mental imagery of the superstars

Can an athlete be too good? Is it possible that you can be so good that you can actually hurt your team? Some people think so, but not John Madden. Madden was the first coach in the National Football League to win 100 games in his first 10 years. His success as a sportscaster has been just as impressive as his results in coaching.

One Sunday afternoon, Madden and his broadcast partner Pat Summerall were covering a Washington Redskins game.

Summerall, who had been a kicker in the NFL before he went into broadcasting, commented that punter Reggie Roby, who had been released by the Miami Dolphins and picked up by Washington, had been criticized for outkicking the coverage. He kicked the ball so high and so far, critics claimed, his teammates couldn't get downfield in time to tackle the punt receiver.

"They said the same thing about my kicker when I was coaching," Madden said. "I told him to go ahead and kick the ball as far as he could, and if they couldn't cover it, I'd go get some guys who could. Some receivers complained that my quarterback threw the ball too hard," Madden continued. "I told him to throw it as hard as he needed to, and if they couldn't catch it, I'd go get some guys who could."

Madden's record-setting performance over a 10-year period should be enough to silence any critics.

Do whatever it takes to be the best you can possibly be, and find other players who are willing to do the same.

Effective mental rehearsal

To help them to be the best they can possibly be, many athletes study films of their past performances. Studying game film has been a standard practice in sports for almost as long as there's been film. And now, with the advent of low-cost, lightweight video cameras, virtually all athletes can see themselves in action in order to analyze their performance and make improvements. At the end of this chapter, you will learn how to conduct this kind of review and analysis at your level whenever you desire - using the Silva Three Scenes Technique.

After the review and analysis is completed, athletes go onto the field, into the gym or onto the court and begin their physical practice.

There's a mental equivalent to this physical practice - a technique you can use to mentally simulate physical practice.

- At your level, you can imagine that you are at the place where you practice or compete.

- Then you can imagine yourself performing the way you desire.

- You can imagine yourself improving and reaching your goals.

- You can also get your feelings involved, which will make your programming even more powerful.

You will learn how to do all this with the Silva Mental Rehearsal Technique at the end of this chapter.

In Chapter 1, you read about field hockey players who improved dramatically when they incorporated mental training, along with physical training, into their routines. They spent as little as two-and-a-half minutes at their level and made tremendous improvements in their shooting skills.

But can a technique that helps teenage students improve also work for professional athletes?

Well, it did for Freddie Benavides. He used Silva techniques to help him make it to the big leagues. Here is his story.

Local athlete makes it to the major leagues

Freddie Benavides had a dream. Like a lot of youngsters, he wanted to be a professional baseball player. He's been playing the game for as long as he can remember. "I just enjoy doing it," he said. "I like to make all the good plays. Of course, it's nice to have all the attention."

But Freddie had no role models because nobody from his hometown of Laredo, Texas, had ever grown up to become a major league baseball player. Following college, Freddie was drafted by the Cincinnati Reds organization. In February of 1991, after spending a year in the Cincinnati Reds minor league farm team in Nashville, Freddie was looking for any kind of help he could get. While at home in Laredo, he and his wife Violeta attended the Silva Method Basic Lecture Series.

Freddie and Violeta started programming. They used visualization and imagination at the alpha level to program to get hits. They programmed for Freddie to be a better infield player. They programmed for him to get called up to the big leagues. That last one was a long shot; the Reds had an all-pro shortstop, one of the best in the game. But Freddie and Violeta kept programming for him to make it to the big leagues.

"After the class I was into it," Freddie recalled. "We programmed during spring training a lot, and during the season we tried to do it.

"But I was really struggling. I'd never struggled like that. I was giving up on it, but Violeta kept pushing me. She would program. She would try to do it."

For a while, Freddie recalled, it looked like his career might be coming to an end in Nashville.

"There was a time that they said he was finished, that he couldn't play," Violeta recalled. "He was trying to be positive. I was trying to be positive - talk to him, help him," Violeta said.

"I'd tell him, 'Forget about everything else, today you're going to get a hit.' And that day it wouldn't happen. He would come home again depressed. Then the next day, he'd say again, 'I'm going to get a hit.' And he didn't do it again. It got to the point that it had been said so many times, he told me, 'Violeta, nothing ever happens.' It got very frustrating for both of us."

But baseball is a game of frustration, and only those who can cope with failure can succeed.

"In baseball," Freddie explained, "you succeed 30 percent of the time. You need to get a hit three out of 10 times, and you're considered a great hitter. That's 30 percent - a .300 hitter. You fail seven times, so you are going to fail the majority of the times at bat.

"It's just one of those types of sports," he continued. "It's a game of failure, really, because 70 percent of the time you're failing as a hitter. That's why baseball is tough."

Even though Freddie and Violeta got discouraged, they continued to program. Then the big break came. On May 12, 1991, three months after completing the Silva Method course, they got the call: The Reds' starting shortstop had been injured and was out for a couple of weeks. Two days later, Freddie's dream came true: He was in the game.

"He wasn't called up because he was hitting," Violeta said, "but because somebody got hurt, and they needed somebody to help. And he was great over there. He hit great."

When the starter came back, Freddie went back down to the minor league farm team in Nashville.

"That's my role - filling in," Freddie said. "But hopefully I opened a lot of eyes. I said, 'Well, I'll get called back up again.' It worked out pretty well." He did get called back up and contributed as a utility infielder, able to play any position in which he was needed.

He opened some more eyes with his play that season and was signed by the new Colorado Rockies expansion team, a team for which he could be a starter.

On opening day of the 1993 season, Freddie Benavides was in the starting lineup for the Colorado Rockies.

The following season he was signed by the defending world champion Montreal Expos - the best baseball team in the world.

All this from a player that the big league scouts said could not play for a top-tier team.

Ed Bernd Jr. sat next to a major league scout one day while flying back from a course in Las Vegas. The scout mentioned that he remembered evaluating Freddie. He said he felt that Freddie did not have the talent to play for a top-tier team, but he might be good enough to play for a second-tier team long enough to qualify for a pension - six seasons. "I'm sorry," he had said, "but that's all I see for him."

The mental game is the key to success

Freddie and Violeta agree that their programming helped make the dream come true.

"We just kind of did it, and it clicked," Freddie recalled about those difficult days in Nashville. "I got called up to the major leagues, and I guess the confidence level went up. We started setting goals, and we both started reaching goals.

"I started hitting the ball well - brought my average back up. Everybody has slumps. You just have to get out of it. There's a lot of pressure, trying to get up to the big leagues - a lot of stress."

When it comes to being successful in the big leagues, the mental aspect of the game is the key, Benavides said. "They say the game is 90 percent mental. It's true," he emphasized.

You've got to do your programming and preparation ahead of time, Freddie emphasized. If you don't program until you are in a bind, it is too late. You have to program until it becomes automatic.

"Once you step to the plate, you've got to clear your mind, just see the ball and hit the ball, and let your muscle memory take over," Freddie said. "A lot of repetition, muscle memory, and then your mind works. I was thinking too much at the plate, and nothing happened.

"I was trying to be all mental, to use positive visualization. You can't," he added.

Freddie says that he usually programs once a day - "at night when we're ready to go to sleep. We use visualization. We imagine reaching all the goals we set. I imagine being at bat, hitting line drives, base hits, stuff like that."

Freddie Benavides proved that he has something inside him that has taken him far beyond where his natural talent could. He may not have had any role models in Laredo when he wanted to play major league baseball, but now he is serving as a good role model for anyone who wants to reach his or her goals.

Visualization and imagination

Let's take a moment to review some terminology:

•   You see with your eyes. Any time you attempt to focus your eyes, even if they are closed, your brain will speed up to the beta frequency.

•   To visualize means to recall something that you have seen, or imagined, before. When you recall what something looks like, you are visualizing. It is not the same as seeing.

•   Imagination is thinking about what something looks like that you have never seen or imagined before.

You *see* your coach with your eyes.

When you remember what your coach looks like, that is called *visualization*.

If you imagine your coach getting drenched with the water bucket after you win the championship, you are using your *imagination*.

Later, when you recall the image of the coach being drenched, you are visualizing, because you are recalling something that you have experienced before.

The secret behind successful visualization

Many superstar athletes express the importance of visualization to their success.

In the classic book *Psycho Cybernetics*, author Maxwell Maltz mentions a *Time* magazine report in which golfer Ben Hogan describes how, when he is playing in a tournament, he mentally rehearses each shot just before making it. He makes the shot perfectly in his imagination - "feels" the club head strike the ball just as it should, "feels" himself performing the perfect follow-through - and then steps up to the ball and depends upon what he calls "muscle memory" to carry out the shot just as he has imagined it.

Another golf pro, Jack Nicklaus, claims that hitting good shots depends 10 percent on his swing, 40 percent on his setup and 50 percent on his mental picture. And pro golfer Jane Blalock told *Woman's Day* magazine, "I go into the locker room and find a corner by myself and just sit there. I try to achieve a peaceful state of nothingness that will carry over onto the golf course. If I get that feeling of quiet and obliviousness within myself, I feel I can't lose."

Meditation and visualization have also become quite popular in a sport very different from golf - rodeo riding. Champion bronco bull rider Larry Mahan told author Jack Ludwig in *Games of Fear and Winning,* "I try to picture a ride in my mind before I get on the bull. Then I try to go by the picture."

Several other athletes tell how visualization and meditation fit into their routines:

• Fran Tarkenton, who broke most passing records during his National Football League career, reported that he would spend the entire week before a game going through every aspect of it in his mind.

• "I try to do some form of meditation every day," basketball star Bill Walton told an interviewer.

• During the 1984 Los Angeles Olympics, you could see Dwight Stones, a gold medalist, standing with his head shaking and bobbing before he attempted his high jump, according to authors Steven Ungerleider and Jacqueline Golding in *Mental Practice Among Olympic Athletes.* According to this book, Stones explained, "My success in the jump was directly related to the image of my body clearing the bar. When I didn't get the proper visual picture on my personal screen, I would shake my head and erase it until the correct image emerged."

While these athletes did not use the Silva techniques, the principles they used are the same. Their visualization worked for them because they are probably among the 10 percent of the population who are natural alpha thinkers, even though they may not realize it. In fact, that is one of the problems: These superstars will tell you that all you need to do is visualize, believe and concentrate, and you will be as successful as they are - without realizing that their visualization, belief and concentration are done at a different dimension than that used by 90 percent of the population.

If not done at the alpha level, visualization is not enough. The only people who succeed with these athletes' techniques are the natural alpha thinkers - and people like you who have learned to enter the alpha level and apply their techniques at this level.

Now that you can enter alpha, you are ready to learn specific visualization techniques to help raise your performance to a higher level.

Preprogram the technique to work for you

Before we give you the techniques, let us explain how you will "install" the programs.

In order to use a personal computer, you need to install a program - a set of instructions - into the computer first. Then when you want to use the computer, you turn it on, call up the program that has been installed and use it.

Programming yourself works the same way:

• First, you turn on your biocomputer by entering the alpha level.

• At that level, you "install" the technique.

• Then when you need to use the technique you have programmed, you enter your level and call it up.

Here is how to "install" the various techniques you are about to learn:

1. Enter your level with the 5 to 1 method.

2. Tell yourself mentally that any time you desire to use the Silva Three Scenes Technique (or any technique you desire to install), you will be able to do so in the following manner.

3. Then mentally go through the steps of the technique.

4. Remind yourself that you can enter your level and use this technique any time that you desire.

5. Count yourself out of your level.

Jose Silva's 3- Scenes Technique

In order to solve a problem or reach a goal with the Three Scenes Technique, you must first enter your level. Once in your level, imagine that you are in a room where you can watch videos of your performance. Imagine that there are three video monitors in this room. They are placed at such a height that you must turn your eyes upwards slightly, about 20 degrees, to look at them.

The first monitor, directly in front of you, is numbered Monitor Number 1. The second monitor is to the left of the first one - towards your left - and is numbered Monitor Number 2. The third monitor is still further to the left and is numbered Monitor Number 3.

On the monitor directly in front of you, Monitor Number 1, project an image of the problem or the condition that you desire to change. Project an image of yourself looking or performing a certain way that you would like to change. Study this problem image.

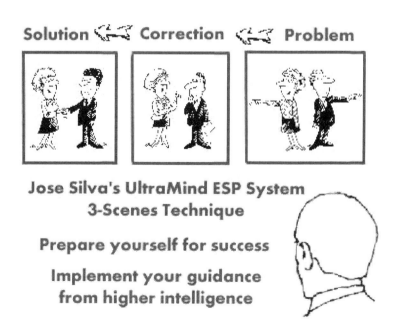

Now, in Monitor Number 2, imagine yourself doing what is necessary to correct the problem.

Mentally picture yourself doing the exercises necessary to bring about your desired end result, and imagine the desired changes beginning to take place.

When you are programming in Monitor Number 2, the center monitor, recall how you feel as you begin to exercise, and imagine your body beginning to respond the way you desire.

As you continue to visualize yourself exercising, recall how you feel when you are halfway through the exercise.

Feel and imagine your muscles growing, becoming more firm. Sense unwanted fat being burned as you expend energy.

Feel and imagine your body performing better than before.

Imagine how you look and feel as you complete your exercise.

Imagine the feeling of your muscles responding to the exercise, growing larger, stronger, firmer.

After you have visualized and then imagined yourself exercising and developing the kind of physique and skills you desire, then direct your attention to Monitor Number 3, farthest to your left, and imagine yourself the way you want to be - your desired end result. (If you have already created such an image when using this technique previously, then use that image.)

You may wish to recall an athlete you admire, and imagine yourself equaling and exceeding this person's development. Imagine people praising you for your achievement, and imagine these people using you as a role model and imitating the good things you have accomplished.

In the future, any time you happen to think of your project, visualize the "solution image" you have projected onto Monitor Number 3. Once you have created the image of yourself the way you desire to be in Monitor Number 3, you simply recall this image in the future. Recalling something you have imagined is what we refer to as visualization.

An important note:

The first time you use this technique for a particular problem, begin with Monitor Number 1, but after that, when you program, begin with Monitor Number 2 - unless you have noticed improvements with that particular problem.

As you notice improvements in your body or performance, be sure to alter the "problem image" in Monitor Number 1 accordingly.

You may program with this technique prior to every training session, workout or athletic event.

Silva Star Athlete Mental Rehearsal Technique

Before you perform this exercise at your level, you must actually go to the place where you practice and go through a practice session. Have your coach with you, guiding you through each part of your practice correctly.

As you go through each movement, pay special attention to how you feel physically and impress this feeling upon your mind so you'll remember how it feels. This is what we mean by establishing points of reference.

Make an impression of how it feels when you are one-fourth through the movement. Make an impression of how it feels when you are halfway through the movement or exercise, then again three-quarters of the way through and again at the completion of the movement.

For example, if you want to improve your golf swing, first you will make an impression of exactly how it feels physically when you address the ball. How does it feel when you start your backswing? How do you feel halfway through your backswing?

At the top of your backswing? Make these impressions throughout your swing, as you are actually swinging the club. When you do this, have your coach there to make sure that you are doing it correctly.

Repeat this for every movement: your chip shots, putts and so on.

Keep making these impressions as you go - impressions at each step. Later, recall the feeling, and you will be there, feeling as though you have practiced, as though you had actually done the movements.

Once you have made the impressions physically, you can practice any time you desire, even lying in bed. By doing this, you get the benefits of practice, but without fatiguing your body.

While at your level, you will bring back and visualize the feeling that you had when you performed the movements physically, and your body will respond the same way.

Practicing at level

After you have made these impressions physically, you are ready for your mental practice.

Enter your level and project yourself mentally to the place where you practice or compete. Notice your surroundings.

Once you have projected yourself mentally to the place where you practice or compete, imagine yourself performing the way you desire. Imagine yourself improving and reaching your goals.

This technique differs from the Three Scenes Technique in that you are not observing a picture of yourself performing, but you feel as if you actually are performing.

Notice how you feel as you make each movement. Imagine the feeling of your body responding and becoming stronger, more flexible and better at performing the movements required of your sport.

Imagine your timing improving, along with your athletic skill. Imagine your mental faculties becoming so keen that you can automatically predict any move anybody makes and outperform them.

You can play out a complete practice session or a competitive event with your imagination in this manner. At the end, imagine yourself being congratulated for your performance.

In order to make strong impressions of the special feeling of success, whenever you have a success, as soon as possible, enter your level and review your performance. Recall how you felt when you were successful. This will help you to be even more successful in the future.

Chapter 7

Advanced techniques

While taking a shortcut across a field, track star Jim Shorts noticed that a bull was coming his way. He began to walk faster. The bull, noticing this, began to trot towards Jim. Jim broke into a run. The bull began to run, also.

When the bull was gaining rapidly, Jim spotted one lone tree. He figured he just barely had enough time to get to the tree - much less climb up it - before the bull got to him. But there was a bigger problem: The lowest branch on the tree was 20 feet above the ground.

Jim was a good athlete, but he had never jumped that high before. Of course, he'd never had to jump that high before, so maybe he would have enough adrenaline to do it.

When Jim got to the tree, he leaped up into the air with all his might - and missed the branch. But it didn't matter; he caught it on his way back down!

How to achieve more than you ever dreamed

Would you like to know how to train and compete at peak efficiency at all times? Would you like to learn how to motivate yourself to perform to the best of your ability - to call on a power deep within yourself to bring out your best at any time?

There might not always be a bull available to motivate you. But you can have your own personal trainer or coach with you at all times - mentally - using a technique developed by Jose Silva especially for athletes.

This technique involves creating a Mental Coach, who will always be with you when you are planning and making decisions, training, practicing and competing.

A second technique developed by Jose - Dream Control - will help you get information about how to train better, perform better and correct mistakes.

Athletes often say their dreams have given them valuable information.

Golfer Jack Nicklaus, for example, had a dream that helped him recover from a slump during a tournament:

"I was hitting them pretty good in the dream, and all at once I realized I wasn't holding the club the way I've actually been holding it lately," said Nicklaus, as quoted in William C. Dement's book *Some Must Watch While Some Must Sleep*.

"So when I came to the course yesterday morning, I tried it the way I did in my dream, and it worked. I shot a 68 yesterday and a 65 today."

Nicklaus added, "I feel kind of foolish admitting it, but it really happened in a dream. All I had to do was change my grip just a little."

Basketball Coach Hector Chacon of Laredo's Martin High School once dreamed about a new defense, a surprise strategy his team could slip into the game in the final quarter. The team would then go back to their regular defense once the other team realized what was going on.

Chacon put his new "mosquito defense," as he called it, into the game, baffled his opponents and won a championship for his team and accolades for himself as coach of the year.

You can learn to remember your dreams and then program dreams to provide you with information that you can use to solve problems, just as Jack Nicklaus and Hector Chacon did.

But first, here's how to use the Mental Coach technique that Jose Silva created for the Silva Star Athlete System:

Jose Silva's Mental Coach Technique

Take a moment now to think of someone you admire, someone whose accomplishments inspire you to achieve greater things yourself.

Who inspires you?

Who do you consider a hero? Perhaps it is a sports star. Or maybe a parent. Or a coach, a scout leader, a teacher, a trainer, a friend.

Perhaps you know more than one person who has inspired you, or who could inspire you. Which one could help you the most?

What has this person done or said that has inspired and encouraged you?

If your role model is a sports champion, then perhaps you have read articles about this person or seen him or her on television. What could this person say to you, to encourage you?

Now, how would you like to have your own personal coach - to be with you whenever you desire, to help you, to advise you, to motivate you and to encourage you to do your best and exceed your goals?

Your Mental Coach can have all the characteristics of someone you know, combine the best characteristics of several people or possess characteristics you have created yourself because you feel they would be most helpful and inspiring in your Mental Coach.

Your Mental Coach will be your own creation and will do anything you ask to help you, so use your imagination to create what you want most.

This is one of the most powerful techniques ever devised to help you reach deep within yourself for inspiration, motivation, creative ideas and guidance.

When you use your Mental Coach, you will really be using the wisdom that you already have within you to help you achieve your goals.

When you are planning your training, you can ask your Mental Coach for guidance.

When you are training or competing, you can imagine your Mental Coach there with you, encouraging you, telling you, "Come on, you can do it! Just a little more, one more time! Go for it!"

Imagine how valuable it will be to have someone like this alongside you during your workouts. Imagine how valuable it will be to talk over your goals, training routines and nutritional program with someone knowledgeable.

Of course, you are using your imagination for all of this.

You may have to imagine both sides of the conversation - what you would ask and what your Mental Coach would answer. But the answers may surprise you.

The ideas that come to you, that you think of at level, when using this technique, may be ideas you never expected, thoughts you never thought before.

To create your Mental Coach, enter your level as you have been taught. Once you are at your level, think of the person whose confidence and courage you admire. You can use your memory of this person as a Mental Coach. Your Mental Coach can help you achieve superior performance whenever you desire.

Whenever you are training, practicing or competing, recall your Mental Coach, and imagine that your Mental Coach is right there with you, encouraging you, guiding you, helping you to do your best. Whenever you desire, you can enter your level and talk with your Mental Coach. You can ask for guidance in your training, nutrition or any other subject and then imagine what your Mental Coach would advise you.

Use dreams to get information & solve problems

There is no such thing as a problem without a solution. There are only problems for which we don't yet have enough information in order to know the solution.

Dreams are one way to find out such information. We saw that idea in action when Hector Chacon had a dream about a new defense and used that defense to help his high school basketball team win a championship.

Have you ever had a dream that contained information that helped you correct a problem? Have you ever had a precognitive dream - a dream about something that then happened the next day or within a few days?

Many people have had such dreams, and scientists assure us that everyone dreams, though not everyone remembers their dreams. Using the Dream Control technique, you can learn to remember your dreams and then "program" a dream that will contain information to help you solve a problem.

Dream Control involves three steps:

1. Learning to remember one dream each night.

2. Learning to remember several dreams each night.

3. Learning to generate a dream that you can remember, understand and use for problem-solving.

A typical sleep-and-dream cycles, last about 90 minutes. After you fall asleep, you spend most of the first cycle in the very deep delta brain wave regions and have a very short dream at the end. In the second cycle, you do not go as deep, and you have a longer dream at the end. In the final cycle, you do not go very deep, and you have a long dream at the end.

If you wake up too early, you will not remember your dream. If you wake up in the middle of a dream, you may be confused.

If you wake up at the end of a dream, you can remember, analyze and interpret it.

Before we give you the specific instructions for Dream Control, let's discuss a few things about understanding your dreams.

Dreams are very personal. We each have our own unique experiences in life, and so each of us adopts unique patterns of symbolic expressions for the events of our lives.

You won't learn about the meaning of your own personal dream symbols by reading a book on dream interpretation. You can learn about the symbols in your dreams by keeping a dream log or a dream diary.

When you awaken with a dream, write down a brief account of the dream. Be sure to write it down as soon as you have it - transfer it to the physical dimension or you may lose it.

In the morning when you awaken, enter your level and ask yourself, "How could this dream relate to what has been happening in my life?" This will help you to understand what your dreams mean.

Now, if you want to use dreams to help you solve problems, follow these instructions:

The Silva Dream Control Technique

Dream Control is a mental technique that you can use to practice remembering dreams. It will help in your development of mental control. Use this technique when you are in bed and ready to go to sleep.

Dream Control Step 1. To practice remembering a dream, you will enter level as you have learned.

Once at your level, you will mentally tell yourself, "I want to remember a dream, and I am going to remember a dream." You will then remain at your level and go to sleep from your level.

You will awaken during the night or in the morning with a vivid recollection of a dream. Have paper and a pencil ready to write it down.

When you are satisfied that Dream Control Step 1 is working, go on to Dream Control Step 2.

Dream Control Step 2. To practice remembering dreams, you will enter level as you have learned.

Once at your level, you will mentally tell yourself, "I want to remember my dreams, and I am going to remember my dreams." You will then remain at your level and go to sleep from your level.

You will awaken several times during the night or in the morning with vivid recollections of dreams. Have paper and a pencil ready to write them down.

When you are satisfied that Dream Control Step 2 is working, start with Dream Control Step 3.

Dream Control Step 3. To practice generating a dream that you can remember, understand and use for problem-solving, you will enter your level as you have been taught.

Once at your level, mentally tell yourself, "I want to have a dream that will contain information to solve the problem I have in mind." State the problem and add, "I will have such a dream, remember it and understand it."

You will then go to sleep from your level.

You may awaken during the night with a vivid recollection of the desired dream, or you may awaken in the morning with a vivid recollection of such a dream.

You will have this dream, remember it and understand it.

Chapter 8

Triggers and other ways to get "in the groove"

A young soldier ran out of bullets during battle. His sergeant told him to keep shooting and to shout, "Bangety-bang! Bangety-bang!" each time he pulled the trigger. The soldier did this, and to his surprise, enemy soldiers fell in front of him.

But then one enemy soldier didn't fall. "Bangety-bang! Bangety-bang!" the young soldier shouted even louder, but the enemy kept coming towards him. Eventually the enemy got to him and pushed him over. As the enemy was walking over him, the young soldier heard the enemy muttering, "Tankety-tank! Tankety-tank!"

Learning to sense danger

You are learning to use your level to help you accomplish anything you desire. But when you are training or in the heat of competition, you often do not have the opportunity to sit down, make yourself comfortable and count yourself into your level.

Not to worry, though. Jose Silva has developed techniques that you can use to help you achieve the state of mind that you desire, any time, any place, under any circumstances.

There may be a lot of pressure and action in a championship game, but conditions don't get any worse than on the battlefield.

In 1965, Jose Silva developed a technique to keep his son Tony - and other members of Tony's squad - safe on the battlefields of Vietnam.

Remember the Three Fingers Technique from Chapter 5? You learned how to preprogram yourself at your level to relax whenever (out of your level) you bring together the tips of your first two fingers and thumb. Some people refer to this as a "trigger mechanism."

You can program similar trigger mechanisms for a wide variety of purposes. That's what Jose Silva did when Tony was drafted and ordered to Vietnam.

"It would be difficult to keep the tips of your three fingers together when you are fighting or firing a rifle," Mr. Silva said. "So we programmed a different way."

Instead, he had Tony press his little finger into the palm of his hand. This is what happens naturally when you make a fist. It is also an easy position to hold when you are firing a rifle - your forefinger is on the trigger, and you can hold the tip of your little finger against the palm of your hand.

Tony programmed so that whenever he held the little finger of either hand against the palm of that hand, he would be more intuitive and aware of any dangerous situation. (We'll talk more about anticipation and intuition in the next chapter.)

How did the technique work? It worked great! Tony tells a story about coming to a fork in the road and selecting one path over another and learning later that there were Vietcong soldiers waiting to ambush them on the path they avoided.

Along with his own son, Jose programmed about 30 young men from Laredo. The area to which they were sent had such a bad reputation that when new soldiers arrived, the paperwork was prepared for their Purple Hearts, with only the date left blank. But all of the young men from Laredo, using their "Little Finger in the Palm of the Hand Technique," came home safely.

You can program yourself in a similar manner.

You can use the Three Fingers Technique, or the Little Finger in the Palm of the Hand Technique, and preprogram yourself for the state of mind that you desire.

You can even use a sound if you like:

Ring a bell, like Pavlov did to train his dog. Preprogram yourself at your level so that every time you hear the bell ring, or hear your school's fight song, or somebody says, "You the man!", you will perform the way that you desire.

Here's how Betty Perry, a Silva lecturer in Florida, used a trigger mechanism to help a college soccer team win a national championship.

What a trigger and a little mind training can do

The Florida Institute of Technology (FIT) has a very good soccer team. Rick Stottler, the coach of the FIT soccer team and a Silva graduate, knows the power of the mind and wanted to have every tool possible available for the young men on the team. At Rick's request, Betty Perry presented a three-hour workshop on visualization and imagery to the team. Betty was more than willing to work with them.

The workshop focused on identifying each individual's feelings at moments of peak performance, whether on the field or off.

Once all were aware of how they felt when they were in charge of a situation, a trigger was set in place and tied to actual game situations.

They programmed that the letters F-I-T would invoke the feelings that they wanted to have in a game situation.

Teamwork and individual performance were both emphasized.

And an end result - winning their division in the NCAA national championship - was programmed.

They won the NCAA Division 2 Championship on December 7. On December 10 Betty had the opportunity to talk with some of the members of the team. She asked one of the players, named Jackson, if he felt the workshop helped the team.

Jackson was enthusiastic in his response. He recalled how he had been informed by the team physician on November 6, the day of the workshop, that he needed knee surgery and would not play for the rest of the year. That was when Jackson decided to use Silva visualization and supervised exercise for his knee. He was able to play the last four games.

When asked about the trigger mechanism that was programmed, he again was very positive. Giving an example of how effectively it worked, he told Betty, "In the championship game, FIT was down by one goal. The fans began to shout F-I-T (the trigger), and I felt an extra spurt of energy and more teamwork."

Betty told Jackson that he can use the same trigger before exams or for any other area of his life.

It was exciting to know that a three-hour workshop was sufficient to teach these young men, who had little or no previous knowledge of the Silva techniques, to use the material to enhance their natural abilities and teamwork.

In fact, Betty learned from coach Rick Stottler that the workshop had affected the young men to an even greater extent than imagined. Rick called her two months after the team won the championship to tell her about one of the players, named Collin, who was in an accident during the Christmas holiday. He was thrown through the windshield of his car and received many injuries, including cuts from glass shards in his eye.

While in the hospital, Collin heard the doctors talking. They were saying that it was indeed unfortunate that he would probably lose the sight in his eye.

He called the doctors over and informed them that he wanted to hear none of their negative talk. He knew his eye would be fine, he would have good vision and all would be well. (He was right.) Rick heard about this from Collin's mother, who had called from England to ask what sort of training in positive thinking the team had received. Rick told her about the single evening workshop that the team had attended.

Betty recalls that when the workshop had concluded that night, after just three hours with the team, she was not certain how many, if any, of the players would actually believe much of what she had presented.

Obviously, they got a lot out of it.

It is true that when you plant seeds, you never know which ones will sprout.

Programming a special state of mind

Have you ever noticed that there are some days when everything seems right?

You have plenty of energy, every movement you make is graceful and powerful, you feel like you have enough endurance to go on all day long, weights seem lighter, distances seem shorter and you are performing perfectly.

In competition, athletes refer to this as being "in the zone" or "in the groove." Movements are easy and natural, and success is easy to attain.

How would you like to be able to perform like that any time you desire? If you could, every workout would be a real joy, wouldn't it?

Well, you are about to learn a technique Jose Silva taught Ed Bernd Jr. to help him get "into the groove" when practicing Olympic weightlifting movements. You can use it to help yourself get "in the zone" or "in the groove" whenever you need it.

As with any kind of training, the more you practice this technique, the better it will work for you. You can use your Mental Coach that you developed in Chapter 7 to help you.

Advanced Performance-Enhancing Technique

Being "in the groove" is a state of mind. You want to prepare yourself so that you will be in this special state of mind when you get into the gym, onto the court or onto the playing field.

Recall a time when you were "in the groove," or "in the zone," when you performed perfectly, when everything you did was right, when you could feel yourself achieving your best, when you knew that you could achieve everything you desired. You can recall a training or practice session or a competition.

Recall exactly how you performed, and exactly how you felt - physically, mentally and emotionally - when you had this special state of mind.

You want to be able to recall that same state of mind again when you go into the gym, onto the court or onto the playing field.

Here's what to do so that you can recall that feeling whenever you need to:

At your level, recall that time when you felt that "in the groove" state of mind.

Program yourself so that any time in the future you need to have this same state of mind, all you need to do is imagine your Mental Coach prompting you to get into this special state of mind.

Use those words, "special state of mind," as a trigger mechanism to help you get into that special state of mind, in which you will be just as successful again - even more so every time after that - whenever you need to be.

What's the perfect time to program yourself to have this special state of mind that will help you perform better? And how can you determine this perfect time? Read on.

Best Time to Program Technique

At night, when you are in bed and ready to go to sleep, enter your level as you have been taught. Program that you will wake up automatically during the night or in the morning - at the best time to program yourself - so that with the aid of your Mental Coach, you can invoke this special state of mind whenever you need it. Stay at level, and go to sleep from your level.

The first time you wake up, sit up, bow your head slightly, turn your eyes slightly upwards (keeping them closed), enter your level as you have been taught and do your programming.

Recall a time when you were training, performing or competing and you had this special state of mind. You were "in the groove," you were performing perfectly, everything you did was right, your actions were easy and natural, you felt that you were achieving your best and you knew that you would accomplish what you desired.

Then program the following: In the future, whenever you desire to invoke this same special state of mind in order to be just as successful again - and even more so every time after that - you will imagine your Mental Coach encouraging you and reminding you to invoke this special state of mind.

Then imagine yourself performing perfectly with this special state of mind, and imagine your coach encouraging you and reminding you to have this special state of mind.

Practice makes perfect

Every time you perform in a superior manner or have a successful training session, enter your level and reinforce the experience by reviewing what you did and how you felt. Program for future training sessions to be just as good when you get into this special state of mind.

Here are some basic guidelines for using this "special state of mind" technique:

The night before you are going to need this special state of mind for a training session, a performance or a competition, program yourself to wake up automatically at the best time to program.

Then go to sleep from your level.

The first time you wake up during the night or in the morning, program yourself to have this special state of mind during the event.

Program yourself again just before you start your training session, performance or competition. Take a few moments to enter your level and program yourself just as you did the night before.

When you are training, performing or competing, recall this special state of mind, and imagine your Mental Coach there with you, encouraging you and reminding you to recall this special state of mind. Bring back that special feeling - that "knowing" that you are going to succeed. Recall it. Get back "in the groove."

Then take it for granted that you are going to perform the way you did when you were very successful - and even better than before. Every time you do this, you will achieve superior results.

Eventually, when you have practiced this enough times and you are very familiar with that feeling of being "in the groove," it will become automatic. All you will need to do is recall that state of mind of being "in the groove" - and you will be there.

Chapter 9

Developing anticipation

After listening to muscle man Harry Chest go on and on about his great strength, a slender young man spoke up:

"I'll bet you 20 dollars that I can wheel something in a wheelbarrow from one end of this block to the other, and you can't wheel it back."

"How big a wheelbarrow?" the weightlifter asked.

"Just a standard size."

"Well, you go ahead and put anything you want to into that wheelbarrow, and I'll push it twice as far as you do," Harry boasted.

They got a wheelbarrow and took it to the street corner.

"Okay, Harry," the young man smiled, "get in."

How intuition can help you

The ability to correctly anticipate what your opponent is going to do gives you a definite edge in competition. In fact, the ability to use your intuition to get information and to anticipate future events is the real secret to outstanding success in every area of life.

If you can use your intuition to sense the best training routine, you will get into better shape more quickly and easily than if you are limited only to random guessing.

Any time you can sense what other people are thinking or what they are likely to do, you know exactly how to prepare so that you will be ready for them.

Imagine sensing what someone is willing to pay for your services. You'd know exactly what price you can negotiate.

Imagine sensing what opposing players' game plans are. And imagine being able to send a message to your teammates - to let them know mentally what you are going to do next.

Basketball player Walt Frazier said that he and teammate Bill Bradley could do this. "Sometimes he has passed the ball before I've taken the first step. It's like telepathy," Frazier said in the book *Clyde*, which he wrote with Joe Jares.

Many athletes use intuition

There are ·many real-life examples of athletes who use intuition:

• Sportscaster Frank Gifford often speaks of the great quarterbacks in the National Football League having the ability to "sense" when a tackler is rushing up behind them and moving out of harm's way at the final moment.

Gifford's broadcast partner Dan Dierdorf agreed during a broadcast on December 31, 1994, noting that when he asked the great ones how they knew to move, they said they didn't know it was just instinct.

• Race driver Emerson Fittipaldi has talked about how premonition works for him. When asked how he knew how fast to go into a corner during the Indianapolis 500, Fittipaldi told interviewer Charlie Rose on the Public Broadcasting System, June 3, 1993, "You must know what the car will do before it does it."

• Muhammad Ali made many accurate predictions about his fights. He often ignored the advice of his trainers and fought the way he felt he should.

• Soccer great Pele said he played his first World Cup game in 1958 entirely in a trance, as if the future were unfolding before his eyes. Pele's team won, largely due to his efforts, according to Peter Bodo and David Hirshey, authors of *Pele's New World*.

- Middle linebacker Ray Nitschke said in his book, *Mean on Sunday*, that Cleveland Brown fullback Jim Brown "had a sixth sense that told him how the defense would react."

- Pitcher Sandy Koufax wrote about the extraordinary rapport he had with catcher John Roseboro in his autobiography, *Koufax*. "Not only did we have the same idea at the same moment," he said about one risky decision about what pitch to throw, "we even had the same thoughts about what could happen back in the clubhouse" if it turned out to be the wrong decision.

Olympic fencers sense opponents' strategies

To help his fencers develop a strategy, Andrzej Wojcikiewicz, a sports psychologist and former coach of the Canadian National Fencing Team, used a special technique taught in the Silva UltraMind ESP System.

This technique allows you to experience what another person is experiencing by imagining that you are putting his or her head over your own, as though you were putting on a helmet.

"This was used by some fencers before unusually difficult bouts in order to instinctively plan the correct strategy for the fencing match," Wojcikiewicz explained.

"One fencer imagined putting on the head of a world champion before a match, got the feeling, took off the helmet' and then fenced the match with a great success."

Know when to shoot

Lance Miller, an international shooting coach trained at the United States Olympic Training Center, said that the most important things in the Silva Method to help his athletes are visualization, mental rehearsal, stress management and intuition.

"Why intuition?" Ed Bernd Jr. asked him. "There's no need to figure out your opponent's strategy or anything like that."

"Are you kidding?" he answered. "There are things beyond a shooter's control that can affect his or her accuracy."

"Like what?" Ed asked.

"Like the wind," he answered. "The wind at the target may be different than the wind at the muzzle of the gun. And the wind can change suddenly.

"If you can somehow use your intuition to help you determine the exact instant to squeeze the shot off, you can improve your score."

The athlete cannot detect other factors objectively, Miller said. "Despite the excellent quality control in the manufacture of ammunition," he said, "you could have a nick in a bullet that you can't see with the naked eye, or a smaller powder charge.

"The athletes need to be able to sense this. I tell my guys and girls that if everything doesn't feel right, don't shoot. When they learn to project their minds to detect problems, this will help them tremendously."

Miller is teaching his athletes how to use some of the Silva Method techniques to help them in their quest for world and Olympic championships.

The same idea applies to other sports as well, where variables such as wind or precision manufacture of equipment could be factors that influence the success of the athlete's effort.

Intuition can be taught

In a research study presented at the American Educational Research Association's 1988 annual meeting, Dr. George Maycock of Appalachian University in Boone, N.C., demonstrated that college students who learned the Silva

Method "showed a significant increase" in their intuition.

A group of 30 students who took the Basic Lecture Series were asked to complete three tests before and after they completed the training:

1. The HCP Profile Test, a test to determine left-brain (logical) versus right-brain (intuitive) dominance.

2. The HCP-PSY Test, a test to determine beliefs and experiences about intuition.

3. The Intuitive Potentials Test, a test developed by Dr. Maycock to measure a person's potential for being able to intuitively, or clairvoyantly, detect information

The results of these tests were compared to those for a control group of 30 individuals who did not take the Silva Method training but were instead enrolled in an education course, a regular college course in research methods.

"The individuals who completed the Silva Method training," Maycock reported, "showed a significant increase in scores for all three tests. This showed that they tended to become more right-brain or intuitively oriented, their beliefs became more positive toward intuitive thinking and their potential for intuitive thinking improved.

"Individuals in the control group who did not participate in the training showed no significant gains in scores on any of the tests."

According to Maycock, 83 percent of the Silva students showed gains in intuitive abilities. Of the five students who did not show gains in intuitive attitudes, four of them (13 percent of the test group) were already functioning in a high intuitive mode before the training, as their scores on the tests they took before the course indicated.

"It was also found that those individuals who were left-brained or logic oriented prior to the training tended to benefit the most, since the Silva Method training enabled them to become more intuitively oriented or more balanced in their thinking styles," Maycock noted.

"One researcher," Maycock continued, "found that 70 percent of gifted or high IQ students were predominantly intuitive, while only 39 percent of students in regular classes were intuitive.

"If intuition has been shown to be useful for creativity and success, then both teachers and their students need to be trained to fully use their intuitive abilities.

"The present research study using the Silva Method shows that a training program does exist that can improve right-brain intuitive abilities," Maycock concluded.

Athletes as artists and clairvoyants

Dord Fitz, an art teacher/historian who organized the first commercial Silva Method course for Jose Silva in Amarillo, Texas, in 1966, taught art to ordinary people as a method to help them develop their clairvoyant abilities.

Before he had even met Jose Silva or discovered the Silva Method as a straightforward way to teach people to develop their clairvoyant abilities, Fitz had always insisted, "You cannot be a great artist unless you are also a great clairvoyant."

While Fitz was teaching art at the University of Alabama, he became friends with legendary football coach Bear Bryant. Bryant sent his football players to Fitz's art class, not because it was an easy course, but because they benefited so much.

"The great athletes were also great artists," Fitz said.

As Dord Fitz suspected, this great right-brain ability which produces art, clairvoyance, intuition, creativity - makes people champions in any field. But you do not need to take the roundabout pathway of learning art in order to develop your clairvoyant ability - you can do it with the Silva techniques.

Putting clairvoyant abilities to the test

In the new Silva UltraMind ESP System, we use a very direct method for demonstrating students' clairvoyant abilities. We have to, because we promise to give students their money back if they are not satisfied. We don't depend on artistic ability or tests like those used by Dr. Maycock to determine attitude and brain hemisphere dominance.

Instead, we use a method called "case working" to find out whether the students can sense information not available to their physical senses and to verify their accuracy.

In case working, the Silva student is given the name and age of someone who is not present and whom he or she doesn't know, then uses his or her mind to sense what kind of health problem that person has.

The names of the subjects do not come from the instructor but from other students in the class; they are people outside the class whom the students know.

When the students are able to obtain the information not available to their physical senses, they know they have learned to use their intuition. How accurate are the participants in the Silva courses?

Approximately 80 percent!

Students take turns working each other's cases. Before the conclusion of the Silva UltraMind ESP System, every student has the opportunity to work at least 10 health cases.

Once they have verified that they were accurate at sensing the information, they imagine the subject in perfect health. You can learn how effective this is by reading Jose Silva's book *You the Healer*, published by H.J. Kramer.

Words of wisdom from an intuitive thinker

Jose Luis "Pepe" Romero has played competitive sports all his life and has worked for Silva International all of his adult life - since 1972. He currently serves as Director of U.S. Lecturers for Silva International.

Pepe says intuition helps him remain competitive against players half his age. At a Sports Power Workshop at the 1994 Silva International Convention in Laredo, he related the following about his experiences as an intuitive player:

"You always hear that the professionals are focused; they are in the zone.' The reason that they are at that level is because they are able to go into alpha and use it to do the things they need to do to be successful.

"You are constantly going into alpha - in and out, in and out. Your brain dips into alpha approximately 30 times every minute, for very short periods of time.

But do we use it? Are we able to use it?

You need to learn to use alpha - how to use it so that you can be able to extract the information that you need, whatever you need from alpha.

"A few years ago I heard an interview with Larry Bird, one of the top players in basketball. During the interview they were asking him, How is it that you can make those no-look passes, without looking, without knowing who is behind you, and make them perfectly?' He said, I see the play develop before it happens.'

"What is he doing? Visualizing. He is doing it while he is physically moving around. You can learn to do those things, too.

"You can develop your intuition so that you can use it any time without having to stop and do a countdown. Intuition is very good because it can help you in sports, or in anything in life, to be able to anticipate. If you can anticipate what the opponent is going to do - this is true in business and in family life - if you can anticipate what your child is going to do, would that be helpful to you? Of course it would. In sports, it is the same thing.

"I am active in sports, softball primarily, and basketball. At my age, I need to have an advantage to be able to be out there and participate competitively.

"In softball, I play in the outfield. Normally they have kids there in their teens and 20s who are very fast, who can move and catch.

"One game last season I was playing center field. It seemed like everything was falling in place. I could actually picture the ball right before the batter hit the ball, and picture in which direction it was going. I was getting such a good jump on it that even though I don't have the speed that I used to have, that anticipation helped me make the plays.

"You can do that, when you learn to develop and use your intuition."

Intuition is a natural God-given ability

Most people have flashes of intuition. Have any of these events happened to you?

- The phone rings and somehow you know who is calling.

- You have a dream that helps you solve a problem. Or you dream about something, and it happens in the next day or two.

- You guess what someone is going to say before they say it. Or you guess what they are going to do before they do it. This happens often with close friends.

- You automatically do the right thing at the right time or say the right thing without knowing why you said it.

Most people say they have had such experiences. Techniques developed by Jose Silva can help you further develop these natural intuitive abilities on your own in order to perform better in sports and in every other area of your life for better health, success and happiness.

How to develop your intuition

The fastest way to develop your intuition is with a Silva UltraMind ESP Systems instructor who is specially trained to guide you both verbally and mentally so your mind knows exactly what to do.

You can also learn from recordings, and on your own if you stick with it. You can use the Silva UltraMind ESP System Complete Home Seminar, available at www.SilvaCourses.com.

Jose Silva can teach you things - even in the pages of this book - that you can do to increase your intuition. The most obvious thing that you can do to increase your intuitive abilities is to be aware of when you have an intuitive experience and reinforce it at your level.

Let's say that you are participating in a sporting event, or some other activity, and you get the feeling that something is going to happen.

Then it happens.

You were correct.

Your intuition was functioning.

As soon as possible after this event, enter your level and review exactly what happened - especially how you felt when you were thinking about the possibility of it happening.

Soon you will learn to recognize this special feeling, so that you can take advantage of it.

You might even learn how to evoke this special feeling and

cause it to happen when you need to use your intuition.

You can do this at any time.

- The phone rings and you guess who it is before you pick it up.
- You are thinking about someone and they call or come by.
- You must make a decision, but the evidence is not clear on which choice to make. So you enter your level and select one choice, and it turns out to be correct.

Whenever you do any of these things, enter your level at your earliest opportunity and review the event, especially how you felt.

Your intuition will guide you in the right direction - towards the winner's circle.

Section 3: Specific training routines

Now that you know how to enter your level, as well as basic programming techniques, you may go on to read any chapter in the remainder of the book. The chapters that follow cover a wide range of topics in the field of fitness, athletics, appearance and health:

• The chapters in Section 3 offer specific guidance for fitness and sports.

• Section 4 includes techniques for your health and well-being.

• Section 5 includes subjects that do not fit into the other categories, including information that parents and coaches can use when working with young people.

Pursue any of the topics that you desire. You can always come back to other topics later, as you need them.

Chapter 10

Training for fitness

- *Beating around the bush is not an acceptable exercise.*

- *Running your mouth off about not having time to exercise won't get you in shape.*

- *Skipping workouts is no substitute for skipping rope.*

- *Jumping to conclusions... well, you get the idea: Getting in shape involves using your body.*

The recipe for fitness

Yes, getting in shape involves using your body, but when you use your mind in addition, you can get into shape even faster. Every person - from world-class athlete to the average person - should have four goals in a fitness program:

1. Flexibility. Stretch and limber up. Flexibility is associated with youth, stiffness with old age.

2. Endurance. Practice exercises that cause you to breathe heavier than usual for 20 minutes.

3. Strength. Exercise against resistance to give you a reserve of strength.

4. Coordination. Develop your timing and coordination with activities such as sports or dancing.

There are three more factors to be considered in order to help you get into shape and stay in shape:

1. Nutrition. Put quality fuel into your body to build the strong healthy muscles and organs you desire. You can learn how to use the alpha level to help you determine what foods

you need and to get the greatest nutritional value from the foods you eat (see Chapter 18).

2. Relaxation. Get sufficient rest, relaxation and sleep to recuperate and grow stronger. You will learn how to avoid burnout and determine how much rest and relaxation your body needs in Chapter 17.

3. Mental. Motivation, positive thinking, mental rehearsal and programming at the alpha level are necessary to give you the success you desire.

The overload principle

According to legend, a young man named Milo began lifting a small calf every day in order to become stronger. As the calf grew, so did Milo's strength, until eventually he was lifting a full grown cow. This was the birth of "progressive resistance" exercise, which is still used today. There are three parts to this kind of exercise:

1. Overload. To improve yourself physically (in terms of appearance, endurance, strength and athletic skills) you must do a little more than you are accustomed to doing.

2. Rest and recovery. Give your body time to rebuild.

3. Overcompensation. After your body has recovered and come back to where it started, it will add a little more strength for reserve. This is how we grow stronger.

Physical conditioning is as simple as that: Do a little more than usual, then rest and give your body time to recover and then overcompensate. You might not be placing enough load on your body, or you might not be giving your body enough time to rebuild and overcompensate.

If you do not grow stronger when you increase the load, then try going the other way: Give yourself more time for rest, recovery and overcompensation.

Of course, numerous other factors are involved in becoming a completely fit person. Besides the physical aspects, there are psychological factors, social considerations, mental conditioning (which is very important) and spiritual development. The Silva techniques you are learning in this book can help you in all of these areas.

As we discuss physical training, please remember that you should see your doctor and have a medical checkup before you begin any physical activity that exceeds the level to which you are accustomed. Let your doctor know what you plan to do, and listen to the guidance that this professional offers.

When Ed Bernd Jr. was 5 years old, he had polio. Dr. Robert L. Bennett, a pioneer in the field of physical rehabilitation for polio patients, helped Ed to learn to walk again. Dr. Bennett also taught him a lot of things about exercising and training, many of which are being passed on to you in this book.

As a teenager, Ed went to Dr. Bennett and asked for an exercise routine, because he still had some lingering effects from the polio.

Instead of giving Ed a calisthenics routine - which he said nobody did anyway - Dr. Bennett recommended that Ed "go to a hardware store and get any of the spring systems or a weight set, and follow the instructions."

Ed fell in love with weights and has continued to use them for the last four decades. By 1975, weighing about 175 pounds, he was able to do a squat (deep knee bend) with 305 pounds on his shoulders - nowhere near a record - but not bad for someone who lost the use of many of the muscle fibers in his legs at 5 years old.

A year later, he had another outstanding success: eliminating the pain that still persisted in his legs from polio by adapting the Silva Headache Control Technique, which you will learn in Chapter 15.

Flexibility

Most trainers recommend that you spend sufficient time stretching and warming up before you attempt any intense exercise. This is good advice. Even more important is to never, never overdo it. Be patient. You do not achieve flexibility by force; you only injure yourself when you try to force it, and this slows your progress.

Do your stretching by relaxing, not forcing your body.

Recall the relaxation exercise you did in Chapter 5, and practice relaxing your muscles until you relax into the position you desire. This is what is taught in Hatha Yoga. Hatha Yoga takes the approach that you can discipline your mind by learning to control your body.

You can also use physical discipline to help you develop mental discipline, as well as use your mind to help you to loosen up your muscles. Over time, your flexibility will increase - no matter what your age.

Contrary to what some people believe, large muscles do not keep you from having great flexibility. Just look at what super heavyweight Olympic lifters can do: hold 300 pounds overhead while in a deep (lower-than-thighs-parallel) squat, with their buttocks only inches from the floor, their upper body leaning forward and the weight held well behind their head. That's real flexibility in the ankles, knees, hips and shoulders.

And think of how Olympic lifters hold a heavy "clean": 400 pounds on their shoulders with their wrists bent well back and their elbows so flexible that their hands are actually positioned outside of - and down past - their shoulders!

Looking at these lifters, with their massive legs, arms, chests and shoulders, provides ample evidence that having large muscle mass does not inhibit great flexibility.

You can develop great flexibility, too. Just remember to concentrate on your muscles and allow them to relax into position.

Endurance

Advice about endurance (aerobic) training has changed through the years.

For a while the experts said that the more intense the training was, the more effective it would be.

Then they said that additional research showed that lower intensity would produce just as much conditioning, while being easier on the feet and joints. So how do you know what is best for you?

You use the same principle we've been discussing: Overload your system - even add a little bit extra as a safety factor - then rest so that your body will recover.

But don't do too much.

Doing too much simply causes fatigue, and your body spends all its energy repairing damage and does not have anything left for overcompensating and adapting to even heavier work.

To learn what is best for you, enter your level and analyze the situation.

Consider various kinds of endurance exercises. Outstanding endurance exercises include jogging, aerobics, bicycle riding, skipping rope, riding a stationary bike, walking, swimming - something you can do for 20 minutes or more that will cause you to breathe heavier than usual. Wind sprints would not qualify. Weight training is not aerobic, unless it is something like circuit training, where you switch from one exercise to the next without any pauses or rest in between.

When selecting an exercise, consult your coach or trainer, and consider your own personal needs, your fitness level, any problems with your body, etc.

Jogging, for example, can be hard on your knees and ankle joints, so if you have problems in these areas, you should probably choose another activity.

For some people, walking is a relatively strenuous activity. For others, an hour of jogging is relatively comfortable. As always, consult your doctor before starting any exercise program.

But in the end, *you* have to make the final decision for *you*.

So once you have gotten advice from the experts, enter your level, analyze yourself and your needs, and determine what you think is best for you. Then do it.

But wait - you're not done yet.

After you go out and train, you need to measure your progress.

If it is satisfactory, continue.

If not, enter your level and analyze the situation again.

Do you feel that you should make some changes? Perhaps you should train harder or select a more difficult activity. Or maybe you should select an activity with less intensity.

One Silva graduate named Paul G. wanted to get into shape, so he went out and ran several times a week. But Paul, who was 40 years old, could only run about a mile, and that was in about eight minutes. His younger friends used to tease him that they could walk a mile faster than that. And they could!

Worst of all, Paul could not detect any progress. After three years of training, he still could seldom run much farther than a mile. And his time did not improve. And when he checked his pulse, his resting heart rate still remained at about 72 beats per minute.

After Paul learned the Silva Method, he decided to use the alpha level to see if he could find anything that might help him improve his condition.

At his level, Paul realized that he was running almost as hard as he could and that he could not seem to slow down and pace himself. Thus, he was exhausting himself.

He wondered, while at his level, if a less intense activity might be better for him. So he bought a bicycle.

As a youngster, Paul had loved riding a bicycle. As a middle-aged adult, he liked the idea that with the bicycle he could exercise while sitting down.

This thought made him feel a little guilty, like maybe he wasn't doing enough, but his Silva lecturer had advised him to go ahead and act on the idea he got at his level and see what kind of results it brought him.

The results were spectacular. Paul would ride the bike for about 45 minutes at a time, much longer than he had been running. His pulse rate immediately after riding the bike was not going as high as when he had run.

But after a month of riding the bike three or four times a week, his resting heart rate had dropped from 74 beats per minute to an outstanding 62 beats per minute!

Strength

It is nice to have a little more strength than you need. It makes tasks so much easier. In fact, it is very natural to have a little more strength than you need. Your own body tells you that. It is the overload and adaptation principle that we have been talking about.

For some people, deep knee bends and push-ups are sufficient to build a reserve of strength. But for most people who are serious about being in good shape, some kind of progressive resistance exercise (weight training) is appropriate.

One thing to be careful of: Weight training is very intense. You can overdo it very quickly if you are not careful. Please remember the information in Chapter 4 about different body types and the appropriate training routines for each type.

If you're the average person, the kind of exercise you do is less important than the fact that you do exercise. But there are some guidelines you should follow.

First, unless you are very advanced, or have a very high metabolism, it is usually best not to train with weights on consecutive days.

Also, when you are using weights to build up strength, it is best to use only the big, heavy exercises.

• Work your upper body with military presses or bench presses, exercises which any weight trainer or gym operator can show you how to do correctly.

• Work your back with deadlifts or power cleans, or work on the lat machine. Avoid back injuries by exercising your back regularly.

• Exercise your legs with squats. Your legs are your foundation. They say that the legs are the first thing to go on an athlete, so the stronger your legs are, the longer your career. A trainer or gym operator even the instructions you receive with home fitness equipment can show you the correct way to do any of the exercises recommended in this paragraph.

You should avoid small exercises with light weights. The little high repetition exercises are used to help you decrease size in order to increase definition; they are not for building muscles.

A few safety tips:

- Always breathe when exerting yourself. If you hold your breath, you will restrict the blood flow through your neck to your brain, and you might pass out. This is not desirable when you are holding a heavy weight. So, grunt and groan if you need to let the air out as you exert yourself. Let the neighbors wonder what the noise is all about; that's better than losing consciousness and having the weights fall on top of you!

- Also, you should not train alone. Use spotters. Weight lifters who have trained alone have died when they could not raise the bar after doing a set of bench presses, and it rolled back onto their throats, crushing the windpipe.

- When you are training alone, do not put the outside collars on the bar. Leave them off, so if you get stuck, you can push up on one side of the bar and the weights will fall off of the other end, allowing you to free yourself. Learn from an experience Ed Bernd Jr. had:

Once he forgot to set the stops on his power rack while doing bench presses, and the bar - with more than 200 pounds loaded onto it - rolled back across his throat. There was no time to think, just to react, and he started shoving as hard as he could with both arms.

One side of the bar lifted, and the big Olympic plates fell off the other end. Then the bar tilted back the other way, and the weights on the other end clanked noisily to the floor - allowing him to throw the now-empty bar off of him. If collars had been holding the weights onto the bar, he wouldn't be here today to write this book!

- When lifting the bar off the floor, as in the deadlift or the heavy clean, you can use straps wrapped around your wrist and around the bar to ease the strain on your hands, allowing you to lift more weight. Your trainer can show you how this works.

Just remember, if you use straps, use short ones, just barely long enough to go around the bar, so that if you let go, the bar will fall freely.

Several years ago, a lifter training in Ft. Lauderdale used long straps that wrapped around the bar several times. As he lifted the bar overhead, he lost his balance and released his grip. But the straps, which were still wrapped around the bar, did not come loose. He fell along with the weight. His elbow hit the platform with the weight still in his hand, causing severe injury to his elbow and arm.

• Also remember, when lifting weight off the floor, keep your back flat. You can do this by selecting a point high up on the wall in front of you and watching it. This will keep your head up and your back in the correct position. Have your trainer or coach check out your form from time to time.

As always, gather information at beta, but do not make your decisions at beta. Remember that your brain operates much more efficiently at 10 cycles per second (alpha), so enter your level, analyze all of the information that you have and make your decisions at alpha. Then test them at beta, and keep making adjustments by making decisions at alpha and acting on them in beta, until you find the best method for you. It is much faster this way than trying to make decisions at beta and also act on them at beta. That would be like an athlete using only one leg instead of two.

Coordination

Now it is time to take that strong, fit and flexible body out and do something with it. Use it. Have fun with it.

You can take part in recreational activities like golf, bowling or tennis. Or you can engage in competitive sports. Dancing can be a great exercise, as well as a lot of fun and absolutely wonderful for your social life.

So get out and move your body. Enjoy the rewards of the work that you have done. Not only will it be fun, it will be good for you, too.

Trust your inner wisdom

Take Jose Silva's advice:

Nobody else knows you as well as you know yourself. You have within you everything you need to be healthy, happy and successful.

Enter your level every day, for five, 10 or 15 minutes.

- Relax.
- Deepen your level.
- Go over your goals.
- Analyze problems.
- Make decisions.
- Program to help yourself and others.

Practicing going to level once a day is good, twice a day is very good and three times a day is excellent.

Remaining at your level for five minutes is good; 10 minutes is very good; 15 minutes is excellent.

At your level, analyze all of the information you have from books, trainers, coaches and other players, then make your own decision about what is best for you. Should you exercise more? Should you get more rest? Trust yourself.

As you work out, notice the progress that you make. Let the results that you get guide you in your future programming and in your exercise routines.

When you are satisfied with your progress, continue doing what you have been doing. Continue programming in the same manner. If you are not satisfied with your progress, enter your level and analyze all of the information that you have. Make the decision whether to continue with what you have been doing or do something different.

You may need to change your training routine to train more or to train less.

You may need to spend more time at level or less time at level.

You may want to try using a different Silva technique.

If you are not getting any results at all, then review the instructions and the formulas.

Jose Silva invested 22 years of his life and a half-million dollars of his own money working out these formulas.

Every word is included for a specific purpose.

So use the formulas as he has given them to you.

Until you begin to have success with them, follow Jose Silva's instructions exactly as he has given them to you. Then if you want to experiment to see if you can improve your results, feel free to do so.

Nobody else in the world is exactly like you. You are unique, and you have something unique to offer to the world. The best way to program - for you - is relative to your personality, your attitudes, your goals, your energy, your experience and many more things.

Learn to use your intuition and your own good judgment. This is what champions are made of.

Chapter 11

Program yourself to win

Boxing instructor Bruiser Butts asked his new pupil, "Now that you have had your first boxing lesson, do you have any questions to ask?"

"Just one," the dazed pupil said. "How much is your correspondence course?"

The winner within

A winning attitude cannot be forced from the outside. It must come from within you. That's why it's so important for you to learn to use the alpha level so you can convert your subconscious into an inner conscious level that you can use to change your attitudes, beliefs and performance.

You've been "psyched up" before. But do you know how to do it reliably, any time you desire? Superstars do. They are usually the "naturals" at functioning at the alpha level, so that they are able to achieve maximum performance on demand.

Now, with the Silva techniques, you have a way to prepare yourself for maximum performance. In this chapter, you are going to read testimonials from people who have done just that, for a wide variety of competitive events. And then you will learn Jose Silva's techniques for programming yourself to win during your training and practice sessions.

Italian martial arts champion reveals her training secrets

Vidheya (Giuseppina Del Vicario) used the Silva techniques to help her become the Italian national champion in tai chi chuan, a title she held for three years until she retired undefeated in 1992. She was the overall champion not the women's champion. She was one of the few women who competed against both men and women.

Vidheya holds a fifth degree black belt in tai chi chuan and a fourth degree black belt in shao lin chuan, the only woman with such degrees. She holds one of the highest rankings in all of Italy. She was the only woman in competition in shao lin chuan and rose to a very high position in that sport, as well.

To watch her perform is to admire a work of art. She weighs less than 100 pounds. When she is not competing she has a buoyant personality and frequently flashes a beautiful smile.

But when she performs, she is transformed into something else. Her face takes on a frightening seriousness, a reflection of her total concentration and focus.

The exquisite movements of her body are in stark contrast to the intensity of her expression. Her balance, her flexibility and her graceful athletic movements all combine to create a masterpiece.

"You must love what you are doing," she says with a characteristic simplicity and clarity of thought. "Otherwise you will not have enough desire, belief and expectancy to continue."

Discipline and a childhood dream

Vidheya fell in love with martial arts when she was 8 years old, but her father was opposed. "He said it was of no use, that there was no occupation in it," she explained.

When she was 18, she took up judo. Then her natural intuition led her to a master teacher who was perfect for her. "I was looking in the yellow pages for a school where I could learn tai chi," Vidheya said. "Then I saw a name, and I knew immediately that this was my master."

She joined his classes and began to work hard. "He trained

me like a man," she said. "I loved it. The first year, I got up at 5 a.m. every day to train. You must train physically and learn to discipline your body and your mind. If you discipline your body, this will influence your mind," she explained. "And if you discipline your mind, this will influence your body."

Besides her martial arts training, Vidheya also practiced meditation. Then in 1985 she learned about the Silva Method and attended the Basic Lecture Series. She immediately began to use the techniques. "It is much more pragmatic than anything else I had found," she said.

"I practice my martial arts every day," she said. "I do the same thing with my Silva techniques. Repetition is the best way to increase your skill. If you practice every day, you condition yourself to do it every day.

"You must practice your mental techniques just like you would practice any physical skills if you want to become good, if you want to become the best," she said. "Eventually, you reach a point where you don't need to think about it any more. You just do it automatically. It becomes a part of your life. Martial arts is a discipline," she continued. "The Silva Method is a discipline as well. If you have no discipline, you get no results."

Managing energy during training and competition

Vidheya described the three phases that competitors typically go through as they gain experience in competition:

1. As a novice competitor, you may get nervous and lose your energy.

2. Then, you learn to concentrate on yourself, to turn your energy inward.

3. You gain the ability to use the energy of the people watching you. Their energy helps you perform even better, she said.

"During competition, I concentrate on myself first. I unite with my interior energy," Vidheya said. "I concentrate on an image of myself. I don't care about the other person. If you worry about the other person, you are lost."

She added, "In a big meet, when there are a lot of people in the audience, you cannot have any fear. You must imagine in your mind that you are alone.

"When you have fear, the first thing that happens is confusion of mind. The first symptom of fear is in your breathing. So take a deep breath. Learn how to breathe deeply, so that when you need to, you can take deep breaths until you feel your body relax, and then your mind is under control again."

During matches, Vidheya folds her hands in the salute that she was taught by her master. She uses this gesture as a trigger to help her relax. "I entered my level and programmed that every time I do this, it will help me to control my breathing," she explained. "I do this at the beginning and the end of each movement. It helps me to catch my breath, and to make sure that my mind is under control.

"We can control ourselves, or we can be controlled," she said. "I practice every day so that I can be in control."

Using visualization to correct mistakes

"If I do not do a movement perfectly," Vidheya said, "then I go to my level and visualize until I can visualize doing it perfectly. I use my master as a model. He shows me how a movement is to be performed, so I visualize the image of him doing it until I can picture it mentally, and feel it, and know that it is perfect. Then I do it physically.

"When I am training, I have in mind a mental picture of my master. He shows me how the movement is done. I keep this picture of him in my mind. During competition, if I had a clear picture in my mind of myself performing the movement perfectly, then I would win," she recalled.

She described how to correct mistakes. "You can go to your level and recall your mistakes," she said. "Try to find out what is happening at the moment you make the mistake. Was it something in your mind? Was it the way you made the movement?"

Use the Three Scenes Technique, and make a good study of the problem in the first scene. Then in the next scene, imagine correcting the mistake and doing it right.

Recall the image of your master, of your coach. Repeat it over and over until you feel that everything flows easily. In the third scene, imagine yourself doing it perfectly. Then as soon as you can, go to the gym and do it physically.

"You cannot do it all with willpower alone," she emphasized. "Use both will and imagination. They reinforce each other. Imagination gives you much more willpower."

The importance of focus

"When you practice tai chi, you are at your level," Vidheya said. "One of the first things they teach you is not to focus your eyes on anything specific when you are doing your movements. This makes sense because when you focus your eyes, you cannot be at level. When you defocus your eyes, you can be at your level. Then everything that you visualized will happen. And you will also be able to react instinctively.

"When you are first learning, you must focus on what you are doing. But after you practice and practice and practice, you no longer need to focus. You can defocus your vision and let the movements flow naturally.

"It is the same when you learn the Silva Method. At first you must practice, practice, practice, until it finally becomes automatic."

Keeping the rewards in perspective

Athletics can bring you rewards on many levels. Getting in shape makes you feel better and gives you the pride of accomplishment. Sports activities give you an opportunity to socialize with other people. That's why activities from daytime bowling leagues to local weekend golf tournaments to more physical activities like softball and flag football are so popular. Recognition, appreciation, fame and, often, monetary rewards come to those who take sports seriously and excel at them.

But extremism and obsession about athletics can create problems. Vidheya looks at it from this perspective:

"Too much attachment to the rewards is not good because it makes you dependent on something outside of yourself," she says.

"Too few attachments to the rewards means that you have no interest and will not continue your efforts.

The middle ground is the most difficult way, but it is also the best."

4 hours of mental training bring victory

A four-hour workshop and some follow-up help were all that it took to propel the Lady Tiger Volleyball Team at Martin High School in Laredo, Texas, to their first district championship in 17 years.

At the beginning of the 1990 season, nobody picked the Lady Tigers to win the district. But they had a weapon in their arsenal that nobody else knew about.

All of the players, with their parents' consent, had attended a four-hour Silva Athlete Training Workshop presented by Martin High School's veteran basketball coach Hector Chacon. Volleyball Coach Carmela Gonzalez had asked Coach Chacon to present the workshop to her players. She also attended the Silva Method 40-hour Basic Lecture Series so that she could help her players even more.

The athletes learned how to enter their level, the Mental Housecleaning technique (see Chapter 2) and the Silva Mental Rehearsal visualization technique (see Chapter 6). It paid off. They won eight of their 10 district games and the district championship. Two of the Martin volleyball players were named to the six-member 1990 All City Volleyball Team. Four other schools landed one player each on the squad.

Chacon said the two games the team lost had been games before which the players had not gone to level. "Every time they went to their level and programmed, they won," he said.

Non-winner becomes a winner

Silva graduate Goeff Bruce of Burlington, Vt., was one of the top winners in the highest-stakes pro ski racing event of the season at Winter Park, Colo., according to a story in the March 1982 issue of Ski Racing. The 29-year-old skier took home a large share of the $60,000 purse from the Colorado meet by winning the giant slalom race, the opening event of the First of Denver Cup pro ski racing series.

"Bruce has been a non-winner in the pro circuits prior to this season," the story noted. But, the article continued, Bruce now uses a new mind game.

"All I did," Bruce said, "was program myself to win. The Silva Method teaches you through visual imagery to help yourself eliminate any negative thoughts, and ski racing is so mental. I just tell myself I am going to win. I imagine myself winning."

Success in tae kwon do

Silva Method lecturer Judy Qua of the Philippines has a number of sports success stories in her book *Everyday Miracles and the Silva Method*. One is about 18-year-old Ma Fatima Da Luz, who turned her clumsiness into success even before she entered a tournament. This is how she describes her experience:

"An avid participant in my weekly tae kwon do class, I was delighted and excited when my head coach announced that I would compete in a tournament sponsored by the Hong Kong Tae Kwon Do Federation in August 1992. I managed to gain my mother's permission to go.

"However, negative thoughts were seriously impeding any progress I could have been making, because I had not worked on my performance. Therefore, I decided to employ the Silva visualization technique to eliminate this hindrance.

"First I visualized myself as I was: timid, lacking confidence and aggressive though clumsy. Then, I visualized myself as I wanted to be: powerful, aggressive, agile. I repeated this programming daily for a whole month.

"The result was that I did get my cup after all. But a note of warning to all practitioners: Be specific when you are programming. Since I didn't specify what prize I wanted, I ended up with the silver instead of the gold! But it still worked for me - I got something!"

Improved health, sports skill, business, quality of life

Judy Qua also tells of the successes Raju Mangharam experienced after he attended a Silva seminar in March 1988 in the Philippines. Here is his story:

"My mother, who lives in India, has been a diabetic for 10 years. One chronic problem is her constant loss of voice over several days. Last April she had a similar bout, but it went on for two weeks and she had to be hospitalized. I was informed she had bled or spat blood.

"I decided to do caseworking' on her. The news that she had regained her voice in full and had been discharged by the doctors surprised many who thought it was a seemingly miraculous recovery.

"As of this writing, my mother is in excellent health and hasn't had a recurrence of any illness, especially the loss of voice." (In Chapter 18, you will learn how to use your mind to speed recovery and to remain healthy.)

Mangharam continues:

"I took up two sports, tennis and bowling, after the Silva course. I learned with the use of the Silva visualization technique to play tennis well in four months, compared to the average eight to nine months needed by most people. I was even drafted by the Indian Chamber of Commerce to be part of the team composed of veteran members with 20 to 25 years of playing experience. I haven't won any tournament as yet, but I have been described as pro' in rating standard, giving every competitor a worthy challenge.

"Also with the visualization technique, I learned bowling in one month - what would take beginners six to eight months to master. I averaged 180 points per game for eight weeks and then started hitting 200 and over. I recently won a singles and a doubles competition.

"My business of importing and marketing electronics products has flourished after Silva. My Three Fingers Technique has helped me gain some eight to 10 more department store customers. My public relations is much better and customers are the ones calling for more supplies. The Three Fingers has further aided me to become more relaxed, remain calm and composed during traffic and other stressful situations.

"I have observed that my relationships with co-employees, family and fiancee have greatly improved to mutually satisfying levels. And I'm very pleased and happy over so many things. I believe in the Silva Method. I practice regularly and earnestly."

Father and son both win competitions

Ernesto O. Uy and his son John Paul both used Silva Method techniques to win two very different kinds of competitions.

The father entered a shooting competition. "There were three categories of competition," he said. "In the first two, I became champion because I had programmed using the Silva Method that I would be the best. In the third course, I changed my goal to achieving perfect Alphas (the center of target with highest scorepoint). Guess what? I got 24 Alphas and one Bravo.

"I just programmed myself minutes before every course, using the Silva Method technique. And lo and behold, it really worked!

"Another occasion Silva was put to use was September 2, 1991," Uy continued. "During the school foundation day, my son John Paul was one of the contestants for a declamation contest. Just before he stood, I told him to relax and use the Silva Method. He closed his eyes for a while, then he went on stage.

"He seemed to have heard a voice instructing him to look for his teacher. So he scanned the audience from left to right, slowly, very slowly. As he did so, he felt something from his head going down to his feet, not unlike going to the alpha level. He finished his declamation without missing a word. And he was adjudged the champ."

Team wins championship against all odds

Albert L. Laurel, a businessman who has since moved to Hong Kong, told Judy Qua how he used the techniques when the basketball team for which he played had a rough season.

"This year's basketball tournament was a tough, high pressured one for our team, although we were the back-to-back champions," he said. The team's six-foot-three center and coach had both left to work abroad.

"Until three weeks before opening rites, no other coach was willing to take on the pressure of coaching a defending back-to-back champion," Laurel explained.

Making things even more difficult, half of the players in the lineup were taking evening classes that conflicted with most games and practices. The team also had limited funds for practice-related, medical and other expenses. Then, after two wins, the team's center-forward was injured and had to rest for the remaining seven games.

"Knowing these odds against us," said Laurel, "I used the Silva visualization technique to program myself to play a well-rounded game. Now, I wasn't a dominant player on the team since there were certainly younger and more high-jumping players in the group. I seldom even attempted a shot in a game. I was what you might call a role player.

"However, during the championship game I was able to get an important rebound, then drive in past three opposing players for a lay-up at the opposite end of the court. This really sent the crowd shouting and cheering. After a few seconds, I did it again!

"In just under two minutes and cold from the bench, I scored four critical points and sent the crowd into a frenzy all throughout the rest of the game.

"Needless to say, our team was able to bag the Grand Slam crown at the end of the tournament. Against all odds with a little help from Silva," Laurel concluded.

World Series MVP benefits from the Silva System

Can a superstar benefit from the Silva techniques? Russell "Bucky" Dent told us that he did - and that he has recommended the techniques to some of his young players.

Dent and several of his Chicago White Sox teammates took the Silva course with instructor Rich Hero during spring training in 1975. A pitcher on the team had attended the course the previous year, and it had helped him so much that the club decided to try the course during spring training. The class was even featured on the CBS television program *60 Minutes*.

Dent said that the visualization technique helped him with his concentration. "It sharpened it," he said. "It improved my hitting and fielding, and it helped me to relax before the pressures of a game."

It must have worked, because in 1978, playing for the New York Yankees, he was named Most Valuable Player in the World Series.

Dent said that he goes to level for 10 to 15 minutes several times a week. "I visualize what I'm going to do or how I want to react." He added that he spends time at his ideal place of relaxation "to calm myself down."

She could accomplish anything

Before we move on to specific techniques and guidance, we would like to tell you how two more athletes used the Silva Method techniques to succeed.

The first, Dana Sheets, was thought to be too young and too small to compete successfully. She was a 14-year-old high school freshman when she attended the Silva Method course with her mother in 1966. It was the first class that Jose Silva had ever taught outside of Laredo. Jose made a deal with the participants in the class: He would teach them his method if they would help him with his English. (Things have changed since then: Now the Silva Method is taught in 29 different languages, and Jose Silva lectures in three of them English, Spanish and Portuguese.)

One of Dana's first goals was to make her high school varsity tennis team. Dana approached her tennis coach, but he laughed at her and reminded her that she was only 14 years old and a freshman and weighed only 95 pounds. He suggested that she still come out to practice every day and expect to make the team when she was a junior or a senior.

"Mom," Dana said to her mother, Nelda, "Mr. Silva said that I could accomplish anything I really want, if I use my mind. I really want to be on the tennis team. I'm going to do it!"

Dana and Nelda decided to make the Silva visualization technique the heart of their programming effort.

"The programming included impressing positive statements about the benefits of sports in general and tennis specifically," Nelda recalled. "Then we used the visualization technique to work on problems and solutions. When I say we,' I mean that together we composed the wording. I directed her to level and guided the use of the techniques and impressed the programming," Nelda explained. "Then she continued on her own until she needed a new program."

First they used visualization to correct a weak serve. Dana imagined looking at a mental movie of herself with a strong and perfect serve. When she went to the tennis class, Dana physically practiced what she had mentally practiced.

"After a week or two of working at level every day - 15 minutes each session - mentally practicing a perfect serve and then reinforcing it on the court, the results were obvious," Nelda said.

Next Dana chose to work on her backhand. She repeated the same routine with her ground strokes, overhead and her lob. By the time the coach had tryouts, Dana had perfected several important techniques for championship tennis. She made the varsity team as a freshman.

Starts winning tournaments

Dana's next big project was to win the district tournament. When that was accomplished, her next goal was the regional tournament. She had a lot of anxieties about this challenge, for she was not only going to be playing against senior high school girls who had won the regional title the year before, but against a state champion, as well. Plus she knew there would be a large crowd watching the matches, and she wasn't used to an audience.

Meanwhile, Dana's mother was facing a similar challenge - she was trying to become a Silva Method lecturer. "I was programming to overcome my shyness and fear of public speaking," Nelda said. "I had been successful in imagining that everyone who came to my lectures were there to give me energy and confidence."

So Dana used the same approach. She programmed that everyone who came to watch her play were her fans - that they were there to project energy and confidence.

"I gave her the suggestion that any time she felt anxiety for any reason, she would put her three fingers together and feel strong, confident and feel and play like a champion," Nelda said.

"When we discussed the programming for winning the tournament," Nelda continued, "Dana told me that she wanted to make it to the finals, and she would be happy with that. I suggested that she had a limited goal. Then she admitted that should she win regional, she would be expected to go to Austin to the state tournament, which would cause a conflict with a date she really wanted to keep: She had been selected to be a special server' at the Junior-Senior banquet and she was invited to the prom later.

"So we programmed that she would make it to the finals. That is exactly what happened."

Dana went on to win trophies for the high school tennis team and at invitational tournaments in the Amarillo and Lubbock, Texas, area. She made the University of Texas varsity team as a freshman.

A lifetime of successes

Today, 25 years later, Dana Sheets Coussou and her husband are the parents of two teenage daughters. Dana, an interior designer who owns her own business, is still winning first-place trophies at invitational tournaments. She has won more than 30 first-place trophies the past three years, several at the state level.

Dana still uses the Silva Method techniques. She watches master players at tournaments and on video, then, at her level, imagines that she is duplicating all the winning techniques. Last year, Dana amazed tennis players and fans when she won a state tournament despite what many would consider a catastrophe.

On the way to the tournament, she had stopped at a Houston shopping center. When she returned to the parking lot, her car was gone - stolen - along with her racket, shoes, water jug, "lucky shirt," energy bars and other items. Dana had time to get a replacement racket, shoes and clothes, but not the water bottle and the energy bars. She used her level to program relaxation, a feeling of excitement and energy to win. Doing this, she converted the stress of the theft into positive energy that helped her win the first-place trophy.

And just as Nelda helped her daughter Dana, Dana is now helping her daughters, who both play tennis. The eldest, Jill, learned the Silva Method from Nelda when she was seven.

When she entered high school, Jill became the first freshman in the history of Kelly High School, in Beaumont, Texas, to make the varsity tennis team.

"Regular practice, clear goals and some support from family and other Silva Method graduates can help you make your dreams come true," Nelda said.

Mental techniques are ageless

Our final story is about a man who was thought to be too old to keep up with the younger players.

"I play slow pitch softball in a very competitive league where most of the players are younger than myself," said Gary McMonagle of Mineral Ridge, Ohio. "As the natural speed and agility of youth begin to fade, I find I must use my mental abilities more to stay ahead.

"On the afternoon before each game," he continued, "I go into level and imagine myself playing flawlessly. Visualizing myself prepared at shortstop, I imagine myself moving fluidly to the left, picking up a hard ground ball, throwing accurately to first base. The next play I move to the right, skillfully field another ground ball, throw accurately to first.

"Then I charge a slow rolling ball, scoop it up quickly and throw accurately to first. And finally I leap up for a high line drive, time it perfectly and come down with the ball in my mitt.

"Always in level I do each play to perfection, performing without error and hearing the congratulations of my teammates.

"With batting I take it one step further. The difficulty with slow pitch softball is that the bat is swinging horizontal, while the ball is coming down almost vertical. So while I'm at my level, I imagine myself using my Three Fingers Technique.

"I walk up to the plate, touch my three fingers together while taking a deep breath and say, 'slow motion.' Then from when the ball leaves the pitcher's hand until it crosses home plate, time appears to be slowed down so it takes about 30 seconds.

"Even with a vertically falling ball and a horizontally swinging bat, it is difficult to miss such a s-l-o-w moving object. And hit! I mentally picture the ball being lined into the outfield and falling in for a base hit. In the actual game, I can only achieve the time distortion about one-third of the time. But one-third of the at-bats being guaranteed hits does wonders for the batting average!

"At season's end," McMonagle concluded, "I always have one of the highest averages on the team and for the past three years have been voted by my fellow players to represent them on the All-Star Team. Thanks to Silva!"

Some pointers from Pepe

Jose Luis "Pepe" Romero has played competitive sports all his life and has worked for Jose Silva at Silva International, Inc., since 1972. Along the way, he has learned some valuable tips about using the Silva Method to stay competitive, even in one's 40s. At Ed Bernd Jr.'s request, he presented some of his experiences and suggestions in a workshop at the 1994 Silva International Convention in Laredo. Here is an excerpt from his presentation:

"Visualization can help you to motivate yourself to work out... to motivate yourself to go out and actually participate, take part in the activity, in the game. It can help you to prepare, and it can help you to correct your mistakes.

"In everything in life, you need to prepare yourself mentally. You hear that 90 percent of the time, it is a mental thing - the mental game. You also need to do the physical things. But sometimes, what do we do? Get home, sit down, turn on the television. How do you motivate yourself to go out there and do the things you need to do to prepare yourself? Use the visualization techniques. Imagine yourself doing the things.

"One of the best ways to motivate yourself is to visualize your successes. Visualize the times when you accomplished something good... when you won the game, when you did something spectacular. Those will help you to motivate yourself to go and work out.

"How many time have you said, 'Gee, if I had just done this, we would have won the game'? You can prepare yourself by using the Silva Mental Rehearsal Technique. Imagine yourself doing the things that you need to do. Imagine yourself doing the right things.

"If you have made a mistake, acknowledge it, and correct it. That's all you need to do. By the time you get to the physical part, you will have already played the game. You will have already won the game."

Now here are 10 recommendations for improving your practice routine, as developed by Jose Silva.

10 Ways to Use Your Mind to Improve Your Practice Sessions

In order to get the most benefit from the Silva Method techniques, it is important that you establish a regular practice routine. Mental practice is just as important as physical practice. The following 10 recommendations will help you thoroughly prepare yourself to reach your fitness and athletic goals.

1. Take time to practice deep relaxation at least once a week. Set aside enough time to practice the progressive relaxation exercise that you learned in Chapter 5. This will accomplish a couple of things for you. First, it will help you establish and maintain a deep level of mind. Second, it will be valuable to you when you encounter high-pressure situations. When you have practiced enough, you will be able to relax your body simply by

recalling that feeling of deep relaxation.

2. Establish a regular mental practice routine, and go to level at least once every day. The best time to practice is in the morning when you first wake up. The second best time is in the evening before you go to sleep. The third best time is at noon, after lunch. To practice once a day is good, twice a day is very good, three times a day is excellent. Five minutes of practice is good, 10 minutes is very good and 15 minutes is excellent. Practice even when you don't really need to; this way, going to level will become so automatic that you will be able to go to level at any time, no matter how stressful the circumstances.

3. Remember: While it is important to first identify any weaknesses or mistakes that you want to correct, you want to spend most of your time imagining yourself performing correctly. Review the instructions in Chapter 6 from time to time.

4. Remember to get your feelings involved in your programming. First, have your coach or trainer work with you to make sure you are doing the movements correctly. Check your balance, your timing, your form. As you perform correctly, notice how your body feels at various times. For instance, if you are practicing your golf swing, notice how your body feels as you address the ball, how it feels during your backswing, at the top of your backswing, as you bring the club down, as you strike the ball and as you follow through. Then later, at your level, recall all of these feelings, to help you perform better. The same applies to every exercise and to every sport.

5. Whenever you program to correct a mistake or a weakness, or to become even better at what you do, follow up by doing it physically after you do it mentally. After you program your golf swing, remember to go out and practice the swing. Physical practice reinforces your mental practice, just as your mental practice reinforces the physical.

6. Program for your teammates and friends to perform well. As long as you imagine a perfect performance, you will benefit.

7. Remember what you learned about positive thinking in Chapter 2: Positive thinking is thinking about what you want. Your belief system is very important. If necessary, program yourself at your level to be more positive. Avoid negative statements, and say positive things. Give yourself a chance to perform correctly and win. Do not fear making mistakes, but think about doing your best and performing correctly. When you do make mistakes, "cancel-cancel" them, and immediately imagine yourself performing correctly. Get used to doing this while training and practicing, so that when you are competing it will be natural and automatic, and you will do it without having to stop and think about it.

8. Remember that "mental toughness" is nothing more than keeping your attention on your goal, your desired end result. People who think about mistakes are not mentally tough. People who dwell on errors will make more errors. Practice being mentally tough by "cancel-canceling" your miscues and thinking about performing correctly.

9. Increase your desire by thinking about your goal. Think about such things as getting into great shape, winning the championship and feeling proud of your accomplishments when your friends and family praise and compliment you. Review Chapter 3 for a more thorough discussion of motivation.

10. When you are preparing for competition, spend some time at level thinking about what your opponent might do. Do not let them surprise you; make it a fair competition. Use your creative and intuitive ability at your level and look at things from your opponent's point of view. If you can anticipate what your opponent's strategy is, then you can prepare for it. This will make the contest more equal and fair; it will be decided on athletic skill rather than trickery.

Chapter 12

Using mental techniques in competition

After his track career was over, long-distance runner Willie Ketchum became a long-distance truck driver. He continued to be a winner, as the following incident demonstrates.

After several hours on the road, he stopped at his favorite truck stop, went into the restaurant and asked his favorite waitress for his favorite meal: thick steak, baked potato with all the trimmings, chef's salad with the special house dressing and homemade hot apple pie with a big scoop of ice cream melting over it.

Just as the waitress was bringing over the meal, four grubby, mean-looking motorcycle punks swaggered into the diner. They spotted the truck driver, went over and sat themselves right down at his table.

One took his steak, picked it up and began gnawing on it. Another took the big salad, poured the whole pitcher of dressing over it and started shoveling it into his dirty mouth. The third took the potato, smashed it up with the sour cream, cheese and bacon bits and started cramming it into his mouth. The fourth dug into the homemade hot apple pie, the ice cream running down his scraggly beard.

Willie sat for a moment, looking at their taunting expressions. They were bigger than he was, and stronger. But Willie was a champion - he knew how to win.

He got up without saying a word, went to the cash register, paid his bill and left. They could hear his big 18-wheeler pulling out of the parking lot.

"Boy, he sure wasn't much of a man, was he?" one motorcycle rider sneered at the waitress.

"No," she answered with a shake of her head and a glint in her eye. "And he wasn't much of a truck driver, either. He just ran over four motorcycles as he was driving out of the parking lot!"

Outwit your opponents

Physical skills can put you in a position to win. But to become a champion, you also need mental skills. You must use your mind to help you give your best performance. To maximize your workouts and your performance, you must visualize your goals, and you must do this visualization at the alpha level.

With practice, you can learn to do this visualization even during competition. And you can also learn how to predict what is going to happen so that you will have time to prepare for your opponent and develop a winning strategy.

Top athletes tell how they play the mental game

Top athletes have used visualization and imagination to help them perform better for years. They are the lucky few who are natural alpha thinkers. In this book, we have provided reports from many of them about how they play the mental game.

Legendary golfer Ben Hogan is one of them; he talked about how he used his imagination during matches long before Jose Silva had perfected his mind training system.

Time magazine reported that when Hogan was playing in a tournament, he would mentally rehearse each shot just before making it.

He makes the shot perfectly in his imagination - "feels" the clubhead strike the ball just as it should, "feels" himself performing the perfect follow-through - and then steps up to the ball and depends on what he calls "muscle memory" to carry out the shot just as he has imagined it.

Now let's hear how some modern athletes have used Jose Silva's scientifically researched and proven techniques in competition to help them perform better and win. Then we will get some more tips and guidance from Jose Silva.

Silva techniques help Olympic fencers

Sports psychologist Andrzej Wojcikiewicz found several ways to use the Silva Method techniques in fencing competition. He even helped athletes learn how to use their intuition to figure out in advance what their competitors had in mind so that they could be prepared for it.

Wojcikiewicz is a highly respected sports psychologist and coach who already had a lot of experience both in fencing and in sports psychology when he first encountered the Silva Method. He was the national Olympic coach in fencing in Denmark from 1972 to 1977. In 1978 he became the coach of the Canadian national fencing team. He earned a Master of Science degree in sports psychology from the University of Ottawa in Canada in 1984. Five years later, he attended the Silva Method Basic Lecture Series.

He was so impressed with the potential for the Silva Method in sports that he attended the Silva instructor training program, and in 1990 he taught the techniques to most of the national team fencers, as well as key national coaches.

"First of all, this had an extremely strong impact on the team harmony and team skill levels," Wojcikiewicz said. "This was probably a major factor in the success of the Canadian sabre and epee [two types of fencing foils] teams in the 1991 World Fencing Championships in Budapest, Hungary, and the success of the epee team in the Barcelona Olympics in 1992.

"We used visualization, expectation and all the rest," Wojcikiewicz said. "But during the match, the Three Fingers Technique was the most frequently used technique. We used it to help us relax and also to get more adrenaline going, to get into the fighting spirit."

Wojcikiewicz said the team used the visualization technique to train in technical skills as well as to program the outcome of competitions. For intuition, they called upon a special technique that is taught in the Silva UltraMind ESP System. This technique allows you to experience what another person is experiencing by imagining that you are putting their head over your own, as though you were putting on a helmet.

"This was used by some fencers before unusually difficult bouts in order to instinctively plan the correct strategy for the fencing match," Wojcikiewicz explained. "One fencer imagined putting on the head of a world champion before a match, got the feeling, took off the helmet' and then fenced the match with a great success."

The Canadian team, which had been ranked only 12th in the world, rose rapidly through the rankings and finished far better than expected in the Olympic Games the following year. The year after they finished the Silva course, they rose from 12th place to sixth place. They went to the Olympic games in Barcelona and came within one touch of the medal round.

Silva techniques give young gymnast an edge

At age 11, Natalie Lacuesta was the youngest and least experienced gymnast on her team, and it was her first year on the team. She needed some way to steady her nerves and improve her concentration.

Natalie's mother, Dr. Evelyn Lacuesta, took her to the Silva course on the advice of three sisters-in-law.

"They are graduates of the course," Dr. Lacuesta explained, "and had been telling me for a long time that we should take the course."

So in order to give Natalie an extra edge, they took the course. Natalie subsequently won the U.S. Junior National Rhythmic Gymnastics Championship, beating out the older, more experienced competitors. By the age of 13, she had been ranked number one in the nation in rhythmic gymnastics, junior division, for two consecutive years.

Her next goal was to compete in the 1996 Olympic Games in Atlanta, GA. When Natalie inquired about trying out for the Olympic Games, she learned that her age worked against her.

While everyone was impressed with her accomplishments, the rules specify that only senior division athletes can try out for the Olympic team - and you must be 15 years old to join the senior division. Natalie wouldn't turn 15 until a couple of months after the Olympics were over. Once again, programming came to the rescue. With hundreds of Silva graduates in the Chicago area programming for her, she won a chance to try out for the U.S. Olympic Team. Unfortunately for Natalie, only one athlete would be selected, and the committee selected one of the older girls.

Mental practice has paid big dividends for Natalie when it comes to competition. When she is standing at the edge of the mat, ready to begin her routine, she is relaxing and programming.

"I go to my level to relax before I go on the mat," she said. "It helps me to focus on my routine more and to keep my nerves down. I use my Three Fingers Technique to calm myself down and to concentrate on my routine," she said.

Then, with the image and the feel of a perfect routine imprinted strongly in her mind, she proceeds to give a championship performance and shows everyone why she is ranked number one in the nation. She often programs before going to her practice sessions. "Before I go to the gym," she said, "I do the Long Relaxation Exercise, and then I go through my routine in my mind."

She also programs every evening. "I program that when I am doing my routine, I stay focused, I stay relaxed and am not nervous."

Black belt at age 57

Richard D. Grater of St. Louis, Mo., is the first person older than 35 to earn a black belt in the karate studio where he trains.

"For several years, the Silva Method has been very successful for me in programming for physical results," he said. "This year, after training for seven and a half years, I passed my black belt karate test at Tracy's Karate in St. Louis. It was the first time anyone over 35 had achieved a black belt in any of their local studios. My age was 57 at the time."

Grater used the Silva visualization and Three Fingers techniques in order to overcome physical exhaustion. Even though the black belt test took three and a half hours, Grater felt that his five years of having used the Silva Method (ever since his third brown belt test) made the test less difficult. "Prior to using Silva, I had a very difficult time with the physical requirements at the lower (elementary) levels. After applying the information from the Silva basic course, I was able to breeze through these lower levels easily and do well on the advanced belts.

"In addition, I programmed for the Senior Olympics in St. Louis and won men's volleyball for three years, plus I won the running long jump this year.

"In the National Senior Olympics, also held in St. Louis, I made the mistake of programming for third in the running long jump. Guess what I placed? Third! To keep from getting second I had a foul on my best jump. If I had programmed to do my best I would have had at least second. Next year I will be first in this event."

LPGA golf pro programs for fun and success

Sherry Dircks, the head professional at a private country club near Phoenix, AZ, uses visualization and the Three Fingers

Technique to help her have fun - and win - on the golf course.

Sherry is a member of the Ladies Professional Golfers Association (LPGA) Teaching and Club Professionals Division. She took the Silva course in 1988. "I preprogram myself before a round," she said. "Before I leave the house, I enter my level and visualize the round I want to have. I program myself to have fun and to be relaxed.

"Then when I am actually on the course, playing the round, I use my Three Fingers Technique to help me achieve what I programmed for. I put my three fingers together to help me relax. When I put the ball on the tee, I put my three fingers together to help me visualize where I want the ball to go.

"Two years ago I began using a new technique," she said. "When I am lining up a putt, I imagine a big catcher's mitt behind the hole. I imagine that the ball hits it and falls in the cup. And it works."

Dircks teaches her students to focus on the target - where they want the ball to go - instead of focusing on the ball. "When you focus on the ball, you tend to chop down on it," she said.

"Of course, you have to look at the ball, but if you focus on the target the green - then it is easier to hit the ball towards the target. That's what the really good players do. Instead of focusing on the ball, they focus on their swing, where the clubhead goes."

She explained, "When you are not focusing your eyes, you can be at the alpha level and you can visualize what you want to achieve. I'm sure that this is what the great golfers do.

"This is true in other sports as well," she pointed out. "When you first learn to shoot a basketball, for instance, you concentrate on the ball: how to hold it, the movement of your arms and wrists. After you have mastered the movements, then you learn to focus on the basket.

Pro golfer wins when he takes his eye off the ball

"You could see Johnny Miller focusing on the target when he won the AT&T Tournament," Dircks continued. "You could see him looking at the hole while he was putting.

"He talks about it on a videotape titled Insights to the Players' Minds, which is part of the series The Player's Course. Miller was having trouble with his putting. He told the interviewer, Chuck Hogan, that he heard a voice that told him to look at the hole when he was putting. The video even includes a film clip of him doing that at the AT&T Tournament.

"Actually, quite a few golfers have done that. Beth Daniels did the same thing when she was having some trouble putting.

"Golf is such a mental game," Dircks noted. "Your mind has to be right in order for your body to do what you want. So I program myself to have a sense of freedom - to have no restrictions. I program that my energy just flows. This makes it much easier to play good, consistent rounds."

Only focus when ready to strike

Jose Silva Jr. - Joe Jr. as he is known at the office - was a boxer when he was in the Navy and is also a black belt in karate. He talks about using a "defocus point" when fighting.

"If you focus on one part of a person's body," Joe says, "you won't see another part of the body in time to react to an attack with that part of the body. If you are watching the person's eyes, you may not see their foot move in time for you to block it as they try to kick you."

What he recommends is that you look towards your opponent's chest, but do not focus your eyes on the chest. In this manner, Joe says, you can be aware of the person's entire body and can react quickly to whatever he or she does.

You only focus your eyes when you are ready to strike. Then you go back to the defocused vision.

There is another big advantage to using this technique: It makes it easier to be in alpha.

How to be in alpha during competition

Whenever you focus your eyes, or attempt to focus your eyes, your brain goes to 20 cps - beta. Even in beta you still have some alpha output. During the day, while you are in beta, your brain dips into alpha approximately 30 times every minute. But only for a few microseconds. You might be in alpha for three seconds out of that minute.

By practicing the deep relaxation that you learned in Chapter 5 and going to level every day, you will become so accustomed to being at alpha that both the time and the quality of alpha during those brief episodes will improve.

When your brain dips into alpha it will stay there longer. And since you are so familiar with functioning at alpha, you will be able to benefit from even a fraction of a second there. This is how people have hunches or flashes of insight. It helps to explain why they can sometimes do extraordinary things even when they have not counted themselves into alpha.

If you want to have even more alpha functioning with your eyes open, there is a way to do it: Defocus your vision. That is, keep your eyes open, but do not focus them on any particular thing. It is a lot like a daydreaming state. You will still be aware of what is in front of you, but it is like you are seeing things indirectly. You can do this by using the "defocus point" technique that Joe Jr. recommends.

"We have another technique that we call focusing," Joe explains. "You use that when you are going to deliver a blow. You focus on the part of the body that you want to hit. As soon as you are done, you go back to the defocus point technique, so that you can be aware of what your opponent is going to do.

"When you use this technique, you will know what your opponent is going to do before it happens. Everything goes into slow motion."

Many athletes have talked about how the action sometimes seems to slow down in the heat of competition. Perhaps it is more a matter of your brain operating faster when you are at alpha, so that when you are not at alpha, things seem slower.

More victories with the Silva System

Here are a few more stories of success with Silva techniques that Silva lecturer Judy Qua collected for her book, *Everyday Miracles and the Silva Method*.

Eugene L. Velasco, the assistant vice president of a stock brokerage firm in the Makati Stock Exchange in the Philippines, used the visualization technique to lead his team to victory in a "sportsfest" held by the group of companies for which he works.

"I am not actually sports minded, and I was not very enthusiastic about the event," Velasco admitted. "Thus, we were considered by everyone else as the most likely loser of the event, even though we had some good players on our team.

After completing the first weekend of the Silva Method, I thought I'd try an applicable technique to make our team win an event," he said.

Velasco imagined using a green headband (his team was the green team) to encourage team spirit and easy team recognition and help enlighten the minds of the members.

At the next group meeting, the team's captain proposed the idea of using green headbands and contributed money to buy them.

Then Velasco mentally pictured the team in joyous triumph, having won the championship, and receiving the championship trophy during the awards night.

"Amazingly, we won the first game of the event (a marathon course). And during the subsequent games, although we experienced some losses, we continuously maintained the leading position.

"All throughout the games," Velasco said, "I noticed how we had caught the members of the other teams by surprise as they were not expecting us to lead in the games. Our team was energetic and had a strong, fighting spirit. After each game, only our team cheered a lot no matter what the result was.

"I participated in only one event where our team also made it to the number-one slot. What I did was move around during the games talking to the members and imparting to them a positive mental attitude. I continuously asked them to think only of number one and to cancel any negative expectations.

"At any rate, our team's victory created the strong impression on other teams that physical practice is not all there is to win the event," said Velasco.

Rafael "Paeng" Nepomuceno described how he used the Silva Method to help him win his third World Cup of Bowling victory.

"I have been practicing the Silva Method for three years now," he said. "After I took the course, I also had a few private sessions with Judy Qua to help me manage my nerves.

"In 1992 I had the chance again at the World Cup in Le Mans, France. I was able to realize my dream of winning the World Cup for the third time, the first person in the world to do so, through the Silva Method.

"My mental programming is quite simple: I just used a lot of feelings, and, of course, my desire was strong and intense. I also concentrated on my belief that I could do it and that I expected it. It was that simple.

"During the World Cup competition, I imagined surrounding myself with white light to shield myself from all opponents. In the process I broke four world records. In previous years, different people held the world records at different times, and this was the first time that one bowler surpassed all in one tournament. I led by 551 pins, the biggest winning margin ever in the World Cup.

"So from day to day I reinforced my visualization to stay in the lead," said Nepomuceno. "It was as if I was untouchable."

Joel E. Paner told Judy Qua how he used the Silva Method in December 1991 when his tennis club had an exclusive doubles tennis tournament.

"The problem is that my partner and I were not really top caliber players," he said. "I didn't belong to the top five of the 20 who were playing, and my teammate was only a beginner, having just learned the game only six months before.

The rule applied in elimination was the knock-out system, meaning that if you lose one game then you're out."

Every night before a match, Paner used the Silva visualization technique to imagine that the last point of the match always counted in his and his partner's favor.

He also imagined their opponents congratulating them as the winners. During the match he used the Three Fingers Technique for a good, powerful return of serve.

"It worked. I was able to break the serves most of the time," Paner said.

"We were able to win our first two matches and so were able to advance into the semifinals wherein only three teams out of the original 10 were left to fight it out. Again I used the same techniques and was able to eliminate one team to qualify for the championship finals."

When he was about to play for the championship match, he visualized that cherished situation wherein the organizers were handing the championship trophy to him and his partner.

"What was imagined in my mind was actualized in the awarding ceremony," Paner said.

Winning at board games

The same mental techniques that help you win physical contests can help you win other kinds of competitions as well, as the following story from a back issue of Silva Newsletter, the official publication of Silva International, Inc., demonstrates.

Vernon Ball said he used Silva techniques to help him win a world championship in one of the world's oldest games - backgammon.

He won the Eighth Annual World Championship of Backgammon held on Paradise Island, Nassau, Bahamas in 1977.

Experts in the field said that Ball, who had played backgammon a little more than two years when he won the world title, has a revolutionary style and is the most exciting personality that the game has ever had.

Ball said that for him, a crucial plan in the game is a matter of intuition, and the Silva Method enabled him to heighten his intuition.

So remember, whenever you want to come out on top - in sports or in any other activity - use your Silva techniques to help you do it.

And for more help, here is Jose Silva's guidance on programming in the heat of competition.

10 ways to use Silva techniques in competition

In the previous chapter, you received guidance on how to program yourself ahead of time, during training and practice, to be better prepared for competition. There are many ways that to use the Silva techniques to help you in actual competition:

1. The night before competition can be a stressful time.

Enter your level and relax, and program yourself to remain relaxed.

Use that feeling of relaxation that you have while you are at level as a point of reference, so that you can recall that feeling later when you need to relax.

Use the Sleep Control Technique in Chapter 16 to help you get a good night's sleep.

2. Use your level to calm your nerves just before competition.

Anticipating an event is often more stressful than the event itself. Even some professional athletes get sick and throw up shortly before competition. Use your level to correct this.

- Identify the problem in the first monitor that you get too tense.

- Identify the solution in Monitor Number 2 having all the energy you need but not too much tension.

- And in Monitor Number 3, imagine yourself going into competition ready to perform at the very peak of your ability.

3. During breaks in the competition, use your visualization techniques to correct any mistakes and imagine yourself performing perfectly when you get back into competition.

Close your eyes or defocus your vision, and recall the feeling of being at your level.

You can also preprogram yourself that when you use the

Three Fingers Technique, you will be at your level so that you can program.

Practice ahead of time, so that when you are in a high-pressure competitive situation you will be able to program yourself in only a matter of seconds.

4. At halftime, or whenever you have a long enough break, count yourself into your level, review your mistakes and cancel-cancel them.

Then review the things you did well and reinforce them, especially recalling how you felt.

Then program to perform correctly in the second half and win.

5. Use a trigger mechanism, as you learned in Chapter 8.

You can use your Three Fingers Technique to help you perform better, or a phrase, or the cheering of the crowd.

Preprogram your trigger mechanism at your level ahead of time, and expect it to work for you during competition.

6. Stay focused by canceling out any distractions and thinking about what you want to accomplish.

If you make a mistake and it helps your opponent, then mentally or verbally say "cancel-cancel," erase the image of the mistake and start thinking about what you want to accomplish.

This is what is meant by "mental toughness."

7. Recall the feeling of succeeding, of winning.

Recall how you felt mentally, emotionally and physically when you were performing exceptionally well, when you were "in the zone."

Use the "special state of mind" technique that you learned in Chapter 8. Call on your Mental Coach to help you, as you learned in Chapter 7.

8. Be careful about trying to "psych out" your opponent.

Remember Mental Housecleaning in Chapter 2. Any image that you put into your mind will make an impression on your brain. And signals from your brain control your body.

Wish your opponents well, and make sure that you do a little better than they do.

9. Help your teammates stay focused and positive by encouraging them.

Do not tell them what *not* to do; tell them what *to* do.

Beware of the word "don't."

Instead of saying, "Don't miss the ball" or "Don't blow the play," tell them to "Hit the ball" or "Hold your position."

Review Chapter 2 on Mental Housecleaning, and program yourself to make only positive statements when competing.

10. When you've got your intuition going for you, use it.

If you correctly anticipate what is likely to happen, then use this success to help you have even more successes.

Even in the midst of competition, if you can take a moment to put your three fingers together and program the feeling that you had when you correctly anticipated the event, this can help you to anticipate more events.

After the competition is over, enter your level, review all of your successes and reinforce them, especially how you felt, so that you can use this to have even more successes in the future.

It is easier to detect - anticipate - what another person is thinking or planning to when they are there with you. That's because the physical part of your aura extends about 8 meters out from your body. Now that you are aware that you can detect information this way, you will find it easy to do.

Chapter 13

Post-competition programming

Two golfers who had sliced their balls into the rough searched for them for a long time. Finally an old lady who had been watching them called out, "I hope I'm not interrupting, gentlemen, but would I be cheating if I told you where they are?"

Failure is best forgotten

Perfect games are rare. So are perfect practice sessions and perfect training sessions. Whenever you have one of them, you remember it. So do your friends. People talk about it. You enjoy it. It builds your confidence.

It is always good to fill your consciousness with memories of these successes. It is not good to dwell on mistakes and failures. We talked about that back in Chapter 2.

After you have identified the problem and figured out what went wrong, it is time to let it go and move on. It is good to go to your level after your performance so that you can correct mistakes, cancel them out and reinforce your successes.

Here are some ideas on how to do this from athletes who have been doing it for a long time.

Post-competition evaluation and programming

Bruce Schneider of East Brunswick, N.J., uses all of his experiences - both the successes and the mistakes - to help him improve his athletic performance.

Schneider, a big, powerful man who plays slow pitch softball, was an average player when he first took the Silva course. But he had a dream. "I wanted to play on one of the best teams and be one of the top players in the country," he said. "I wanted to be good enough to be listed in the U.S. Slow Pitch Softball Association's Directory."

So that's what he programmed to happen, and it all came to pass.

"Softball is a highly mental game," Schneider explained. "Once you have the basic talent and determine what type of player you are best suited to be (a lot of people try to be something they are not and do not end up enjoying the game as much as they should), then your mental abilities take over - to a degree that we may never understand.

"Your mental abilities, once increased, can help you in every aspect of your life. I know, because I've done it myself:

I went from being an average player to batting cleanup on the fourth-ranked team in the world," he said. The strongest hitter is usually the one selected for the "cleanup" position - the fourth up at bat - so he has a chance to score any of the first three batters who may be on base.

"My first year playing in the top league in the northeastern United States, I hit three home runs," Schneider recalled. "Through programming with the Silva Method techniques, I raised that to an average of 17 or 18 per year.

"But I was not satisfied. One guy, who was a national legend in the game, held the record with 29 home runs. I visualized myself hitting more home runs. I watched videos of myself and other players hitting home runs. I worked out with weights and programmed myself to get the feeling of making a perfect lift so that I could grow stronger. And my home runs increased every year.

"I finally broke the record. In 1991, I hit more home runs than the guy who had become a legend. The record was 29 home runs. In 28 games, I hit 37 home runs, and I had 91 runs batted in."

Every experience an opportunity to improve

"Very few people take advantage of their recent learning experiences," Schneider said. "You just played a game or tournament; now what? There are very valuable exercises to help you benefit from what you have just accomplished, whether the results were good or bad.

"First, let us say you were successful.

"The most important thing here is to figure out why so you can reproduce it. Did you practice the pre-game techniques? What was going through your mind during the game? Try to remember as many details as possible. Make sure you "file" this experience so you can recall it and benefit from it the next time. Remember how you felt after your success, how your teammates reacted, how you felt in the car on the way home.

"What if you played poorly? No experience is ever a losing one. You can get a great learning experience from your failures. Actually, the word failure is a poor one. The only failure would be to not learn something from your mistakes. Analyze the events from before and during the game to see if you can pinpoint why things went wrong. Were you nervous? If so, you need to relax more and believe in yourself. Remember the magic word: confidence.

"After you figure out what went wrong (if you could), then mentally correct these mistakes. Relax and visualize yourself in the game again. Only this time fix the outcome and perform in your mind the way you wanted to. There are many benefits to doing this. One is to erase any negative thoughts and reprogram yourself to think only positive thoughts.

"The mind is a resource that few people ever tap into to help them get what they want. Remember that we use only a small percentage of our brains. Who knows what will happen when we learn to use more?" said Schneider.

A library of successes

"My greatest success story using a Silva technique," Schneider recalled, "involves a technique that I have used time and time again. I simply go to level during a pressure situation and visualize a previous success. I have a library' of successes that I make withdrawals' from when I need them."

Schneider was playing softball in a World Series qualifier tournament when he found himself at bat in the bottom of the last inning. His team was down two runs and had two runners on base, with two outs. "This is the ultimate pressure situation," he said.

"If I swung and missed, we were out of the tournament!"

But he had practiced going to level so much that he was able to get to his level, even during this pressure situation. "I took a deep breath, relaxed my body, defocused my vision for a moment and recalled the feeling of being at my level," he said. "Then I visualized my previous best success. I had been up three times already that game and hit two home runs and a single. So far, I was the hero of the game.

"I had been in a similar situation and came through with a hit. I coupled this memory with the success I had already had in the game and was able to feel a great deal of power.

"I always try to get my feelings involved," he said. "This time the feeling was so strong that I knew I would succeed... and I did!" Schneider's teammates carried him off on their shoulders after he hit his home run.

"It was an incredible experience. This, then, became my point of reference' whenever I need to recall what it feels like to be successful. I can recall the sights, sounds, feel and even the smell!

"Now, before any pressure situation, I imagine that I have

just accomplished my feat again, and it almost always leads to another success. The key, of course, is being able to do this at the alpha level.

Practice your mental training just as much as you do your physical training, so that you can do it easily and automatically even in high-pressure situations."

3 steps to greater success

Schneider uses a "before, during and after" technique to help him become a better player:

1. "I go to level and prepare for an event by imagining myself performing perfectly. I include all the feelings and sensations. I want to create a feeling of accomplishment before I even start."

2. "During the game I let go. I put myself on autopilot and trust my programming."

3. "After the game, I evaluate what I did at my level, mentally making any corrections that are necessary. I find there are valuable lessons to be gained from mistakes. Great athletes are able to learn from mistakes and not dwell on them. Of course, I also reinforce my successes and replay them over and over in my mind."

Programming for better workouts

For successful training routines, Schneider recommends the Silva Awake Control Technique, which you will learn in Chapter 16. Here is how he uses it:

"At my level, I tell myself mentally that I feel tired and weak, that I don't want to feel tired and weak - I want to feel energetic and powerful. I tell myself that I will count from 1 to 5, and at the count of 5, I will feel energetic and powerful. Then I do it. This always works."

He also uses the Three Fingers Technique: "Sometimes when I am training with weights, I put my three fingers together, close my eyes and visualize the perfect lift. Once I feel that I have already accomplished this lift, I do it. I know this works, because it so very often does - and this keeps my belief and expectancy very high. Most of my personal bests were accomplished with this method."

10 Post-event strategies to improve your performance

Now here is Jose Silva's guidance on what you can do after you have completed your performance, training or competition to help you continue to improve.

1. Some coaches and sports psychologists will take videos of their players in competition, cut out all the mistakes and have the players watch the edited videos that show only their successes.

You can do the same thing at your level. In fact, you can do even better: "Cancel-cancel" mistakes and imagine yourself having performed correctly. Combine these revised performances along with your successful actions, and you will have a fabulous "mental movie" that you can review again and again.

2. Remember to review every great play that you made, every success that you had and especially recall the feeling that you had at the time.

Did you have a special state of mind were you "in the zone"?

How did your body feel? Balanced? Strong? Agile?

What was your emotional state? Relaxed? Exhilarated?

Recall these feelings, at your level, and incorporate them into your future programming to help you to be just as successful again and even more successful in the future.

3. Use Mental Housecleaning. Sometimes people get down on you when you make a mistake that causes you to lose. They have a right to be disappointed. And you must be gracious to them, even though they are saying things that may hurt you.

However, without their even knowing it, you can use Mental Housecleaning to help yourself:

When they mention what you did, you can say, "Yes, and I should have..." and describe the positive image that you have in mind. Or you could say, "But remember when I did..." and mention a success that you had. Or perhaps, "Well, next time I will..." and get them thinking about positive events in the future.

If they continue to be negative, then excuse yourself and leave at the earliest opportunity, go to level and recall your successes.

4. Remember that every experience is a learning experience. Remember that Babe Ruth struck out almost twice as many times as he hit home runs, and he is still considered the Home Run King. Remember that the only people who don't make mistakes are the people who never attempt anything.

Give yourself a pep talk at your level.

Call on your friends who are also practicing the Silva Method; they will program for you and help you overcome your disappointment.

Remember what former United States President Teddy Roosevelt said:

"It is not the critic who counts. The credit belongs to the one who is actually in the arena; whose face is marred by dust and sweat and blood; who strives valiantly; who, at the best, knows the triumph of high achievement; and who, at the worst, if he fails, at least fails while daring greatly, so that his place shall never be with those cold and timid souls who know neither victory nor defeat."

5. We have a saying here in the American West: If a horse throws you, get right back on the horse. That's because if you wait, the anticipation of trying again can breed thoughts of more failure. Face your fears immediately.

Program yourself to perform successfully, then go and do it.

Never let the pain of the past, or the fear of the future, keep you from enjoying life today. Program yourself.

When you are nervous about doing something, then enter your level and imagine doing it, over and over again, until you are no longer fearful but are confident. Then go do it.

6. When there are weaknesses that you desire to correct, enter your level and analyze the problem at your level. Determine exactly what the problem is, and then program to perform correctly. Imagine yourself correcting the problem and performing correctly.

7. When you are studying videos of your performance, preprogram yourself that you will use the Three Fingers Technique to help you identify the cause of the problem and to know what to do to correct it:

Enter your level, bring together the tips of the thumb and first two fingers of either hand, and mentally tell yourself, "In a moment, I am going to watch a video of myself performing (mention the event and the date). While watching this video, I will have superior understanding and the ability to detect problems and to know how to correct them." Then open your eyes and watch the video.

Use your Three Fingers Technique while watching the video. After you have watched it, enter your level, use your Three Fingers Technique and analyze your situation, so that you can determine what to correct and how to correct it.

8. Use new information to your advantage. After every training or practice session and after every competition, you

have gained additional experiences. You now have more information than you had before. Use this new information to help you:

Enter your level and analyze how you performed, and determine whether you might have performed better if your preparation had been different.

Did you over-train or under-train previously, and thus hurt your performance?

Were there certain things that you neglected to do?

Or things you did that were unnecessary?

Use this information to help you improve your training and practice sessions.

9. Your body heals faster at alpha. Spending 15 minutes at alpha strengthens your immune mechanism.

Whenever you have worked hard and especially if you have sustained any injuries, enter alpha for 15 minutes and imagine yourself overcoming the strain and injuries (if you have any) and regaining perfect health.

There is more information on injury recovery and health maintenance in Chapter 19.

10. Give your body enough time to recover from the extra load you have placed on it, but do not use this as an excuse to be lazy and take too much time off.

At your level, analyze the situation and determine what is best for your body at this time. Consult with your Mental Coach.

Remember, the alpha level is the best level for making decisions. Then act on those decisions, and let the results that you get guide you in your future programming.

Section 4:

General Self-Improvement Techniques

This section of the book includes a variety of techniques for your health and well-being. Review the contents and select any subject area that you want to work on.

For information on an audio-video home study course, please visit www.SilvaCourses.com and check out our Choose Success program.

The section after this one includes subjects that do not fit into the other categories, including information that parents and coaches can use when working with young people.

Chapter 14

Develop success habits

Jack was depressed as he and his wife, Jill, left church following a particularly blistering sermon by Rev. Stone.

"All those things he talked about," Jack said, "drinking, smoking, goofing off when I should be working, I'm guilty of all those things. That makes it seem like my life is worthless."

"Nobody's life is worthless," Jill said.

"Even mine?"

"Even yours," Jill answered. "Look at it this way: You can always serve as a bad example. You'd be perfect for that!"

A powerful lesson from a real-life "bad example"

Old jokes can lose their humor with the passage of time. Before you laugh too much at the joke above, think about baseball player Mickey Mantle. As we were writing this book, Mantle was receiving a liver transplant that was needed to save his life. He died a few weeks later.

"I had it all," Mantle said to a television audience a month after the transplant, "and I threw it all away. I was finished when I was 36." Speaking from his hospital bed, he shrugged and said, "This is a role model? Don't be like me."

The baseball great said he ruined his liver from too much alcohol. Drinking was the thing to do in the 1950s, and Mantle did it very well. A valuable saying comes to mind: It is good to learn from your mistakes, but it is even better to learn from other people's mistakes.

There is no excuse for people to engage in bad habits that ruin their health and their lives. Superstar athletes are dying from using recreational drugs. Others are dying from using performance-enhancing drugs - steroids.

And there is no doubt about it: Cigarette smoking not only hurts athletic performance, it kills people every day.

An even more powerful tool

Habits start as cobwebs and become cables, according to a Spanish proverb. They are hard to break. This can be bad news or good news, depending on what your habits are.

If your habits include drinking, smoking, doing drugs and ducking work, they will hurt you. But if they are good habits, you can win championships, earn fame and fortune and have all of the good things you want in life.

Author Ed Bernd Jr. says he had both kinds of habits. Fortunately, he survived the bad ones. Now he programs himself to have good habits that help him reach his goals. You can use this same tool. Here's what he learned after making a lot of mistakes, then studying with Jose Silva.

The anatomy of a habit

What are habits?

Habits are simply repeated patterns of behavior that are easier for you to continue than to change. In other words, once you get used to doing something, any effort to change and do something else is very threatening. If you are accustomed to losing, the prospect of winning can be very threatening - so threatening that you find a way to lose.

The good news is that once you understand this, you can turn fear into victory by using the extra energy that is generated to your advantage.

Let's discuss how this works. Habits are powerful because

they build on a natural human trait: our fear of the unknown. Apprehension is triggered anytime we encounter something new. This apprehension creates energy that you can use to help you achieve your goals or it can become a fear that makes you want to crawl in a hole and hide. The choice is yours. You can use this energy any way you desire.

Flight or fight response

To help you better understand how this energy works, let's go back to a time before recorded history, when your ancestors had to survive in the jungle, without tools or weapons, living by their wits.

Imagine them walking through the jungle, and they hear a rustling in the bushes nearby. That noise could mean one of two things. Perhaps it's a small animal, like a rabbit, that they can catch and eat. Maybe it is a large animal, like a tiger, that wants to catch and eat them.

It is all a matter of survival. Catch the rabbit and eat it, and you will survive longer. Outrun the tiger, and you will survive. Either way, your ancestors needed a big burst of energy. The people whose bodies could generate the most energy in the shortest amount of time during an emergency were the people who survived.

Their descendants - that includes you - inherited the characteristics of their ancestors, including the ability to create a lot of energy when something happens that they are not expecting.

Somebody quietly walks up behind you and startles you when they speak.

The coach gives you a new assignment that you have not prepared for, and you become nervous, wondering if you can handle the job.

Your coach, boss, parent or spouse asks, "Why did you do that?" and you tense up, wondering if they are angry.

In any of these situations, and countless others that come up every day, you can use your Silva Method techniques to help you maintain control, so that you can choose to use the energy the way that you desire. Take a deep breath, and as you exhale, relax. Then use the energy that has built up to deal with the situation.

This is especially appropriate in training and athletics. The energy that builds up is in the form of a faster heart rate, tense muscles, rapid breathing, adrenaline released into your bloodstream things that prepare your body to do additional work. Use it. Use this extra energy that you don't normally have to help you perform better than you normally do.

Little steps to success

How can you get rid of bad habits and create good new habits?

Jose Silva has developed strategies to help you make the changes a little at a time. Small changes are usually easier to make than big ones. Let's look at some specific examples, and then we will teach you the techniques Jose Silva has developed.

The first step to getting rid of a bad habit is to always enter your level and analyze the problem.

If the problem is cigarette smoking, for instance, then analyze and determine when you smoke the first cigarette of the day. Is it when you first wake up? With your cup of coffee? While you are on your way to work?

Program yourself, at your level, to smoke the first cigarette one hour later than this time.

You are not depriving yourself of the cigarette, you are just changing the habit. In effect, you are developing a new habit by smoking the first cigarette one hour later. And it is easier to break a new habit than an old one. An old habit is so familiar that it can be very difficult to part with. It is like a long-time love affair, and breaking up can be difficult. So do it little by little.

You can change habits in other ways, too. For instance, smoke a different brand of cigarette. This makes it a new habit, which will be easier to break.

Break your habit in 30 days

The following technique is so powerful that it can help cigarette smokers, drinkers, heroin addicts and others end their habit in 30 days. We've personally met and talked with four people who said they were on heroin when they took the course.

They were so addicted that they would go into the restroom and inject heroin during the breaks in the course! They got off of heroin in 30 days with this technique. Two of those people were so grateful that they became Silva lecturers, and one of them won the President's Cup, the top award that Jose Silva presents to lecturers.

How did people, so addicted, kick their terrible habit? They did it at level first. Let's say smoking is the habit you want to break. Here's how you would do it:

- First, mark a date on a calendar, 30 days from the present.

- Then enter your level and tell yourself mentally that on that date you will stop smoking and will never smoke again in your life.

- Enter your level every day and reinforce this programming.

When the 30 days are up, you will not want to smoke anymore.

You can apply this technique to any kind of habit.

Creating new habits

You can gradually create new habits in the same manner:

If you want to get into the habit of going to level every morning when you first wake up, then in the beginning you might have to remind yourself to do it. You might have to rearrange your schedule a bit in order to do it.

Make it easy on yourself by going to level for just five minutes. When this becomes effective, then begin staying at level for 10 minutes.

When this is easy and natural, increase to the recommended 15 minutes.

Use Your Mind to Get Your Body Going

If you have wanted to get into shape but just haven't been able to get started yet, then do it the easy way: at level.

Even couch potatoes can do it. Stay on the couch or in your easy chair, but turn off the television set. Enter your level. Imagine yourself working out, exercising, getting into shape.

Do this every day for 30 days. Imagine your body responding. Imagine people complimenting you on your improved appearance and increased energy. Imagine how good you feel. Imagine how you get through each day easier, with less fatigue, and how you have more energy in the evening.

Make the changes on the inside first. Then it will be easy to get up and get your body involved.

After you program yourself at your level for 30 days, you will be just as comfortable with the new habit you formed at your level as you are with the old habit, the physical habit. It is simply up to you to choose the habit that you want.

Now here are Jose Silva's techniques for helping people to stop smoking, drinking and using drugs.

Stop Smoking

Whenever you wish to reduce or quit cigarette smoking, enter your level and, at your level, analyze the problem. Determine when you smoke the first cigarette of the day, then program yourself at level to smoke it one hour later.

When that becomes effective, program yourself to smoke the first cigarette still one hour later, and continue to make these changes by programming at level, until you smoke only a few cigarettes a day. It will then be a simple matter to stop smoking altogether.

You can also program yourself to smoke only one cigarette per hour on the hour. When this has become effective, then program yourself to smoke only on the even hours. After this has taken effect, it will then be a simple matter to stop smoking completely.

You can also program yourself at your level to stop smoking altogether 30 days from the date of your initial programming. You can mark a date on a calendar, 30 days from the present, and tell yourself mentally that on that date you will stop smoking and will never smoke again in your life. Reinforce this programming for this purpose at level daily, and it will be so.

Tips that will help in your programming at your level:

1. Change cigarette brands frequently.

2. Do not inhale the cigarette smoke. Go through the habitual motions of raising the cigarette to your mouth and breathing in deeply, but do not inhale the smoke.

3. Program that three deep breaths will stop the immediate desire to smoke. Fill your lungs with clean air, not smoke.

4. Stop smoking for the sake of your loved ones. Set a good example for your children. Think of how sad your loved ones will be if you die because of your habit.

Control, Reduce or Eliminate Alcohol and Drug Habits

To help you control alcohol and drug habits, do the following three times a day:

Enter your level and, at level, tell yourself mentally: "Every day, as days go by, I will have less and less desire to (drink alcohol/use drugs)."

When you have the urge to drink alcohol or to use drugs, get a glass of tomato juice with a liberal amount of hot pepper sauce in it and sip it until the urge passes. (You should consult a medical doctor to make sure that it is safe for you to use the hot sauce.)

Eventually you will lose all desire to drink alcohol or use drugs.

Chapter 15

Self-management techniques

Rodeo cowboy Ben Thrown caught a midnight train to Austin, where the next rodeo was being held.

"Be sure to wake me up in Austin," he instructed the porter. "Sometimes it is hard to wake me up," he added, "so no matter how much I protest, make sure you get me up and put me off the train in Austin, because that's a very important rodeo." Ben gave the porter $20 for his help.

When Ben woke up, it was already daylight. "Where are we?" he asked the porter.

"About 10 miles from Dallas," the porter answered.

"I told you to make sure I got off the train in Austin!" Ben shouted at the porter, and then he proceeded to chew him out with a lot of colorful language.

When Ben had finished and stormed off, the conductor came over to the porter. "I know we have to be courteous to our passengers," the conductor said, "but you don't have to take that kind of language from anybody!"

"Oh, if you think that was bad," the porter sighed, "then you should have heard the man I put off the train in Austin!"

Give yourself a wake-up call

Managing energy is a challenge everyone faces, especially athletes.

When you are busy or have other things on your mind, for example, it is very tempting to skip a workout or a practice session.

Or the night before a big meet, it can be quite difficult to fall asleep.

Some people really dislike getting up and getting started in the morning. For others, it seems like that "second wind" never arrives.

Headaches can also hinder your performance. Once, a National Football League quarterback who had led his team to a Super Bowl victory was forced to leave a critical, nationally televised game because he had such a severe migraine headache that he could not continue.

You can gain control over circumstances like these and perform at a higher level. In this chapter, we will show you how.

Athletes exercise self-control

In the 1960s a field of applied psychology called "psychic self-regulation" was developed in the Soviet Union. It is based on laboratory studies of our human ability to control various physiological processes, including pulse, muscular relaxation, blood pressure and breathing.

Authors Michael Murphy and Rhea A. White reported in their book, *The Psychic Side of Sports*, that the methods developed there were adopted and put to use in sports by some Russians and East Europeans. In East Germany, they had a very effective sports training program that included meditation, autogenic training and hypnosis.

Meanwhile in Laredo, Texas, Jose Silva was teaching people how to lower their brain frequency while maintaining conscious awareness.

Once they mastered that - learning how to convert the subconscious level to an active inner conscious level they could then use techniques that he developed to take control of their physical selves.

Program yourself for success

Let's take a look now at some of the techniques developed by Jose Silva that can help you take more control of your life and improve your sports performance. We will examine some of the physical problems people encounter and provide specific, formula-like techniques to correct these problems.

You will learn to relieve the pain of tension and migraine headaches.

You will also learn a very special technique to program your mind to cause your body to respond automatically - the Silva To-Awake Control Technique, which will enable you to feel raring to go, even after a long night's rest.

First, we will give you the five "Principles of Programming" to establish for you the foundation of how programming works and of how to program yourself for success - in training, practice, athletics and life.

Standard Programming Strategy

Programming is a lot like learning a new athletic technique or a new play.

First, the coach usually tells you that you need to improve your technique or that your opponent is good at doing a particular thing.

In order for you to win, your coach tells you, you need to find a solution to the problem. He tells you what that solution is.

He gives you a plan: a new play, a new tactic, a specific move you can make that will bring you success. The coach probably demonstrates it to you or draws you a picture of it.

Then your coach walks you through it and makes sure you know each movement involved. Then you practice it until you gain both skill and confidence in it.

Eventually, you have done it so many times that you are confident that you will be successful when you use it for real in competition. You believe you will be successful. You expect victory.

If you go back now and review the preceding five paragraphs, you will see that they represent five steps:

1. Identify the problem.

2. Identify the solution.

3. Make a plan.

4. Work your plan.

5. Take it for granted that it will succeed.

We use the same five steps in our mental programming. We refer to them as the "Principles of Programming."

Applying the Programming Strategy

We are going to discuss how to apply these same five steps to relieve some common problems that athletes experience, such as the pain of tension and migraine headaches.

We will also cover a special technique that you can practice to use your mind for programming your body to respond the way that you desire.

You will notice that these techniques include the five steps outlined above.

As you go through the techniques, remember that the more you practice entering your level and the more opportunities you have to practice the techniques, the better you will become at programming.

Also remember that when you use any of the Silva Method techniques, use them confidently. Expect success. After applying the Headache Control Technique, for instance, don't start checking to see if you still have the headache. Act as if the headache is gone as you finish the technique. When you do that, it will either be gone immediately or within a very short time.

Now on to Jose Silva's techniques...

The Silva Headache Control Technique

Doctors advise us that most headaches, possibly 90 percent, are caused by tension. Few are organic in nature. This means that most headaches are under our control. Whether you actually have a headache because of organic reasons or feel a tension headache caused by stress, you can learn to relieve the pain with the Silva Headache Control Technique.

If your headaches are caused by excessive stress, then you will obtain permanent relief by applying the technique. The headaches will occur less and less frequently until your body forgets how to cause them. But if the headaches continue to recur with the same regularity, then you can suspect an organic cause and should definitely seek medical attention immediately.

The Silva Headache Control Technique uses the same five programming steps mentioned earlier: (1) state the problem; (2) state the goal; (3) make your plan to reach the goal; (4) implement the plan to reach your goal; and (5) take it for granted that it works make up your mind and make it happen.

Before you begin to use the Silva Headache Control Technique, the first thing you must do is "install" the instructions of the technique by entering the alpha level and "preprogramming" yourself. Then when you need to use the program, you enter your level and use it. Here is how to preprogram yourself how to install the formula (the instructions of the technique):

1. Enter your level as you have learned.

2. Tell yourself mentally that any time you need to get rid of

a headache, you will be able to do so with the use of the Silva Headache Control Technique.

3. Mentally go through the formula to "install" it into your biocomputer brain.

4. Remind yourself mentally that any time you need to get rid of a headache, you will be able to do so with the use of the Silva Headache Control Technique.

5. Count yourself out of your level.

You can follow these steps to preprogram any technique. Now here is the actual formula for relieving headaches:

Headache Control formula

If you have a tension-type headache, enter your level with the 5 to 1 method. Once at your level, mentally tell yourself, "I have a headache. I feel a headache. I don't want to have a headache. I don't want to feel a headache."

"I am going to count from 1 to 5, and at the count of 5, I will open my eyes, be wide awake, feeling fine and in perfect health. I will then have no headache. I will then feel no headache."

You will then count slowly from 1 to 2, then from 2 to 3, and at the count of 3 you will remind yourself mentally: "At the count of 5, I will open my eyes, be wide awake, feeling fine and in perfect health. I will then have no discomfort in my head. I will then feel no discomfort in my head."

Notice that we have made a change at level 3, from ache to discomfort. We left the ache behind. You will then proceed to mentally count slowly to 4, then to 5, and at the count of 5, with your eyes open, you will say to yourself mentally, "I am wide awake, feeling fine and in perfect health. I have no discomfort in my head. I feel no discomfort in my head."

If you have a migraine headache, apply the same formula,

but use three applications (do the routine three times) five minutes apart.

The first application will take care of part of the problem.

The second application will take care of more of the discomfort.

With the third application, the headache will be gone.

From then on, when symptoms appear, one application will take care of the migraine problem.

As you continue to take care of this problem in this manner, the symptoms will appear less frequently, until the body forgets how to cause them, bringing to an end the migraine problem without the use of drugs.

To correct health problems, controls are applied under a doctor's supervision. Consult your doctor and work under medical supervision.

Correcting the cause of the problem

You might be wondering how we can say that using this technique as instructed will bring the problem to an end and you will stop getting headaches. It must seem as if we are only treating the symptoms and not the underlying tension and stress that is causing the problem.

With almost any other technique, that would be true. A hypnotist can program you while you are hypnotized and get rid of your headache, but he will not correct the cause of the problem. As a result, you will continue to get headaches. Aspirin will correct the symptoms, but not the tension that is causing the headaches.

However, when you enter your level yourself, on your own, and you apply the formula yourself, then what you are actually doing is instructing your mind to do whatever is necessary to correct the cause of the problem. You may not ever be aware of what was done to correct the cause of the problem, but your mind takes care of it.

You can correct virtually any problem in a similar manner. If you are not a good batter, you can program yourself to be a better batter. If you have trouble with your backswing, you can program yourself to correct the problem. You will learn techniques for doing these things soon.

The Silva To-Awake Control Technique

How would you like to be able to program yourself to wake up automatically, at any time you desire, feeling wide awake, refreshed and ready to go? That's what you can do with the Silva To-Awake Control Technique. At the alpha level, you can give instructions to your mind to wake up your body when you desire. Here is how you apply this technique:

At night, when you are in bed and ready to go to sleep, note the present time on the clock, then enter your level with the 5 to 1 method. Once you are at your level, visualize (recall) the clock. Mentally reset the time on the clock to indicate the time that you want to awaken and tell yourself mentally, "This is the time I want to awaken, and this is the time I am going to awaken."

Remain at your level, and go to sleep from level. You will awaken at your desired time, feeling fine and in perfect health.

Remember that you must first preprogram this technique.

Enter level and tell yourself mentally that you can use the Silva To-Awake Control Technique to awaken whenever you desire, without a clock.

Then mentally review the technique and imagine using it.

Finally, before coming out of level, remind yourself that you can use the Silva To-Awake Control Technique to awaken whenever you desire, without a clock.

Chapter 16

Rest and recovery

"Why are you always lying around, instead of doing something useful?" Mary asked her teenage son.

"I try to get plenty of rest during the day, because it helps me sleep better at night," he answered.

What gets in the way of a good night's rest

Exercise - not resting during the day - is what actually invigorates the body and stimulates the organs and glands and helps to get them working properly, which makes it easier to sleep at night. But there are some nights when it is difficult to get to sleep. It may be more difficult to get a good night's sleep when:

- You have over-trained and are stressed out.

- You have a lot of problems on your mind and don't know how to solve them.

- You are expecting a challenging next day.

- You are following a different schedule than usual.

- You are in a different location, on a different bed, in different surroundings.

Whatever the reasons for your inability to sleep, Jose Silva has developed an effective technique to help you get to sleep any time, any place, without the use of drugs.

Doing what comes naturally

Given the choice, you are always better off doing things naturally than forcing your body to respond to drugs. When you sleep at night, your brain waves cycle up and down, faster and slower, like the ebb and flow of the tide, throughout the night. Drugs have undesirable side effects. They interfere with your normal - and important cycles during your sleep and dreaming. That's why a person who uses chemicals to get to sleep usually needs chemicals in the morning, too.

Amphetamines, for example, can give you a feeling of energy. But they have undesirable side effects. The energy you get from them is artificial energy. Sooner or later you have to pay the price. Get high on uppers, and you will crash. As the old saying goes, you can't fool Mother Nature.

In a few minutes, you will learn a technique that you can use to help you stay alert when you need to, without the use of drugs. First, let's consider how you can determine the optimal amount of exercise and training for you.

Training routines of the superstars

As we discussed in Chapters 4 and 10, you can make improvements to your body by exercising it - giving it more work to do than usual - and then getting enough rest to let your body recover, then doing a little bit more. But how do you know how much exercise is appropriate for you?

Perhaps the worst way to decide is by trying out the exercise routines that athletes say they follow in books and magazine articles. Often, though not always, they exaggerate greatly.

Bodybuilders will report that they train six days a week, two or three sessions a day, each session lasting two hours or more. They tell you that they do hundreds of repetitions for each body part.

They can do this, they say, because they exercise different parts of their body on different days, thereby giving one set of muscles a day to recover while they are working different muscles the next day.

Sometimes what they are describing is a routine they use just before a major contest. They are not building any muscle when they do this; they are getting rid of fatty tissues so that their muscles will be better defined when they are on the posing platform. In the process, they also lose some muscle tissue.

They exhaust themselves.

In fact, some bodybuilders who peak at the prejudging during the morning session of a contest will look haggard, drawn and almost sick by the time the evening posing session comes around.

And these are elite athletes. They have practiced for years. They have great genetics going for them stamina and rapid metabolism that make it possible for them to train to exhaustion.

These characteristics are very rare in people. Only a few people have the physical makeup to permit them to train that hard, and even then it takes years of training for their bodies to get used to such a heavy load. Even then, they have been known to exaggerate about the amount of weight they lift and the number of exercises they do when they are interviewed by writers for muscle magazines.

A lot of people started training after watching the movie *Pumping Iron*.

Many people benefited from this training, but just as many did not, because the training did not live up to the expectations that were raised by the picture.

In an interview televised on March 26, 1990, Barbara Walters asked Arnold Schwarzenegger about one of the more memorable lines in *Pumping Iron*. Now that he is married, she wanted to know, would he still be willing to say that hard training feels better than sex? Is it really comparable to having an orgasm?

"I'm a marketing guy," Arnold said. "When I said this, people lined up to try it."

"Then it's not true?" Barbara pressed.

"That's right," Arnold answered. "It's not true."

Arnold Schwarzenegger has inspired a lot of people, but just remember: Use common sense. Check things out at your level. Ultimately, you are responsible for your own life.

When you read stories about people who were small and sickly as children but, through some exercise routine, built themselves up to have fabulous strength, health and energy, just remember that they probably had a good genetic foundation to begin with and that not everyone can duplicate their success. In fact, most people cannot duplicate their success.

That's not to say you shouldn't strive to do your best. You might actually exceed what they did.

But be sensible about it. Enter your level and figure out what is best for you. When you do what is right for you, you can greatly improve the quality of your life.

An unrealistic training routine

Author Ed Bernd Jr. once purchased a set of weights from a man who no longer used them. The man threw in a year's worth of *Muscular Development* magazines. He had not renewed his subscription.

Tucked into one of the magazines was his training record.

The lines were neatly drawn, the days of the week marked and the dates penciled in. He also recorded his weight and measurements; he weighed about 120 pounds, a clue that he might have been an ectomorph and a hard gainer.

The first couple of weeks he made good progress. He was lifting heavier weights, and this effort showed in the increasing measurements of his biceps and other parts of his body. He continued to gain nicely the third and fourth weeks.

By the fifth and sixth weeks, he hit a plateau. He was not able to increase the amount of weight or the number of repetitions he was doing. His muscles were no longer getting bigger.

His training record showed that he began to work even harder.

He started lifting four times a week instead of three.

Then he began to lose ground.

His repetitions went down.

His biceps lost some of its size.

That's where his training record ended. The neat squares representing the days of the week were blank.

And two years later, he admitted total defeat by running a classified ad in the local newspaper and selling the weights.

What did he do wrong?

He tried too hard.

Weight training is extremely intense. It is easy to overdo it. He had plenty of desire. Even when he was obviously exhausted, and his body was regressing, he began to train even harder. Instead of helping, that hurt him even more.

Confused, with no place to turn for responsible guidance, he threw in the towel.

What should he have done?

He should have taken it easy for the first few months. He might have trained in cycles lifting heavy weights one week, then using lighter weights the next week.

As soon as his progress stopped, he should have taken a few days off to give his body time to recover. Then he could begin again.

Ed states, "I've found that if I take one week off after six weeks of training, I come back to my training refreshed and renewed, feeling great, and I make faster progress than before."

The most photographed male body

While we were writing this chapter, there was a brief story on television about a man who was dubbed "the most photographed male model in the United States."

Pictures of his washboard abdominals and chiseled chest have appeared in many major advertising campaigns in magazines and on television, the reporter stated.

Then the reporter expressed disbelief when told that this man trains with weights just three times per week. "It must be great genetics," was the skeptical conclusion.

The reporter obviously did not understand that too much training could have prevented this man from developing such an attractive body.

Genetics does play a part - you must have natural potential. But even great genetics cannot overcome the damage done by a person who overworks and overtrains his body and does not give it sufficient time to recover and grow.

Few people will find any significant benefit in doing more than three or four hard workouts a week.

We will provide a specific weight training routine for hard gainers in Chapter 17.

But now, here are Jose Silva's suggestions for using your level to help you determine what is best for you and his instructions for using his Sleep Control and Awake Control methods.

Making decisions at the correct level: alpha

The alpha level is the ideal level to do your thinking. So enter your alpha level and analyze your body and your training routine. Use the information in this book. Talk with your coach or fitness trainer about your body and what might be best for you.

But do not depend completely on anybody else.

Paul Anderson was kicked off his college football team because he was sneaking out at night and exercising with weights. The conventional wisdom in the early 1950s was that weight training would make you "musclebound" and slow, and most athletes were prohibited from partaking in it. But Anderson decided to stick with weight training. He won the gold medal for weightlifting in the 1956 Olympic games. He weighed approximately 390 pounds.

Was he musclebound? Just look at the position that a heavyweight lifter gets into while doing a two-hand snatch: body doubled up, squatting way below the parallel position, buttocks nearly touching the floor, weight overhead at arm's length, behind the shoulders. It's clear that heavyweight lifters are extremely flexible athletes. And they are very quick. They have a lot of "quick twitch" muscles. Paul Anderson was reported to be able to jump vertically more than 30 inches - quite a feat for someone who weighed almost 400 pounds.

So get information, enter your level and, like Anderson, determine for yourself what is best for your own body. Then put it into practice. Keep a record of your progress. Enter your level and analyze your progress. Make any adjustments that seem appropriate. Notice whether they help you or hurt you, or have no effect. Then use this additional information to guide you in your future decisions. This is a kind of "trial and error" approach that will help you determine exactly what is best for you.

How to be more alert instantly

Here is a technique that you can use when you feel drowsy and sleepy. For instance, if you feel tired when you get home from work, you can use this technique to get you "pumped up" and ready for a workout. The workout itself will stimulate your body, and this will make you feel invigorated.

One word of caution: You do not want to overuse this technique. It is not a substitute for sleep. But it can help you overcome inertia and get started.

This technique can help you pay attention while watching game films or listening to your coach in a long boring meeting. It can also help you when you are driving home, tired and exhausted, after a late-night practice or event.

For safety's sake, you will learn the formula for use when driving late at night when you are drowsy and sleepy. When using the technique in other circumstances, simply modify the wording in the section about pulling over to the side of the road. (Remember that you first want to enter your level with the 5 to 1 method and preprogram this technique - install it into your biocomputer brain.)

Here is the formula:

Jose Silva's Awake Control Technique

Whenever you feel drowsy and sleepy and don't want to feel drowsy and sleepy, especially if you are driving, pull to the side of the road, stop your motor and enter your level with the 5 to 1 method.

At level, mentally tell yourself, "I am drowsy and sleepy. I don't want to be drowsy and sleepy. I want to be wide awake, feeling fine and in perfect health."

Then tell yourself mentally, "I am going to count from 1 to 5.

At the count of 5, I will open my eyes, be wide awake, feeling fine and in perfect health. I will not be drowsy and sleepy; I will be wide awake."

Mentally count slowly: 1, 2, 3. At the count of 3, mentally remind yourself: "At the count of 5, I will open my eyes, be wide awake, feeling fine and in perfect health."

Then mentally count slowly to 4, then to 5. At the count of 5 and with your eyes open, tell yourself mentally, "I am wide awake, feeling fine and in perfect health, feeling better than before."

When necessary, you can substitute the words "tired and exhausted" for "drowsy and sleepy." This is the same 5-step approach we discussed earlier. Use your level to correct problems, any problems you encounter.

Expect the best

Remember that it is important to want the technique to work and to expect it to work. If you apply the technique and start wondering, as you're finishing up, if it is going to work, it may not work. If you start checking to see if you are still tired, you will probably find what you are looking for: a feeling of tiredness.

Instead, expect to feel wide awake. As soon as you open your eyes, take it for granted that you are wide awake. Pretend that you are wide awake if you have to, and you will be wide awake.

How to go to sleep when you want to

Often, trouble going to sleep is due to worry - worry about what you did that day or what you have to do tomorrow. If you can get your mind off your worries, it will be easy to go to sleep.

Some people try counting sheep. But that's a little too interesting. In order to go to sleep, you need to use a technique that is boring. We've got a technique that is so boring it will put to you to sleep right away.

The Silva Sleep Control Technique involves the use of countdowns, which you are accustomed to using for entering lower brain frequencies and deeper levels of mind. The technique also uses the word "deeper," another reinforcing mechanism. It also involves erasing a figure within a circle on an imaginary chalkboard in your mind. You start at the center of the circle, and then you can erase in a circular motion, going outwards until the figure has been erased, or you can erase by following the shape of the figure itself - just as long as you concentrate on not erasing the circle itself.

Sleep Control is to be used when you are in bed and ready to go to sleep. You should complete any other programming that you have first because you will go to sleep while using this technique.

Continue to use this technique until you fall asleep. When your mind knows that you are serious about using the technique until you go to sleep, then you will go to sleep. Remember to use the technique exactly as written. Here it is:

Jose Silva's Sleep Control Technique

Whenever you need to use Sleep Control, enter your level.

Once at your level, you will visualize a chalkboard. Mentally, you will have chalk in one hand and an eraser in the other.

Then, you will mentally draw a large circle on the chalkboard. You will then draw a big X within the circle. You will then proceed to erase the X from within the circle, starting at the center and erasing towards the inner edges of the circle, being careful not to erase the circle in the least.

Once you erase the X from within the circle, to the right and outside of the circle you will write the word "Deeper." When you write the word "Deeper," you will enter a deeper, healthier level of mind, in the direction of normal, natural, healthy sleep.

You will then write a big number 100 within the circle; then you will proceed to erase the number 100, being careful not to erase the circle in the least. Once the number 100 is erased, to the right and outside of the circle you will trace over the word "Deeper." Every time you go over the word "Deeper," you will enter a deeper, healthier, level of mind, going in the direction of normal, natural, healthy sleep.

Then write a big 99 inside the circle. Erase it, and to the right and outside of the circle, trace over the word "Deeper." Every time you go over the word "Deeper" in this manner, you will enter a deeper, healthier level of mind in the direction of normal, healthy sleep.

Continue writing and erasing numbers within the circle on a descending scale - 98, 97, 96, 95 and so forth - until you enter normal, natural, healthy sleep. Write the number, then erase it, then go over the word "Deeper." Continue this, with descending numbers, until you go to sleep.

Whenever you enter sleep with the use of Sleep Control, if someone calls you or in case of danger or an emergency, you will open your eyes, be wide awake, feeling fine and in perfect health.

Whenever you enter sleep with the use of Sleep Control, you will awaken at your customary time, or you can remain asleep for as long as you desire. When you awaken you will be wide awake, feeling fine and in perfect health.

Chapter 17

Nutrition and weight control

Eat, drink, and be merry, for tomorrow ye diet. -William Gilmore Beymer

Whenever there is a conflict between willpower and imagination, the imagination always wins. -Jose Silva

Food for thought

The guidelines for nutrition have changed over time. A generation ago, bodybuilders considered a very high protein diet a necessity. Muscles are made of protein, so they believed that they needed a lot of it in their diet in order to build larger muscles. For rapid weight gain, a drink made up of protein powder and cream was popular.

Now nutritionists are horrified at that kind of protein-and-cream drink. They say that we only need a little fat, a moderate amount of protein and plenty of carbohydrates for energy. Today, bodybuilders consume far less protein than in the past.

Ideally, the carbohydrates that you consume should come from fruits, vegetables and whole grains - not refined sugar.

The problems with refined sugar are well documented in books like *Body, Mind, and Sugar* by E.M. Abrahamson, M.D., and A.W. Pezet (Pyramid Books, 1951) and *Sugar Blues* by William Dufty (Warner Books Edition, Chilton Book Company, 1976).

Read these books and you may never eat refined sugar again. Refined flour has many of the same problems.

But we are not going to get into a long discussion of

nutrition, or the value of various foods, or the number of calories you should eat.

It is common sense that if you want to reduce your weight, you should eat less or exercise more.

Adjust the number of calories you consume to the amount of energy you expend, and you can control your weight easily.

There are plenty of books that go into that subject. Magazines run articles regularly on nutrition and weight control. We're not going to get into that fray.

Instead, we will concentrate on the one topic that we know more about than anybody else: how you can use your mind to help you make the changes you want to your body.

Just a couple of points to cover first.

Know yourself.

If you are large and heavy-boned, there is no sense trying to look like an anorexic fashion model.

If you are slender and small-boned, then realize that you may never have a huge chest.

Remember what we discussed in Chapter 4 about different body types.

Yes, the grass always seems to be greener in somebody else's pasture. Just remember that while you are wasting your time wishing you were like somebody else, he or she is probably dreaming of having body characteristics like yours.

Instead of trying to be something you are not, learn to accentuate your best features. You will be far more attractive when you build on your strong points and feature them than when you spend all your energy trying to hide your weak points. Enter your level and figure out what you can do to emphasize your best features.

Use imagination to boost your willpower

You move in the direction of your dominant thoughts. We explained that when we discussed Mental Housecleaning.

When you think about what you don't want, that's what you get, because that is what you are thinking about.

If you think about depriving yourself of food that you enjoy, then you are going to seek what you are thinking about: the food that you enjoy.

So think about what you do want.

No amount of willpower can overcome the thoughts you have in your mind. Maybe willpower will win out for a short period of time; maybe you'll stick to a diet and lose 10 pounds. But then imagination will take over, and you'll go back to the foods you enjoy.

You can have the body you desire

Do you have to deprive yourself of foods you enjoy in order to lose weight?

Not necessarily.

Let's focus on the word "deprive." That means you are giving up something you desire, which is an unpleasant situation. You can deal with that unpleasant situation in one of two ways:

Go ahead and eat the foods you want. Find something else that you desire more than the food, something that is so much more valuable to you that you will focus on it and will not even think about the food. The food will become a non-issue.

What's really important to you:

- Good health?

- Attractive appearance?

- Being respected and liked by others?
- Winning in competition?
- Being a champion?
- Feeling good physically?
- Feeling good about yourself, having high self-esteem?

Decide what you really want most. Enter your level and think about it.

Once you decide what you really want, program yourself to achieve that goal. Then, in the future, whenever you think about the situation, think of your goal.

You may, for example, want to be in better physical condition and have more endurance so that you can work the long hours necessary to get to the top in business. So you design a healthy diet and an exercise program for yourself.

But naturally, a part of you would still like to continue eating the tasty foods you have become accustomed to. A part of you would like to sit on the couch and watch television instead of sweating through 45 minutes of exercise.

If you think about the things you are "giving up" - the tasty food and the comfortable couch - you will be drawn to them, and all your good intentions will soon become things of the past.

Instead, whenever you think of the changes you have made in your diet and your schedule, remember why you made those changes.

Imagine yourself trim, fit and feeling wonderful, with enough stamina and energy to keep going for as long as you want to and so relaxed at the end of the day that you go right to sleep without any problem.

Imagine how good you will feel every minute of the day.

You are not depriving yourself of anything. You are simply making some changes that will improve your lifestyle tremendously and help you to reach those goals you have set for yourself.

Keep the right thoughts in mind and reinforce them at your level regularly, and you will reach your goal.

Even better, you will keep what you have won. You can take off weight and keep it off when you keep your thoughts on the things that are really important to you.

Hollywood actress Alexis Smith was quoted by the San Jose Mercury News as saying, "Positive thinking works beautifully on a reducing diet. Never think once about what you are giving up but concentrate on what you are getting."

As she grew older, she was often told that she was even more attractive than when she made some of the Warner Brothers movies that are now showing on television. She attributes much of this to the Silva Method.

"The big difference," she is quoted as saying, "is that now I'm in better balance and more in control of myself."

To maximize your results, visualize what you desire - at the alpha level. A weight loss experiment showed how well this works. Two Silva graduates in Denver, Colo., launched an experimental program that showed the reliability of the Silva techniques for those who genuinely want to lose weight.

They organized a workshop for 25 Silva graduates to meet once a week for a month. Among the 15 who attended all of the meetings, the average weight loss was a little more than four and three-quarter pounds. All lost weight. A month later, seven had continued to lose weight, and eight were holding steady. None had gained weight.

Not only was this a painless experience for these graduates, it was a joyous one. Besides losing weight without any hunger pangs or any other discomfort, they also reinforced many of their Silva skills.

Get more value from the food you eat

As you have already been learning through your Silva Method training, the way you use your brain and your mind influences the results you get with your body.

This is certainly true when it comes to nutrition, digestion and assimilation.

To offer a simple example, when you are nervous and tense, your "flight or fight" mechanism is triggered. One of the things that happens in your body is that your stomach stops digesting food; this provides more energy to respond to the threat by fleeing or fighting.

If you are nervous or tense while eating or after eating, your body chemistry is altered, and the digestive process does not function normally. This is just one example of how your thoughts can alter your body's ability to utilize the nutrients you consume.

It can work in the other direction, too. Have you ever known anyone who can gain weight just by thinking of food? How could this happen?

Well, the first step in getting nutrients where they need to go after you've eaten is digestion, which begins in the stomach. While some substances are absorbed through the stomach wall, most pass into the bloodstream from the intestines.

When you think about food, you start the digestive process working, and food that has not yet been absorbed begins to be absorbed. If this happens to be excess food that is assimilated by the body rather than eliminated from the body, it is stored as fat.

As you can see, your brain, which is under the direct control of your mind, is the most important organ in the entire nutritional process for an athlete. The ways that you use your mind will determine how much benefit you receive from the food you put into your body. Here are some things that you can do to help yourself:

Analyze your nutritional needs and your eating habits at your level, and determine what changes might be appropriate.

1. Be relaxed when you eat. Relax afterwards. Then you will digest food naturally and feel satisfied when you have eaten an appropriate amount of food.

2. At your level, program yourself to substitute helpful foods, such as carrots, celery or apples, for foods high in sugars and fats. You can even program yourself to be satisfied by taking three deep breaths, substituting clean fresh air for food. You can program that drinking water will satisfy your desire to consume something.

3. At your level, program yourself to achieve and maintain your ideal weight and size.

4. While eating, imagine yourself at your ideal weight and size. Imagine yourself feeling great, performing the way you desire.

Helping hard gainers gain muscular body weight

For the last 60 years, millions of young men have empathized with the story about the 97-pound weakling who had sand kicked in his face by the big bully. The young man exercised, built up his body, went back to the beach, beat up the bully and got his girlfriend back.

It takes hard work - and smart work - to gain muscular body weight. Sometimes the hardest thing about training to gain muscular body weight is to avoid overtraining. Even with all of his natural potential, Arnold Schwarzenegger has said that he only trained about four times a week when he was a teenager.

You must avoid sapping your energy. You have to give your body time to rest and recover. You need to conserve energy so that it can be used to build bigger muscles after you have exercised. Author Ed Bernd Jr. knows this from experience - that's what he had to do in order to gain weight and strength.

The question is: How can you stimulate your muscles enough to cause them to grow bigger without using up all your energy in the process?

As always, get a medical checkup before starting any new training program. Discuss your goals with your doctor, and make sure there is no medical problem. Then start your program.

Here are the main points to remember:

Do only top-quality exercises, the ones that work the big muscles. That includes presses, bench presses, deadlifts, power cleans, squats.

Avoid biceps curls, calf raises and other small exercises while you are working to add muscle to your body.

After warming up thoroughly, use heavy weights and a limited number or repetitions. When you can press the weight 10 times, add more weight.

Do not do more than three sets of any one exercise. Three sets of 10 repetitions each, with as much weight as you can handle, is plenty.

Train fast. Do not sit around and talk between sets. Do a set of 10 (or fewer). Take a few deep breaths and relax for a few seconds. Then move right on to your next set, either of the same movement, or another.

Your entire workout should not exceed one hour. The less time you spend in the gym, the better. Generally, about a half-dozen different exercises are probably enough.

Do not train on consecutive days. Take at least one day off between workouts.

And that means completely off. Do not go out and play three hours of basketball on your off days.

Let your body rest. Get plenty of sleep - nine or ten hours if you feel like it.

When it comes to eating, use the "shovel method" - shovel as much food into your body as you can. Eat a moderate amount of fat and protein and plenty of carbohydrates.

If you are not gaining muscular body weight, then cut back on your training and increase the amount of recovery time. Train twice a week instead of three times. Reduce the number of exercises you are doing. Do only one heavy set instead of three of each exercise.

Use your level to help you make decisions, and let the results you get guide you in your training. This does not mean you can be lazy; train hard, for short periods of time.

The best muscle-building exercise

Here is one exercise that will stimulate growth throughout your entire body. Researchers say that this exercise appears to trigger the release of natural growth hormone. It is also probably the hardest exercise you will ever do - breathing squats.

Put the bar on your shoulders, with a moderate amount of weight on the bar. If you are in reasonably good condition and can handle it, then load the bar with weight equal to about 10 to 20 pounds more than your body weight. Some trainees load the bar with all the weight they think that they can handle for 10 repetitions.

With the bar on your shoulders, your head held high and your back flat, slowly do a full squat. By slowly we mean to squat down in a controlled fashion. Do not drop quickly, and do not bounce at the bottom of the squat. Pick a spot high up on the wall in front of you and keep your eyes on that spot. That will help you to keep your back flat, so that the tension is on your legs and not on your back. Keep your head high as you come back to the standing position.

Pause after you stand up, and take a deep breath. Fill your lungs. Do another squat in the same manner as the first one.

As you stand back up with the weights, remember to breathe. Let the air out of your lungs. Grunt and groan.

Never hold your breath; that could restrict blood flow and you might pass out. Breathe continuously.

After three or four repetitions, you may be getting short of breath. So take two deep breaths while you are standing. There is no need to rush through this exercise.

By the time you get to the 10th repetition, you may feel like you cannot do another one, as you stand there taking two or three deep breaths. But you can do another one. Now you see why you need to take your time - but not too much time.

The average person will stop after 10 repetitions. Your goal is to do 20 repetitions. If you want to increase your muscular body weight, you will do 20 repetitions.

Of course, the first time you try this, do not attempt to do 20 repetitions. Work your way up to it. Do 10 repetitions the first time. Then in your next workout, do 12 repetitions. Continue increasing two at a time until you get to 20.

Usually 20 repetitions is sufficient to stimulate growth throughout the entire body. Even your arms will get bigger.

Once you are used to this exercise, you might want to experiment with using 25 or 30 repetitions or higher weights. Just remember that you may make better progress by concentrating on your rest and recovery time. Give your body time to recover and grow.

Now let's take a look at the techniques developed by Jose Silva to help people manage their weight.

To Gain Weight

If you desire to gain weight, analyze the problem at your level.

Determine what foods will help you gain weight, and program yourself to eat those foods - and to eat slowly, savoring every bite.

Learn to improve your taste and smell by concentrating on your food as you eat.

Use the Three Scenes Technique:

Visualize yourself, the way you are now, in Monitor Number 1, directly in front of you.

Then in Monitor Number 2, towards your left, mentally picture yourself eating in a manner that will help you reach your goal, and imagine your body responding the way you desire.

In Monitor Number 3, still further to your left, imagine yourself the way you desire to be. Stamp what you want to weigh on one corner of this monitor. In the corner of the other side, stamp the size of clothing you want to wear.

Hereafter, whenever you think of your weight, always visualize the image that you have created of yourself in this third monitor. Do this every time you think of your weight.

To Reduce Weight

Jose Silva has developed the following techniques to help people lose weight.

When you desire to reduce your weight, enter your level and analyze your weight problem. At your level, mentally mark a big red "NO" over every item of food considered to be causing the problem.

Program yourself that hunger between meals will vanish when you eat a piece of carrot, celery, apple or other such healthy foods - or when you take three deep breaths.

Program yourself to leave something on your plate, realizing that you do not need all the food you have taken. Program yourself not to eat dessert.

Use the Three Scenes Technique:

Visualize yourself, the way you are now, in Monitor Number 1, directly in front of you.

Then in Monitor Number 2, towards your left, mentally picture yourself eating in a manner that will help you reach your goal, and imagine your body responding the way you desire.

In Monitor Number 3, still further to your left, imagine yourself the way you desire to be.

Stamp what you want to weigh on one corner of this monitor.

In the corner of the other side, stamp the size of clothing you want to wear.

Hereafter, whenever you think of your weight, always visualize the image that you have created of yourself in this third monitor.

Do this every time you think of your weight.

Chapter 18

The healing power of your mind

God heals and the doctor takes the fee. -Benjamin Franklin

"As I understand it, doctor, if I believe I'm well, I'll be well. Is that the idea?"

"It is."

"Then, if you believe you are paid, I suppose you'll be paid."

"Not necessarily."

"But why shouldn't faith work as well in one case as in the other?"

"Why, you see, there is considerable difference between having faith in Providence and having faith in you."

Your body knows how to heal itself

When you cut your finger, your body knows how to cause the cells to grow back together again.

We're not saying that you never need a doctor. If it is a big cut, the doctor can sew it up so that there will not be a scar. Antiseptics can be used to keep it from getting infected. But the actual healing is done by your own body.

Doctors are often important - even vital - to the healing process, because they can remove any interference to healing so that nature can take its course. They create an environment that makes it easier for the body to heal, and they can keep you alive long enough for the healing to take place.

But the actual healing process is carried out by your body.

You can learn how to help your doctor help to heal your body. There are many things that you can do to speed the healing process besides the usual doctorly advice to "take an aspirin, get plenty of rest and call me in the morning."

We will cover techniques in this chapter to help you relieve pain, control bleeding and hemorrhaging and speed up the healing process.

Most of these techniques are included in the Choose Success home study course available at www.SilvaCourses.com

Visualization at alpha speeds recovery from injuries

The Jose Silva's Glove Anesthesia Technique has helped many people, including former Italian National Martial Arts Champion Giuseppina Del Vicario ("Vidheya" to her fans).

One day during training, Vidheya dislocated her ankle. "I had to control the fear," she said. "My first thought was that I could not continue training. But I wanted to continue training, so I ignored the pain and put the bones back into place. Then I finished my training.

"That night, I knew it would swell," she said. "I had a very strong desire. I was not going to stop my training. So I went to level. I started to feel my leg. I visualized the blood flowing from side to side. After a while, I could actually feel it. Then I visualized a blue light coming into my body and healing it.

"The next day I wrapped my leg and was able to continue my training. I was very happy for this, because it usually takes 21 days for that kind of an injury to heal."

She has had other training injuries. Once she received a blow to her head that caused a very bad cut over her right eye.

"I took a deep breath and got myself under control

immediately," she said. "Then they took me to the hospital. I sat quietly while they worked on it. I told them I did not want any stitches on it. Then the doctor asked me why I was there, and he sent me home. I visualized it healing, and today there is no scar."

Another time she dislocated her elbow when she landed too hard on her hands while doing an acrobatic movement.

"I almost lost consciousness that time," she recalled. "I took some deep breaths to bring myself under control. My master put the elbow back in place. Then I went to the hospital.

"The pain was very constant, all night long," she said. "I didn't want to take any drugs. They always have side effects. So I used my Silva Method techniques to control the pain and to get to sleep. I relaxed and went to very deep levels. I visualized energy going through my body. I imagined a blue light going to my elbow and helping it. I never did take any drugs."

Vidheya added, "We can control or be controlled."

Imagination overcomes athletic injury

A man in Florida, at 35 years of age, had taken up jogging to get into shape. But he began to suffer from severe shin splints, and nothing he tried would correct the problem.

If he ran more than twice a week, his shins were hurt so badly that he could not walk without limping. Experienced trainers told him that they had never known of anyone over 30 who had gotten rid of shin splints, so he had better find some other way to exercise.

Then he learned the Silva techniques. He loved the course and attended every class that was held in his area. This cut into his exercise time, so he decided to make up for it by imagining that he was running while he was at his level. He put in more miles this way than he had ever done physically.

Then, on a holiday weekend, he decided he had to get some real physical exercise. He ran on Friday evening, then again on Saturday, then on Sunday and then on Monday (a holiday).

In the past, four straight days of running would have left him limping badly. What happened this time? He reported that his shins were a bit sore, but no more so than he would have expected, considering that he had not done any running - at least not physically - for more than three months. He continued running several times a week, and he has never had a recurrence of the shin splints.

"That alone was worth the price of the course," he told us, adding, "and I have gotten a lot of other benefits besides that."

Send the messenger back home

How does your body know how to heal itself?

When your biocomputer brain was formed, it was programmed with an original set of instructions. These instructions are part of your biological intelligence, and they are carried out automatically.

But it is possible, at the correct level, to change those instructions - to take them off automatic pilot and assume manual control.

Through research, Jose Silva discovered that a person's healing mechanism can be tricked during hypnosis.

"You can tell the subject that they are going to be touched with a red hot piece of metal," Jose explains. "Then you can touch them with an ordinary pencil, and their body will respond as if it were a red hot iron. The skin will turn red, and a real blister sometimes forms. Somehow, the hypnotist and the subject have influenced the body's healing mechanism to go into action, even though there is no need for it."

He continues, "We can also learn to alter our perception of

pain. Pain is a message that there is a problem. After you receive the message, there is no need to keep the messenger."

Control pain, bleeding and healing

Biological intelligence resides in the theta portion of your brain, at 5 cps. This is the level that hypnotists use to prepare patients to have teeth pulled, even to have surgery, without the use of chemical anesthetics.

You can learn, with practice, to influence biological intelligence. Thus far, you have been practicing entering the alpha level - 10 cps. When you learn to enter the theta level on your own, then you can have access to biological intelligence. Once you learn to enter theta, you can learn to use a technique called Glove Anesthesia to control physiological pain and in many cases also control bleeding and hemorrhaging.

To apply Glove Anesthesia, you do not necessarily need to count yourself into your level. Whenever you are injured, you can simply place your "anesthetized hand" over the injury and expect the pain to decrease and go away, expect any bleeding to stop and expect the healing to be rapid and complete.

With practice, you can also learn to use Mental Anesthesia, that is, the ability to make your pain go away by mentally saying the word "gone."

Entering the theta level consciously

We have adapted a technique originally developed by hypnotherapist Milton Erickson to teach you how to enter the theta level on your own.

It is called Hand Levitation.

Why do we need to learn to enter theta if we do all of our mental programming at alpha? Because the problem that you desire to correct must be within reach. Your mind must be able to get the necessary information about the problem and correct it. If you have never entered the theta level with conscious awareness, then it is closed off to you. It is not within reach. Entering the theta level with conscious awareness opens it up for you and brings it within reach. One of the most common ways of entering theta is through concentration.

When you concentrate on something, and exclude everything else from your consciousness, your brain frequency slows down. When it slows down to theta, then you are at the level where biological intelligence resides, and you can use your imagination to cause your body to respond, for such purposes as eliminating pain, controlling bleeding and speeding up the healing process.

To use Hand Levitation, you sit quietly with your hands in your lap, palms down and stare at your stronger hand.

You imagine your stronger hand rising from your lap all by itself. You imagine it rising up to touch your face. (You will get Jose Silva's complete instructions in a moment.)

When you reach the theta level, your hand will rise all by itself. That is, it comes up without any conscious effort on your part.

The subconscious - which you have actually converted into an active inner conscious level - causes it to rise, at the direction of your imagination. When your hand comes up all by itself, this confirms that you are at your correct level. It confirms that you have lowered your brain frequency all the way to theta. It confirms that you are now able to use your mind to cause a physiological effect in your body.

It is a good idea to practice entering your level with the Hand Levitation method occasionally to make sure that you maintain your ability to enter the theta level with conscious awareness. We suggest practicing entering level with Hand Levitation at least once a month.

Once you have entered your level using Hand Levitation, it is an excellent time to program Glove Anesthesia, which you can use to control physiological pain, as well as bleeding and hemorrhaging, in many cases.

A first aid kit to carry wherever you go

Glove Anesthesia is an excellent first aid technique. If you should happen to be injured, you just place your anesthetized hand on the injured part of your body. The pain will decrease and stop, bleeding will often stop and you will often heal more quickly.

Pain, as Jose Silva says, is a message that there is a problem. After you receive the message and respond to it, there is no need to keep the messenger.

Pain is relative to the mental state of the person who is in pain. You have seen many examples of that. Athletes are often able to continue to compete under conditions that would be painful enough to disable them, as long as they continue to concentrate totally on winning their competition.

An example: One night Ed Bernd Jr. was on the sidelines taking pictures at a high school football game. A player came running to the sidelines, blood pouring from his mouth, down the front of his uniform and onto his shoes, and asked, "Coach, am I hurt?" The coach studied the young athlete's face for a moment, then told him, "No, you're all right. Get back in there." And he did.

Now here are Jose Silva's instructions on Hand Levitation, Glove Anesthesia and programming to speed recovery.

Hand Levitation Technique

Hand Levitation is a mental technique you can use for problem solving and goal achievement.

In order to preprogram the Hand Levitation Technique to work for you, you can record these instructions on an audio recorder, then enter your level with the 5 to 1 method as you have learned. Once at your level, you will play the recording and follow the instructions.

After entering your level but before starting the recording, preprogram yourself that you are going to learn how to enter your level with the Hand Levitation Method.

Once you have completed the routine but before coming out of your level, reinforce this by reminding yourself that you have learned how to enter your level with the Hand Levitation Method, and that in the future, any time you use Hand Levitation, you will enter deeper, healthier levels of mind.

While you are preprogramming the technique to work for you, go ahead and raise your hand consciously, timing the movement so that the back of your hand will touch your face at the appropriate time.

Later, when you are using Hand Levitation to enter your level, simply concentrate on your hand becoming lighter and lighter and moving closer and closer to your face, as it rises higher and higher until it touches your face. If necessary, when you are first practicing this technique, help your hand get started and then let it continue to come up all by itself. Remain positive. Expect it to happen.

When you are ready to begin, assume an erect sitting position, allowing yourself enough room to raise your arm comfortably. Then look at and concentrate on your stronger hand, while both hands rest on your lap, palms down. Here are the instructions that you can record on your audio recorder; be sure pause after each instruction:

While I count slowly from 10 to 1, you will go through a complete cycle of Hand Levitation. When I reach the count of 1, the back of your hand will contact your face, and you will enter a deeper, healthier level of mind. When I begin the count, I will be giving you directions for each descending number.

10. Look at your stronger hand. Keep your eyes focused on your hand. (pause)

9. Cause your hand to feel sensitive, very sensitive. Slowly cause one finger to move, then cause your fingers to separate from one another and at the same time cause your hand to rise from your lap. (pause)

8. Continue to allow your hand to rise in the direction of your face. (pause)

7. Higher and higher. Feel your arm becoming lighter and lighter as the back of your hand draws closer and closer to your face. Your hand may feel as though a balloon is lifting it. (pause)

6. Allow your hand and arm to become still lighter and lighter as you continue to help them rise higher and higher. (pause)

5. Your hand and arm become lighter and lighter as you allow them to rise higher and higher, now beyond the midpoint between your face and your lap. (pause)

4. Raise them higher and higher. (pause)

3. Your hand and arm rise higher and higher and become lighter and lighter, now drawing very near your face. (pause)

2. Higher and higher. Your hand is almost touching your face. (pause)

1. The back of your hand now touches your face. Close your eyes, take a deep breath, and while exhaling, return your hand to its resting position on your lap. (pause)

You may now continue with your programming.

Glove Anesthesia Technique

Once you have developed the Hand Levitation method for entering your level, you can program the Glove Anesthesia Technique. Glove Anesthesia is a mental technique that you can practice to develop control over physiological pain and, in many cases, control of bleeding and hemorrhaging.

Glove Anesthesia is the development of a feeling on your less strong hand. Any feeling other than the normal will be considered Glove Anesthesia - a feeling of coolness or coldness, a tingling sensation, a vibration, a numbness as though your hand is asleep, feeling as if you are wearing a leather glove, feeling that your hand is made of wood or feeling as if you have no hand. Any out-of-the-ordinary sensation is suitable for Glove Anesthesia.

In the instructions given below, consider your anesthetized hand to be your cold hand. Also in the instructions, you will be asked to test your other hand for anesthesia. You can do this by pinching it gently or feeling it with your other hand. Does it feel cold? Is it less sensitive to the touch?

If you wish, you can record the following instructions for Glove Anesthesia onto an audio recorder and play it back after you have entered your level with the Hand Levitation method.

We will now program Glove Anesthesia.

At this time, imagine placing your stronger hand into a container of hot water that is next to your chair. (pause) The water is hot, and you can stand the temperature. Bring back a memory of having your hand in hot water - any time that you can recall vividly. (pause) Feel the steaming hot water between your fingers. (pause) Feel your hand pulsing with heat. (pause) Now lift your hand out of the hot water and let it rest on your lap. (pause)

Now place your other hand into an imaginary container of ice water with cracked ice, standing by your side. (pause) Recall a time when you had your hand in ice water. (pause) Feel the ice water and cracked ice between your fingers. (pause)

Allow your hand to remain in the ice water for several moments and imagine it getting colder and colder as you review some of the projects that you are programming for. (pause)

Now, keeping your eyes closed, lift your hand out of the ice water and hold it over and behind your head, keeping your hand from touching your head. (pause) Let your hand dry and get colder in this position. I will tell you when to bring it down. Continue to keep your eyes closed.

As soon as you learn to develop Glove Anesthesia, and after testing it and becoming satisfied with the results, start practicing the transferring of this anesthesia to other parts of the body. First practice transferring this anesthesia from one hand to the other by placing the anesthetized hand over the other hand for a few seconds, then test the other hand for anesthesia.

When this has become effective, practice transferring the anesthesia from either hand to any other part of the body. This is done by placing either hand over that part of the body and holding it in that position for a few seconds.

Finally you can learn, by practicing, to program yourself so that by concentrating on any discomfort and mentally saying the word "gone," the discomfort will be gone.

Now bring your hand down, place it on your lap, and test it for coldness and insensibility with your other hand. (pause) Now remove all abnormal feeling from your hand by rubbing it three times with your other hand, from the wrist toward the fingers, bringing all feeling back to normal. (pause) Your hand now feels as it did before this exercise.

You may reinforce the effects of this technique by practice.

It is fine to use Glove Anesthesia to control pain and speed the healing process, but remember that we are not doctors and that any time you are dealing with your health, work under your doctor's supervision.

Use your imagination when doing this programming. A vivid imagination will make it happen.

Some people, in order to get Glove Anesthesia to work for them, have gotten containers of hot and cold water and actually placed their hands into the water before they programmed so it would be easier to recall the feeling when they were at their level programming this technique.

Remember that you do not want to leave your hands anesthetized, so rub your anesthetized hand with the other hand, as though you were removing a glove, rubbing from the wrist toward the fingers, to remove all abnormal feeling.

Hastening the healing process

We have included two different pain control techniques for you in this book:

• Glove Anesthesia, which is an excellent first aid technique, and

• Headache Control (in Chapter 15), which is excellent for dealing with chronic physiological pain.

Of course, consult with your doctor for medical treatment, if necessary, for the condition that is causing the pain.

To speed up the healing process, you can use visualization. You can use the Three Scenes Technique that you learned in Chapter 6 for healing:

1. In the first scene, you have the injury.

2. In the second scene, you see the treatment you are getting for the injury ice packs, heat, whirlpool, physical therapy, etc.

3. In the third scene, imagine the injury healed.

Remember that after you have started your programming to heal this injury, you do not need to go back to the first scene again unless there has been a significant change. In that case, incorporate the change into the image in Monitor Number One, then continue programming with the other two scenes.

In some instances, time is the only remedy. In that case, you need only two scenes:

1. In the first scene, directly in front of you, visualize the injury.

2. In the second scene, towards your left, visualize yourself healed.

In the future, whenever you think of the problem, visualize the image that you created in the second scene, perfectly healed. Keep this image directly in front of you. Your subconscious knows what to do to bring about the healing.

Section 5: Additional Topics

This section includes additional topics that you can refer to as the need arises.

Topics include training under special circumstances, biofeedback equipment, student athletes, athletes' responsibilities and advice for parents and coaches.

Chapter 19

Training under special circumstances

Murray had been a great athlete. One day Joey saw him sitting at a bus stop, crying.

"What's wrong?" Joey asked.

"My wife died," Murray answered.

"Oh, I'm sorry. When did she die?"

"Twenty years ago."

"And you still miss her so much?" Joey said.

"It's not that," Murray sobbed. "Now I live with a beautiful 25-year-old girl."

"Well, why are you crying?" Joey asked.

"I forgot where I live!"

Exercise is for everyone

Everyone from young children to the very elderly can - and should - exercise to keep both the body and the mind healthy and fit. Most sports have youth competitions as well as seniors' events. The Special Olympics and other competitions exist for people with various kinds of disabilities.

Everybody can find a way to benefit from exercise.

We won't go into detail about how much or what kind of exercise is appropriate. That information is readily available from books and magazines, trainers, coaches and doctors.

But some of Jose Silva's research can give you additional information to help you determine exactly what you should do in your particular situation.

The 7-year itch

Jose Silva's research revealed a correlation between brain frequency and a person's age for the first 21 years of life. We seem to go through life cycles of approximately seven years each, Jose observed.

Infants tend to function more at the delta brain wave frequency than at any other frequency. They spend a lot of time sleeping. They have not yet mastered language and logic, which are left-brain, beta functions. When they focus their eyes, their brain frequency goes to 20 cps. With vision defocused, the frequency is lower.

Up to the age when a child loses its baby teeth and gets its permanent teeth, the overall average brain frequency is in the delta and theta ranges. Getting permanent teeth seems to signal a change of life. The child is now going to school. The alpha part of the brain matures and becomes prominent.

Until the onset of puberty, the overall dominant brain frequency is in the alpha range. This 7-14 cps functioning correlates to the child's age - approximately 7 to 14. During this second life cycle, the child is very creative and imaginative - characteristics of the alpha level.

Puberty signals a third life cycle. The child matures. So does the brain. Now the beta frequencies, 14 to 21 cps, become prominent. In nine out of 10 people, logic takes over, and imagination, creativity and intuition are often left behind. At age 21, the person is considered a mature adult and can drink, vote and own property.

Jose Silva calls these "anabolic life cycles." During them, you are gaining, you are growing, you are getting better and better physically. And he says that there are seven of these seven-year anabolic life cycles. That takes you to age 49.

When you look at the sports of weightlifting and

bodybuilding, you see examples of people continuing to grow stronger. Several heavyweight boxers, who depend more on strength and power than on speed, have even been competitive during their 40s. George Foreman became the world heavyweight boxing champion in his 40s.

The life cycles that follow those first seven cycles are catabolic cycles - meaning that you end each cycle with less than you had when you started.

If we live through seven anabolic life cycles and seven more catabolic life cycles, we will live for 98 years.

If you stay fit and take care of yourself - and enter your level every day to strengthen your immune mechanism and stay healthy - you should be able to live almost 100 years and die in perfect health.

Physical fitness for your children

A child has a couple of jobs:

1. To learn as much as possible.

2. To exercise the body so that it will grow.

A young child does not have a critical reasoning faculty. A child's brain functions inductively, not deductively. A child's brain is like a sponge.

Whatever you tell the child, whatever the child observes, is taken in and filed in the memory banks of the child's biocomputer brain.

Mental Housecleaning is extremely important when you are dealing with young children because they accept everything that you tell them.

Parents should practice good Mental Housecleaning with their children: Praise them, and encourage the behavior you desire.

It is very easy to say, "If you don't study hard and make good grades, you will not be successful in life."

We want to encourage them to make good grades, but we don't want to program them that they cannot do any better in adult life than they did in school!

Instead say something like, "Learn your subjects so you will be able to do the things you want to do."

We also want to be good examples for them. Children do not have a critical reasoning faculty. They simply accept what is told to them.

You want them to grow up with good habits, with habits that will help them be healthy, productive and happy. So be a good role model for them and let them see you exercise regularly.

If a child sees mommy or daddy lifting weights and wants to join in, that's all right, but keep the weights very light.

A child's small body is already growing very rapidly; it does not need the intense stimulation of heavy weight training. In fact, it does not take much stress to injure a child's immature joints and tissues.

Teenagers can probably handle a sensible weight training program. To be safe, get some professional advice. And if you have any doubts at all, use your level to help you make your decisions.

You can also teach your children to enter and use their level. The ideal time to teach children to enter and use their level is between 7 and 14 years old.

We have special programs to guide you to train your child; information on these programs is included in back of this book.

Fitness training for older people

As you grow older, it is very important to continue to exercise and keep the body fit. When you are going through the catabolic cycles, you need to pay special attention to physical fitness.

You will train differently.

For example, you will not use the hard gainer's routine described in Chapter 17. You do not want to overload muscles and tear down muscle fiber because it will not grow back the same way as when you were younger.

It is generally best for older athletes to train at a much lower intensity and for endurance. For example, instead of doing five squats with 300 pounds on the bar, you might find it better to load 50 pounds on the bar and do 50 repetitions.

Walking is good exercise. To place even less strain on the joints, you can exercise in a swimming pool. Simply going through exercise movements while in the water is excellent because the water offers resistance without placing stress on the joints the way that exercise on land could do.

Stretching and flexibility are important for older people. George Foreman said he thought he was feeling the effects of growing older when he came back to boxing, but then after he did some stretching exercises, he realized that he had just lost some flexibility and this made him think that he was getting old.

Once he regained his flexibility, he felt like he was in his 20s again. And the rest, as they say, is history.

As always, get professional advice and confirm your plans at your level. To help you make the decisions that are best for you, check in with your Mental Coach or use any of the Silva techniques that have worked for you.

Training to help overcome injuries

A well-trained athlete can begin exercising an injured joint very early and can come back from the injury much more quickly than the average person. This is because athletes know their bodies so well. They know the exact effect of every exercise that they do.

Get to know your body at your level.

When you are injured or ill, use your level to determine how - or if - you should be exercising.

You do not want to procrastinate and get too far out of condition, nor do you want to exercise too hard too soon and impede your recovery.

Talk to your doctor, your trainer, your coach and your Mental Coach.

Also remember to use your visualization technique to help speed the recovery from the injury.

Age and injuries couldn't hold him back

Raymond Horn of Houston, Texas, recently wrote to Silva International to tell how the Silva Method helped him - a 79-year-old who had suffered from bleeding ulcers - to be able to run in a 26.2-mile marathon.

"In 1957," he wrote, "I spent 40 days and nights in a hospital with bleeding ulcers. I had a subtotal gasoctomecy - removal of half of my stomach.

"I was determined not to be sick again," he continued. "I started running using the Silva Method to convince myself I could run. I then decided to run a marathon - at 63 years of age - by using Silva. I ran a 26.2-mile marathon in Honolulu, Hawaii. Since that time, I have run 16 marathons in a row."

In a 1991 marathon in Honolulu, Horn placed seventh out of 14 males in his age bracket. "I give 100% credit to using the Silva Method," Horn said.

Horn also had a special message for readers of this book:

"I believe if I could run a marathon, you, the reader, can too. I am 79 years of age. You need to train for six months and use the Silva Method every day. I was never considered an athlete in high school or college."

Now, here is Jose Silva's guidance about training under special circumstances.

7 Training Tips for Special Circumstances

1. Whenever you are working with children, remember that they are collecting information about everything they observe and everything they hear. Be positive with them, and give them good examples to follow.

2. Make things fun for children. Encourage them, but do not push them too hard. Lead them. Avoid placing too much strain on their young, maturing bodies. Get expert guidance, and use your level to help you make decisions.

3. Teach your children how to visualize what they desire. Have them close their eyes, and they will probably be functioning at the alpha level. Information on where to get help with this process is included in the back of this book.

4. Encourage older people to continue to train and remain fit. They should not try to keep up with young people but should train more for endurance than to build more strength. Get expert guidance, and use your level to help you make decisions.

5. Encourage disabled people to exercise and participate in sports. Physical exercise can be a great morale-booster and confidence-builder for them. As always, get expert guidance, and use your level to help you make decisions.

6. Much of what's done in physical therapy is just plain, old-fashioned exercise. In order to strengthen and rehabilitate an injured part of your body, you need to exercise it. You want to exercise it enough to stimulate growth, but not so much as to cause further damage or impede recovery. Get expert guidance, and use your level to help you make decisions.

7. Use your visualization technique - and any other appropriate mental technique - to help you, or the person with whom you are working, to succeed.

Chapter 20

Biofeedback equipment

A skeptical athlete visited our web site and read about the benefits of the Silva Trainer 1 Galvanic Skin Response instrument that helps you learn to enter and function at the alpha level.

"Send the instrument," he emailed us, "and if the instrument is good, I will send you a check."

We replied: "Send us your check, and if it is good, we will send you the Trainer 1."

Machinery-aided performance

We are living in an age of high technology, when athletes have many tools available to them to help them learn what is going on in their bodies.

There are machines to measure the amount of force produced throughout a movement.

Other machines track the exact direction and angle of a movement.

Some machines compute acceleration and deceleration. Then there are medical instruments that measure how much oxygen is used, percentage of body fat and much more.

Other instruments, known as biofeedback equipment, can tell you what is happening with your brain and your mind.

Anything that gives you information - feedback - about your body can be considered a biofeedback instrument. This could include a thermometer to take your temperature or an instrument that measures your blood pressure.

Electroencephalographs measure your brain frequency. EEGs are expensive, unwieldy and complicated to use.

A Galvanic Skin Response instrument, or GSR for short, can measure what happens when you use your mind. Specifically, it gives you feedback on your state of relaxation.

Relaxing into the alpha level

Laboratory research has demonstrated repeatedly that you can learn to consciously relax your mind and body, and your brain will slow down, too.

When you use a relaxation method, the amount that your brain slows varies, depending on the method used.

If you use hypnotic induction techniques, for example, your brain will slow somewhat initially, but if you become mentally active under hypnosis (this is called "post-hypnotic response"), your brain will return to rapid beta frequencies, just as though you were fully conscious and physically active.

If you use yoga techniques, the brain will slow to the theta level. Theta is good for learning to control the physical body.

Using the Silva System, you can learn to slow your brain to the alpha frequency, which is in the center of the normal brain frequency spectrum. When you are centered at alpha, you have the most control. Alpha is the ideal level from which to function.

Using a GSR instrument at your level

A GSR instrument can let you know when you have achieved a different level of mind and a lower brain frequency.

Basically, a GSR instrument measures the state of physical relaxation that your body has achieved. It does this by measuring the change in your skin's resistance to a tiny electrical current. The more you relax, the higher the resistance. The more tense and nervous you are, the less resistance.

When you relax and count yourself into your level, you relax your mind and your body, and your brain follows by relaxing into the alpha level. Therefore, a GSR can indirectly indicate that you have entered your level. If you become too excited, you will tense up and no longer be at your level. The GSR will indicate that.

Most GSR's "squeal"; the squealing sound is higher pitched as you relax.

Jose Silva developed and patented a different system. The Silva Trainer 1 instrument is a GSR that emits a beeping sound.

When you first use it, the instrument beeps approximately 18 times per second, slightly slower than the pulsing of the beta brain frequency.

As your body relaxes, the beeping slows.

The concept behind the Silva Trainer 1 is that your brain will then want to follow the beeping sound, and your brain frequency will slow down. The more you relax, the slower the beeping sound and the lower your brain frequency.

Many uses for the GSR

Many doctors are using GSR instruments for pain control. When the patients learn to relax deeply enough, they experience relief from the pain.

GSR's are also helpful in learning. Jose Silva found that his children could learn their lessons more quickly when he read to them at deep levels of mind.

It worked best when they heard a lesson three times, at three different levels of mind. So he would read to them once, then do something else - either bring them out of level or have them do something else while at their level and then read the lesson to them a second time. After doing something else, he would read the lesson to them at level a third time.

This prompted him to invent a special kind of GSR, the Silva Educator. It has the same beeping circuit as the Trainer 1, but it also features buttons that can be set to light, medium or deep.

When the subject has achieved the desired level, the Silva Educator automatically turns on an audio player and plays back a prerecorded lesson. The patent this device received states: "Human concentration turns on an educational program."

The GSR can also be used to help people learn to relax in tense situations, making it of great value to athletes.

Biofeedback and competition

All athletes encounter stress, injuries and days when they just can't seem to do anything right.

One of the biggest challenges facing all competitors is learning to relax enough prior to competition so they do not "choke." Many athletes say they have received substantial benefits from using a GSR instrument to help them learn to relax during competitive situations.

A GSR can help you to get to your level after a stressful day of work, so that you can program yourself for a great workout.

Programming to develop more skill

Relax and enter your level, using the GSR. At your level, mentally play the game. If you encounter any situations for which you do not feel fully prepared, you will often tense up a little bit and the GSR will signal you. Once you become aware of the problem that is causing your tension, you can deal with the situation through programming or practice.

You can make an audio recording of instructions to guide you through the appropriate movements, and turn on the recorded program when the beeping of the Trainer 1 slows to indicate that you are at your level.

If you get tense during a game, make a recording to work on this challenge. Put game sounds on the recording, and with your imagination, sense yourself being totally relaxed during competition.

Injuries often occur because you make a mistake. Your timing is off slightly and you get hurt. Or you fail to see something you should have seen and you get hurt. Or you move the wrong way at the wrong time and get hurt. Or you flinch, hesitate for a split second, and this changes your opponent's timing, causing what normally would have been a clean hit to result in an injury.

You can use a GSR instrument to help you build your confidence in your performance, and thus function better. Visualize yourself performing perfectly, without injuries.

If there is any part of your performance, any part of the game, that you are nervous about, the GSR will signal you. Then you can take steps to correct the problem.

Alpha Sound helps you to remain at alpha

There is one more item worth mentioning. It is not a biofeedback instrument, but it can help you. It's the "Alpha Sound" - an audio recording with a ticking sound that ticks (or clicks) 10 times per second.

The Alpha Sound can help you to remain at your level because your brain can pace itself to this sound. We even have a recording of our standard Long Relaxation Exercise with the Alpha Sound ticking in the background.

The Alpha Sound can be used to help people recover from injuries and illnesses more rapidly. The speaker in an audio player has a permanent magnet with a standing (not modulated) magnetic field. The Alpha Sound recording causes this magnetic field to pulse at 10 cycles per second.

Researchers have theorized that by placing the speaker side of the audio player immediately next to the injured or afflicted part of the body (leaving a quarter of an inch of air space between the speaker and the body so you do not mute the sound), then every cell within the afflicted area gets a magnetic field massage at 10 cycles per second when the alpha sound is playing.

The Alpha Sound recording can be used in this manner three times a day, 15 minutes each time. It should be at full volume. Researchers believe that this magnetic massage stimulates (excites) the subatomic particles. The theory is that after each application, the excited subatomic particles, when resettling, will resettle naturally into the original health state. This is believed to help the body's natural healing process.

You can spend 15 minutes using the audio player with the Alpha Sound to stimulate the subatomic particles in the afflicted area, but then you must allow time for them to settle back down to their normal positions.

Athletes have told us they have corrected various problems with the Alpha Sound. Tennis players say they have gotten rid of tendonitis; joggers say they have banished pain in their joints; trainees say they have eliminated calcium deposits in their hands. And many other people have said the Alpha Sound helped relieve their back pain.

Whenever you are programming for health, remember to follow the instructions correctly. Some people think that if a little bit is good, a lot is better. Not necessarily so. Follow Jose Silva's advice: Allow time in between sessions for your body to correct its problems.

Consult the resources listed in the back of this book for additional information about the Alpha Sound recordings and the biofeedback instruments discussed in this chapter.

Chapter 21

The student athlete

"Are you good at arithmetic?" Golfer Les Strokes asked a youngster who had offered to caddie for him.

"Yes, sir," the boy answered.

"Then how many are four and five and three?" Strokes asked.

"Nine, sir."

"Come on," Strokes said. *"You'll do fine!"*

Intelligence and athletic ability

Would you be surprised to learn that professional athletes are more intelligent than the average person?

Pro football players, for instance, score in the top quarter in IQ tests, according to Michael Murphy and Reah A. White in their book *The Psychic Side of Sports*.

They have to be smart. Just look at how complex the games are at the professional level. In addition, everything happens so fast in professional sports that you have very little time to think.

You have to be smart just to make it to the pros.

How intelligent do you suppose a person has to be to become a superstar?

Becoming a good athlete takes both mental and physical learning. You have to learn the plays, the rules, the strategy. You have to learn to perform the correct actions with your body.

The ability to learn is especially important to student athletes, now that many school districts have instituted "no pass, no play" rules. But even if you are not subject to this kind of rule, it is still valuable to be a good learner because the same skills that make you a good student will help make you a better athlete.

Whether you are trying to figure out batting averages or which pro team is offering you the best financial package, the more educated you are, the better chance you have of arriving at the right answer.

And if you want to go into the business world or profit from your achievements once your athletic career is over, you'd better have enough education to handle the job.

The truth is, the need for learning never stops. With that in mind, we have several tips and techniques in this chapter that you can use to improve your ability to learn and remember what you need to know.

Learning how to learn

Did anybody ever teach you how to learn? Did your teachers teach you what to do with your mind in order to learn something or remember something? Or did they just tell you, "Study harder"?

In this chapter, we'll show you exactly what to do in order to learn more quickly and remember things better.

Scientific research by Jose Silva has revealed that learning is most effective during certain types of brain activity - at certain states of consciousness - that everyone can learn to achieve with just a few hours of instruction and practice.

Jose's background in electronics gave him the key to unlock the door of faster learning.

He discovered that alpha is the ideal brain state for learning the things that you need to know, and beta is the ideal brain state for taking what you learn and putting it into action. Obviously, you will be a better athlete if you use the correct brain state at the correct time.

Research project passes test

In a research project conducted at the University of Tasmania in Hobart, Tasmania, Australia, students raised their test scores by one letter grade when they used the Silva Three Fingers Technique. (We'll teach you how you can do this later.)

"From the results of this study," Dr. Harry E. Stanton wrote in an article that was published in *The Journal of the Society for Accelerative Learning and Teaching* (SALT) in the fall of 1986, "it would seem reasonable to conclude that the Three Fingers Technique is able to facilitate short-term improvement in second-year high school students' examination performance."

The study involved 60 high school students - 34 boys and 26 girls.

These students took eight school subjects in common, and their marks in these subjects at second-term examinations were averaged.

Students were paired on the basis of these marks - one member of each pair allocated at random to an experimental group and the other serving as a control.

At the beginning of the third term, the experimental group learned the Three Fingers Technique.

They were asked to use it to help themselves absorb written material and the information they were given in class.

A week prior to third-term examinations, they reviewed the technique again, particularly as it applied to test taking.

After completion of the third-term examinations, researchers computed the average mark for each of the eight subjects taken in common by the 60 students. This figure was compared to the one derived for the second-term examinations.

The results looked like this:

Experimental Group

Term 2: 63% - Term 3: 72%

Control Group

Term 2: 64% - Term 3: 63%

Those who had learned the Silva Three Fingers Technique improved nine percentage points, while the control group actually dropped one point.

To put it another way, the experimental group improved their scores more than 14 percent of their original scores when they used the Three Fingers Technique.

"The technique is a very simple one which students have no trouble in learning," Dr. Stanton wrote in a report published in the SALT journal.

"Initially, their curiosity is piqued; later their interest is maintained as they find it becoming easier for them to remember the material they read and hear about in the classroom," he continued. "Success breeds success. As students use the technique with increasing confidence in its effectiveness, so they seem to cope more capably with their school work.

"This technique is one which has wide applicability to everyday life," Dr. Stanton said. He described the technique as "a simple conditioned trigger which we can use to focus our faculties. By doing the conditioning while in the relaxed state, our suggestions become more powerful.

"Thus, when we invoke the signal at a later date, it is likely to be more successful in achieving the result we desire. After all," he added, "that is what counts.

"Does the technique actually help us achieve what we want? The results of the study reported in this article suggest that it does, and that further testing of its effectiveness is in order."

How to make stronger impressions on your brain

"In electronics," Jose explains, "you always want to use the circuit that has the least impedance. Impedance is the total opposition to the flow of electrical current. The circuit with the least impedance will give you the greatest power."

It turns out that alpha is the strongest, most rhythmic and most stable of all of the brain frequencies. So it is the ideal level to use when you are using your biocomputer brain.

You will make stronger impressions of information while at the alpha level, which results in a stronger memory.

You can more quickly retrieve information (remember things) when your brain is functioning at alpha.

The brain will do a better job of coming up with solutions to problems when in the alpha state.

Since this has been scientifically documented and experienced by millions of Silva graduates all over the world, why isn't it being taught to every student in every school?

Unfortunately, change comes slowly, especially in big institutions that have invested a lot in their established methodology. Nobody wants to admit that the way they have been doing things for years is not the best way.

However, things are changing.

The Silva techniques were made available to all students in Catholic schools in Guam in the early 1980s. The project was a huge success.

The Silva techniques have been taught for credit in many colleges and universities, as well.

Still, it has yet to be universally accepted in the field of education, so most students have to learn it on their own.

Learning at the alpha level

You have learned that the best way to learn is while you are at the alpha brain wave level. You have also learned that when you focus your eyes, which you do when you are reading, your brain goes to beta. So how can you study while at alpha?

You can do so by preprogramming yourself while you are at the alpha level. Then when you are studying - even though you might not be producing alpha brain waves predominantly - you will nevertheless have an "alpha state of mind."

Later you will learn how you can have an alpha state of mind while actively participating in athletic activity. The more you practice techniques like the ones that follow, the easier it will be for you to learn to maintain an alpha state of mind during competition.

When Jose Silva began his research, he would read to his children while they were at lower brain frequencies, then test them to determine how much they could recall.

You could do the same thing by getting someone to read to you while you are at your level or by recording your lesson onto an audio recorder and listening to it while at your level.

But this isn't always practical. Instead, you could use a pair of formulas Jose Silva developed for use while you are reading a book or listening to a lecture.

Jose also developed formulas that you can use to recall information while taking a test or during a game when you need to remember your assigned move for a play that has just been called.

These formulas are all grouped together under the title of the Silva Three Fingers Technique; you'll learn them in just a moment. First, though, let's hear about how these techniques work in the real world.

Gold medal in elocution contest

Wildan Jan G. Cabactulan, a 10-year-old fourth grader at Southridge school in Manila, the Philippines, reported the following success story. (Thanks to Judy Qua, our lecturer in the Philippines, for letting us reprint this story from her book, *Everyday Miracles and the Silva Method*.)

"I was an honor student in my previous school from up to Grade 1. I transferred to my present school when I was in Grade 2.

"On my first day in my new school, our teacher started writing on the blackboard in script. I looked around and was surprised to see my classmates copying in script! I could already read letters and words in script at that time, but we had not yet been taught in my previous school how to write them.

"My present classmates learned scriptwriting gradually. According to my seatmate, they started writing in circles since they were in Prep. They had plenty of time to practice. But for me I had to do it all at once! I had to adjust to a new school, new teachers and new classmates.

"I had difficulty finishing my notes in the classroom so I had to spend my break time and playtime copying notes from my classmates. During quizzes, even if I knew the answers, I got low scores because I was not able to finish them. For long tests and quarterly exams, I had to go to school on Saturdays. Sometimes, my fingers, hand and wrist would ache. I had to rest them first before proceeding to write again.

"The comments of some of my classmates made me sad. They called me 'slowpoke,' At the end of the school year, I passed all my subjects but didn't make the honor roll.

"One summer vacation (1992), my parents, who are Silva Method graduates, enrolled me in the Silva Method for Children. I was so happy to receive my Silva Workbook, Silva

Pin, Silva Prize and a bag full of new 'tricks' like the Three Fingers Technique, the visualization technique, Glove Anesthesia and many others. I 'leveled' often and used the Silva Method techniques whenever I needed to.

"When school opened, what I visualized came true. The teachers and classmates assigned in my section were good and nice. The bullies went to other sections. My writing improved. My speed improved. I felt better and better. At the end of the quarter I was overjoyed to see my name in the principal's list! I have been in the principal's list since then.

"One time, we had an elocution contest, the 'Battle of the Champions.' The piece was given to us one week before the contest. When I received it on a Tuesday, I was not able to start memorizing it because I had unit tests on Wednesday and Thursday. I only had time to read it Thursday after classes, get the meaning of the difficult words from the dictionary and practice the proper diction and expression. Friday after school up to Sunday morning we had Boy Scout camping.

"When I arrived home Sunday afternoon, I was so tired and sleepy. I went straight to bed. When Monday morning came, two days before the contest, I hadn't memorized a thing. My parents advised me to back out. I didn't want to back out because my classmates and I wanted our class to win and it was too late to get a replacement.

"The piece was *The Charge of the Light Brigade*. It has six stanzas, with five lines per stanza. Using the Three Fingers Technique, I was able to master the piece in just a few hours (Monday evening and Tuesday evening).

"Before the contest and while waiting for my turn during the contest, I felt nervous, so I took deep breaths, exhaled and visualized the numbers 3, 2 and 1. Each time I did it, I felt better and better. When my turn came, the feeling of nervousness was not there any more. I just remembered doing my best. Silva tricks' work! I became the champion and received a gold medal!"

Now we'll tell you how you, as a student, can use Jose Silva's Three Fingers Technique to remember your lessons and much more. (Be sure to preprogram the techniques at your level first.)

How to Improve Your Memory With the 3-Fingers Technique

You can preprogram yourself to use the Silva Three Fingers Technique for a variety of purposes. In the Basic Lecture Series we use it to develop stronger self-programming and to help produce a better memory.

Enter your level as you have been taught. Once at your level, you can program yourself. The first step is to bring together the tips of the thumb and first two fingers of either hand, or both hands. Bring them together to form a circle. A lot of energy radiates out of your body through your fingertips. This technique re-circulates some of that energy so that you can use it for stronger self-programming.

Tell yourself mentally that whenever you bring together the tips of the thumb and first two fingers of either hand, as you are doing now, your mind adjusts to a deeper level of awareness, for stronger programming. Stronger programming of information results in easier recall, producing a better memory.

To Read a Lesson

To read a lesson, enter your level as you have been taught. Tell yourself mentally that you are going to count from 1 to 3 and at the count of 3 you will open your eyes and read the lesson. Mention the lesson, title and subject.

Add, "Noises will not distract me but will help me to concentrate. I will have superior concentration and understanding." Count from 1 to 3, open your eyes and read the lesson.

When you have read the lesson, once again enter level. Tell yourself mentally, "I will recall the lesson I have just read (mention title and subject) any time in the future with the use of the Three Fingers Technique."

To Listen to and Remember a Lecture

To listen to a lecture, enter your level and tell yourself mentally that you are going to hear a lecture and mention the title, subject and lecturer's name. Tell yourself that you are going to use the Three Fingers Technique. Keep your eyes open during the lecture.

Tell yourself that noises will not distract you but will help you to concentrate, that you will have superior concentration and understanding and that you will recall the lecture (mention title, subject and lecturer's name) any time in the future with the use of the Three Fingers Technique.

To Succeed On a test

For test-taking, use this "3-cycle" method of the Three Fingers Technique:

1. Read your test questions the way you always do, but do not spend too much time on any one of them. If you have a ready answer, put it down; if not, skip that question and move on to the next one.

2. To use the Three Fingers Technique, do as you did in the first cycle, but spend a little more time on each unanswered question. When an answer comes, put it down; if not, skip that question and move on to the next one.

3. To use the Three Fingers Technique, read the unanswered question, and if you still cannot answer it, close your eyes, turn

them slightly upward, visualize or imagine your professor on your mental screen and ask for the answer. Then clear your mind, and start thinking again to figure out the answer. (In order to clear your mind, think of an entirely different subject for a moment. For instance, after you imagine asking your professor for the answer, think about the chores you have to do later. Then come back to the question, but this time, expect an answer.) The answer that comes is your professor's. Write it down. Do not turn in a blank paper.

In the third cycle, clearing your mind helps you switch from a "question mode" to an "answer mode." Notice how we tell you to "start thinking again to figure out the answer." If an answer does not occur to you, make one up. You think about what the answer could be. Whatever occurs to you, write it down. You've got nothing to lose you can't score unless you take a shot at it.

Many uses for these techniques

In addition to using these techniques in the classroom, you can use them to help you learn what your coach is teaching you. You have two different formulas that you can use:

1. You can program yourself before your instruction begins and then program yourself again after you have finished, so that you will remember and be able to apply what you have learned.

2. Sometimes you may not have an opportunity to enter your level after the instruction is finished because the coach will take you out for a long practice session right away. In this case, you will want to program yourself at the very beginning, and program that you will have good concentration, will understand and will be able to apply what you were taught when you begin your practice session.

Sometimes one approach is more convenient and better to use than the other.

You can learn to control your temper

Let's take a look at how you can use the techniques for other purposes. You can combine the techniques to accomplish a certain purpose. To control a strong emotion like anger, for example, you can combine visualization with the Three Fingers Technique.

Anger is a negative emotion. It causes stress the heartbeat begins to race, blood pressure increases, body chemistry changes, muscles become tense and rigid. The resulting tension can, in turn, cause a headache. It can also result in an imbalance in gastric juices in the stomach and cause an ulcer. If the stress is not brought under control, even harsher things can happen.

The more control you have over your emotions, the healthier you will be and the more able you will become as an athlete.

The following two techniques can help you deal with anger. The first can help you change the way you approach anger-arousing situations like losing a big varsity game or being told you can't play the position you wanted. The second gives you tools to use when you feel yourself becoming angry.

Reprogram Your Reactions

When you have gotten angry about something and you want to regain control of your emotions, you can enter your level and use the visualization technique you learned in Chapter 6 to neutralize the negative energy you have built up.

Use the two scenes technique.

- In Monitor Number 1, replay the situation the way it happened. This might give you some insight into why you reacted the way you did.

- Then erase the problem image, and in Monitor Number 2, imagine responding differently, without anger. Program that in the future, whenever you encounter a similar situation, you will remain in control of your emotions, the way that you have programmed in that second monitor.

- In the future, if you happen to think of the person or situation that triggered the anger, immediately recall the solution image that you created in Monitor Number 2. Let this be your memory of the way the situation occurred.

Control Your Emotions

In order to help you control your anger, you can incorporate the Three Fingers Technique into your programming.

- First, visualize the problem in the first monitor by recalling a situation when you were angry and out of control.

- Then, erase that image.

- In Monitor Number 2, imagine yourself bringing the tips of the thumb and first two fingers of either hand together, and as you take a deep breath and exhale, you relax and respond without the anger. You are in control. Your body remains relaxed while you deal with the person or situation. While doing this programming, actually put your three fingers together.

- Later, when you encounter a person or situation that starts to make you angry, just bring together the thumb and first two fingers of either hand, take a deep breath, exhale and recall the image of yourself in the second monitor, remaining calm and relaxed. Remember how relaxed you were at your level when you imagined how you would take care of the problem without anger.

Chapter 22

Your responsibilities as an athlete

One day, a lion was awakened from sleep by a mouse running over his face. Rising up angrily, he caught the mouse and was about to kill him when the mouse begged, "If you would only spare my life, I would be sure to repay your kindness."

The lion laughed and let him go.

It happened that shortly after this, the lion was caught by some hunters, who bound him to the ground with strong ropes.

The mouse, recognizing his roar, came up to the lion, gnawed the rope with his teeth and set him free, exclaiming, "You ridiculed the idea of my ever being able to help you, not expecting to receive from me any repayment of your favor, but now you know that it is possible for even a mouse to confer benefits on a lion."

Everyone has a purpose

Jose Silva believes that we were all sent here for a purpose.

"We are not here on earth for a 70-year coffee break," he says in his seminars. "We are not here just to get everything that we can for ourselves.

We were sent here to correct problems and to help convert the planet into a paradise."

Some athletes understand this. Others don't.

While some athletes start their own charitable foundations and spend a lot of time helping people who are less fortunate than they, others brag about how many sex partners they have had or how much money they make with their endorsements.

Without the athletic event, there would be no endorsement contracts. Without opponents, there would be no athletic event.

Great athletes respect and admire their toughest opponents. "I don't want to beat a poor team," basketball coach Hector Chacon says. "I want to beat a good team."

Would boxer Muhammad Ali have been as great a fighter without Joe Frazier? Would he be respected as much?

Just look at Ali today - how he loves people and how much people love him. You know he understands that people are part of his purpose.

A thought from the New Testament is appropriate here:

Much has been given to you, and much is expected of you.

Jose Silva believes that when we use our talent and energy to do the job we were sent here to do, we will be well compensated.

His research and experience seem to prove he is right.

An athlete's responsibility to humanity

How does an athlete help to correct problems on the planet?

By being a good example.

Part of being an athlete is having an audience. When you choose to perform for people and accept the rewards that accompany that, you take on a responsibility to those people.

They support you emotionally.

They applaud you, cheer you, praise you and make you feel good.

There's no question: Being an athlete has many social benefits. Perhaps there are material benefits - if athletics does not become your occupation, it may help you get another job.

Even if you do not compete publicly - if all you do is practice aerobics to look and feel better, or play golf with your friends -

you are still putting yourself in a position in which you can influence people. You look healthy and strong. You act confident. You are relaxed and energetic. People are impressed by you.

Whether you like it or not, you are a role model.

All of us - athletes and those of us who simply try to get ourselves in better shape than the average person have a special opportunity to influence people.

We've all been inspired by athletes. We follow their examples.

When things get tough for us, we strive to overcome obstacles and achieve our goals just as our favorite athletes have. Our attempts to do so help to make us better people.

Great athletes recognize that their talents are gifts and that reaping rewards from these gifts means accepting certain responsibilities.

Benny Parsons, a former outstanding stock car racer, became an announcer for televised races after he retired from racing. When he was inducted into the International Motorsports Hall of Fame in 1994, he spoke eloquently about an idea shared by so many great athletes.

"I haven't had a job since 1968," he said. "I made my living with my hobby. What talent I had was a gift from God."

Referring to his friend Richard Petty, who won more NASCAR races than anyone else in history, Parsons continued, "When we were out there racing, we thought we were just like everybody else. We thought our cars were better. After six years in the broadcast booth, looking down at it, there is a difference.

"That difference is a gift from God."

Superstar athletes and their legacies

Baseball and football are two of the biggest sports in America. Youngsters dream of being superstars in these sports.

Mickey Mantle is a baseball superstar from a previous generation. During an interview on the George Michael Sports Machine television program in October 1994, Mantle was asked what he was proud of most. He answered, "That I was liked by my teammates."

"I'm a team man," he continued. "On my headstone, I wouldn't want them to write that I was a great long ball hitter. I want them to write that I was liked by my teammates."

A year later, after receiving a liver transplant to save his life, Mantle would acknowledge his problem with heavy drinking - and then lose his life to the effects of many years of alcohol abuse. At his funeral, sportscaster Bob Costas referred to Mantle as "the most compelling baseball hero of our lifetime." But a year earlier, Mantle himself had stated, "I wasn't like I should be. I wasn't a good husband or father."

Mantle had not realized, until it was too late, how destructive his drinking was. He didn't know any better at the time. He didn't realize, as a baseball superstar, the kind of legacy he would be leaving behind. He didn't realize how much he would regret his actions.

"This is a role model?" he said in a television interview from his hospital bed. "Don't be like me."

Now you know. Now you have an opportunity to learn from other people's mistakes.

How you play the game

In past generations, athletics offered a way for young people to learn how to get along better in the game of life.

"Baseball is the sport of America," actor Jack Webb said in a Dragnet episode from 1969. "It teaches youngsters fair play."

Unfortunately, the idea of fair play and respect for your teammates, your opponents and the fans seems to have gone the way of the horse and buggy. These days, you see a lot of unpleasant things on athletic fields - players showing disrespect for everything and everybody by throwing temper tantrums, protesting close calls by officials and "trash talking" to their opponents. We see this disrespect carry over to the fans - riots during games and after championships, fans spitting on players as they leave the field.

We all want to be respected, loved and appreciated. In order to get those things, we have to give them. The more we toot our own horns and try to get all that we can for ourselves without any regard for other people, the more unhappy we are going to be with the way we are treated by other people.

Philosopher Harry Emerson Fosdick said, "A person completely wrapped up in himself makes a small package."

How long has it been since you heard anybody say, "It matters not the final score, but how you played the game"?

These days, it seems like many athletes want accolades whether they deserve them or not - regardless of how they played the game. But it wasn't always so.

A winning effort comes up short... momentarily

Richard Petty has been so successful in NASCAR racing that he is known as "King Richard." But he has never let his talent go to his head. In 1958, in a race at Lakewood Fairgrounds Speedway in Atlanta, GA, he got his first trophy. Ed Bernd Jr. was there to see it.

Lakewood Speedway was a 1-mile dirt track, around a lake. The race was 150 laps - 150 miles of racing. At the end, the checkered flag was thrown for Richard's Oldsmobile convertible. Ed watched as Richard sat atop the roll bars and posed for photographers while the trophy girl gave him his first trophy.

The next morning in the newspaper, Ed read the rest of the story:

After the photographers were gone and most of the crowd had left, Richard's father, stock car racing pioneer Lee Petty, came over and said, "I'm sorry to have to tell you this, son, but you didn't win the race."

Richard's reaction: "Oh, okay. Who did?"

Lee said that he had finished ahead of his son.

The old pro - who was the first-ever Daytona 500 winner and is still ranked tenth on the NASCAR all-time winners list with 54 victories and three NASCAR Championships - had a counter on his dashboard. When the scorekeepers recounted the laps, they verified that Lee had, indeed, won the race.

"I know you want a victory," Lee is reported to have said to his son, "but I know you want it to be a real victory."

Richard shrugged it off with the big infectious grin he still has 50 years later, and then went on to win a record 200 NASCAR Cup races and seven season championships.

When Richard was inducted into the new NASCAR Hall of Fame, he noted that the records he broke – most wins, most championships – were his father's records. Richard was one of the 5 drivers inducted into the Hall of Fame the year it opened. His father Lee was inducted the next year.

The story of that race is depicted in the 1972 movie *43: The Richard Petty Story*. Richard plays himself in the movie, and Darren McGavin plays his father. They portray it just the way Ed remembers it, except for some reason, they have it happening on a different race track.

Athletes who inspire us with their honesty and effort

Every sport has these examples of clean competition and fair play. In 1935, Chicago University halfback Jay Berwanger won the very first Heisman Trophy, presented each year to the outstanding college football player. He confirmed a story about an incident that took place during one game.

Berwanger had made a long run down the sidelines. An official was following him and thought that Berwanger might have stepped out of bounds during the run but was not sure. So he asked Berwanger if he had gone out of bounds.

His reply? "Yes."

We are all role models, whether we like it or not. We don't have to be perfect. We don't have to win every time. But we should always make an effort to win. We should always give our best.

Boxer Buster Douglas had his "15 minutes of fame" when he defeated Mike Tyson to become the undisputed heavyweight champion of the world. He lost the title in his first defense. But winning that title saved a young woman's life.

Radio news commentator Paul Harvey told a story on the air about a young woman who was so depressed that she was ready to commit suicide.

Then she happened to see a television report about how Buster Douglas, against overwhelming odds, had knocked out Mike Tyson.

She was so inspired that this underdog - who was still grieving the recent death of his mother - could actually win a great victory, she decided to make another effort in her own life.

She overcame her problems and got on with her life.

Vince Lombardi's creed

People quote football coach Vince Lombardi as having said, "Winning isn't the most important thing; it is the only thing." Those who played for him have said that his actual statement was more like: "Making the effort to win is the only thing that counts."

Lombardi did not advocate winning at all costs. He emphasized character. Read Jerry Kramer's books about Lombardi, and you learn how he valued honesty, fair play and the willingness to give 100 percent to a job you committed yourself to doing.

Lombardi, a religious man who went to mass every morning, said that striving to win "fairly, squarely, decently, by the rules but to win" was all that really counted.

You should win because you are good and because you are willing to pay the price for victory. You are willing to give 100 percent effort. You do everything you can to win. Nothing should distract you from that. Winning "fairly, squarely, decently, by the rules" should be your only concern.

That was Vince Lombardi's message.

Raise the level of the game for everyone

We used to be taught how to be gracious winners and gracious losers - how to show respect for our opponents, the officials and the fans. Sportscaster and former football great Frank Gifford said that he had never known a great competitor who was a good loser.

"You can be a gracious loser," he said on the Monday Night Football telecast, "but great competitors are not good losers."

Winning gracefully is just as important as losing gracefully.

In a social setting, nobody wants to listen to somebody brag about his or her great accomplishments all evening. Likewise, on the playing field, athletes should let their achievements speak for themselves.

Athletes used to just play the game and let the fans enjoy the results. Today, their athletic accomplishments are often overshadowed by their celebrations and dances.

A receiver is expected to catch balls for touchdowns. That's his job. You don't see doctors jumping all around and dancing every time they diagnose the flu and give you a shot for it. That's their job, and they are expected to do it.

Jerry Rice seems to understand this. He doesn't do any fancy little dances when he scores.

He remembers how scared he was when he came into the National Football League and how many people encouraged him and helped him. He talks about it openly.

He says his success is a group effort - a combination of support from parents, coaches, fans and players, his own hard work and his great, natural talent.

For him to dance and show off would be a slap in the face to everybody who blocked for him, for the quarterback who threw him the ball, for all of the people who supported him through the years. He shows respect for all of those other people.

It is okay - important, even - to let people know about your accomplishments. Fans love to see you succeed, and they like it even more when you are happy with your victory.

Genuine excitement over a job done exceptionally well is fun because the fans can enjoy it with you.

But it is disrespectful to everyone who helped out to everyone else who tried hard and gave their very best to show off, brag and act as if you are somehow better than they are.

In fact, without strong opponents to challenge you, you

could never demonstrate how good you are in the first place.

Jack Nicklaus understands that winning through your own efforts is better than thriving on your opponents' mistakes. He demonstrated this at the biannual Ryder Cup competition between British and American golfers.

It was a tight match, the closest in years.

The golfers were on the green at the final hole.

Nicklaus putted first. If he made a mistake, the British could win for the first time in more than a decade.

Nicklaus's ball dropped into the cup.

The British golfer approached his ball next. It was only a "gimme" putt - just inches from the hole, the kind of putt normally conceded by an opponent - but the British player felt the pressure.

If he made the putt, the match would end in a tie. It would be the best finish the British had had in years.

If he missed such an easy putt, it could have a devastating effect on his reputation.

Nicklaus had too much respect for his opponent to wish that kind of humiliation on him. So he reached down, picked up the ball and thereby conceded the putt.

The match ended in a tie, and both men walked away champions.

A new definition of "winning"

In an article from the July/August 1991 issue of *Multi-Images* magazine, published by the Association for Multi-media International, scriptwriter and producer Todd Gipstein tells the moving story of how two disabled athletes inspired him:

Inspiring story

I offer a true story; an event that I personally witnessed and will never forget. It redefined my entire concept of competition and "winning." And it showed me the remarkable power of human spirit, both to endure great hardship and to transcend the moment and achieve a higher plane.

It was the 1986 Boston Marathon. There is no race quite like it. None quite so steeped in history and mystique, with its "Heartbreak Hill" and colorful occurrences over the years.

And marathons have a way of bringing out special qualities in people.

My office was on the same block as the finish line, and that year, I was sitting in the bleachers right at the finish.

It was a cloudy, rainy day. There was a big crowd waiting for the racers to appear at the hill at the top of Boylston Street and struggle down the last half-mile or so to the end.

The first finishers were the wheelchair racers. As we saw the first of them crest the hill and exhaustedly wheel down the homestretch, I marveled at the willpower, strength, and stamina it must take to be able to push oneself more than twenty-six miles. Life in a wheelchair was pretty inconceivable to me, let alone competing in one as an athlete.

Preceded by motorcycle cops with flashing lights and spurred on by the roar of the crowd, the first racer sped by. He'd pump the wheels with his muscular arms, then let the chair glide, then pump the wheels some more.

After the hours of anticipation, the finish happens quickly, in a blur. The first across the line that overcast spring day was Andre Viger, in a time of 1:43:25. He was followed seconds later by George Murray.

And then along came Laverne Achenbach and Ted Vince, streaking down the street, neck and neck, their chairs side-by-side, wheels almost touching.

As they rumbled the last few hundred yards, they swapped leads.

One second, Laverne gave a few quick pumps and pulled a foot ahead of Ted.

Responding, Ted summoned some strength and competitive fire deep within and pushed a little harder on his next stroke to recapture the lead.

We cheered them on to what was sure to be a photo-finish! We cheered not for one or the other so much as in general encouragement.

Ted was ahead.

Then Laverne.

Then Ted again.

Each second brought them closer to the finish line. Just fifty yards to go now. Laverne. Ted. Laverne again. Forty yards. Thirty.

And then it happened. Right in front of me.

They were side by side, dead even. Ted looked at Laverne, who looked back at Ted. They smiled, stopped pumping at their wheels, clasped hands and held on tight. They both raised their free hands in the air in fists and glided across the finish line together.

It was a majestic gesture of sportsmanship and camaraderie. A moment of sublime grace.

I was stunned. Goose bumps prickled my body. A lump of emotion rose in my throat and tears welled in my eyes.

Those two men had fought neck and neck for more than twenty-six miles, but at the end, they'd realized that neither was better; that one finishing ahead of the other was somehow an irrelevance. It was not important. Just finishing the race was all that mattered; and finishing it together, as equal competitors, was still to finish it as winners.

I was trying to grasp their heroic, noble gesture when I heard a disgusted voice behind me. "Now that was stupid! The point is to beat the other guy!"

I turned and encountered a man in a three-piece suit. I started to explain what had happened to him, but thought better of it. Witnessing what he'd just witnessed and saying what he'd just said, he'd never understand. He had a very narrow definition of winning. And it had nothing to do with spirit.

In the Boston Globe that next day, the race results were posted. For the record, Laverne Achenbach finished with a time of 1:51:25; Ted Vince rolled in at 1:51:26.

No doubt the fine Swiss optics that recorded their finish detected a slight discrepancy in their positions as they crossed the line.

Perhaps a hundredth of a second separated them, but something far greater united them.

To its credit, the Globe listed both men as third. Understanding their gesture, the Globe ignored the clock and posted their times as they wanted it - as tied.

I carry the image of that instant with me. I cherish it. Their gesture was impulsive, heartfelt - wonderfully noble.

Laverne Achenbach and Ted Vince triumphed by entering, enduring, and finishing the marathon. But they also triumphed by shedding the pettiness of competitiveness, by celebrating their achievement together.

They showed those of us privileged to see their deed what the spirit of competition is all about.

They conceived a new definition for "winning."

Entertain and inspire people with your deeds

Make no mistake: Professional sports is not just about winning. It is about entertainment - about giving people something that will motivate and inspire them.

If winning was the only thing that mattered to the fans - the people who buy the tickets that provide the money to pay those big salaries - then nobody would attend the games. They would just wait to see who won.

Professional sports is about performing.

Buffalo Bills fans still filled Rich Stadium and support their team, even after four straight Super Bowl losses.

Sure, the most satisfying thing is a win. But it is also satisfying to see people put forth their best effort, to strive in the face of tremendous opposition and to achieve small victories, even if the big victory eludes them.

This holds true in everyday living: We don't always win, but we can always give our best, always put in a performance we can be proud of.

You don't have to be a superstar to inspire people.

A high school athlete who puts forth a great effort, who gives her best even though she does not have the talent to win a championship, can inspire her friends, fans and the people who love her.

For many years, a friend named Johnny White raced stock cars at small tracks around Florida. Even when he wasn't winning, he was always trying.

If he Johnny was running in tenth position in a heat race, he would try to pass and move into ninth position. He would risk wrecking the car even though only the first three finishers get paid in heat races. Johnny would always give his best.

Did the crowd like to see this, or did they only applaud the winners?

Well, at the end of the 1973 season, the fans at Johnny's home track, the Eau Gallie Speedway in Melbourne, FL, voted to award him the *Orlando Sentinel's* Sportsmanship Award - one of the highest honors at the speedway.

Johnny did not need to win a championship in order to inspire people.

Like him, you can inspire people, simply by doing the following:

- *Being in good shape, having plenty of energy and being in good health.

- Accepting compliments graciously.

- Encouraging others to strive to do their best and always doing your best.

- Respecting your teammates, your opponents, your fans and everyone else with whom you come into contact.

- Doing what is necessary to get people involved - like the way Muhammad Ali got people excited about boxing - as long as you do it with respect and love.

Share your success with others

With all of the athletes today who sell their services to corporate sponsors and then use every opportunity to promote the sponsor's product, it was really nice to see what 24-year-old stock car racer Jeff Gordon did when he won the 1995 NASCAR Cup Championship.

In the final race of the season at Atlanta, GA, in November, Dale Earnhart won the race, but Gordon finished high enough to take the championship.

When he was parked in the pits, he climbed through the window, sat on the roof of the car, then lifted a 7-year-old girl up from the crowds of people in the pits and held her in his lap.

With 50,000 people in the stands watching and listening to him, along with a television audience of millions, he faced the cameras and microphones.

"This was just a spectacular day," he gushed. "I know my race car wasn't much today, but it's been a heck of a year. But before I get into that," he said, interrupting himself and turning to the girl he was holding on his lap, "this is Jeriana, and she's got leukemia."

Gordon's crew chief, Ray Evernham, had a young son who has leukemia. This young boy's struggle to survive helped put auto racing into perspective for Gordon. Gordon and Evernham established an organization to help children with leukemia - "Racing for a Reason."

Gordon said to the television audience and the fans at the speedway, "Because of this championship, we're going to donate $25,000 [to the organization]. We've had help from the Speedway Children's Charities, Coca-Cola and DuPont."

Then he looked into Jeriana's eyes and said, "We just want to say, 'Thank you very much.' You're the sweetest thing there is, and we really love you'."

As soon as he had made his point, still holding Jeriana on his lap, he grinned at the sportscasters and said, "We got that championship, man! It's just the greatest thing in the world. I don't know how to describe it..."

You can see the video of that interview on YouTube - on Jeriana's channel. She is grown up now and is doing great.

This young athlete has kept things in perspective. There are things more important than sports - life and death issues that are going on in the world every day. It's gratifying to see someone use his fame to help those who are in need.

As one of the most successful and most popular drivers on the circuit, Gordon is in great demand for public appearances, both for his sponsors and for motivating people. Sponsors have always been important to auto racing, not to give money to drivers for promoting their products but to provide the money needed to build and race the automobiles for this very expensive sport.

Yet with all of the demands on his time - racing, testing, public appearances, traveling all over the country and spending time with his wife and new baby - Gordon made the time to help children with leukemia.

As of 2013, Jeff Gordon was 3rd all time in wins in NASCAR's top series, and 4th in total championships in that series. Is there a relationship between doing good and doing well? Could be.

The importance of respect for life in athletics

Sports used to be associated with promoting health. When Ed Bernd Jr. was growing up, he used to attend the annual Thanksgiving Day game in Atlanta in which the freshman football teams of Georgia Tech and the University of Georgia would play against each other.

The slogan for the game was "Strong legs will run so that weak ones may walk"; the proceeds went to support the Shriners' crippled children's hospitals. As a child with polio, Ed himself had spent a lot of time at those hospitals. If it hadn't been for them, he might not have been able to walk today.

Eventually major sporting events were being sponsored by tobacco companies. Remember the warning on the side of every cigarette pack that cigarettes will harm your health and may kill you.

There are signs that the pendulum is swinging back. Cigarette advertising has been banned from television in the United States, and Congress is considering legislation to prevent television cameras from focusing on the cigarette ads and logos that appear at sporting events.

And then there are athletes like Jeff Gordon, who give us hope that respect and caring still have a place in athletic competition.

Use great champions as role models

Some of the greatest athletes in the history of their respective sports have shown us, through their actions, what they consider to be really important:

• "King Richard" Petty of stock car racing fame was able to shrug off the news that he had not won his first race.

• Jack Nicklaus, the "Golden Bear" of golf, conceded a putt to ensure that a match would end in a tie, rather than giving his opponent an opportunity to humiliate himself.

• Jerry Rice said that his favorite memory of his football career was of his teammate catching the winning pass in the Super Bowl, while he himself served as a decoy.

• Muhammad Ali, the self-proclaimed "greatest" and one of the most beloved athletes in the world today, put on a great act to revive interest in boxing when nobody cared about it. His true character showed through when he gave up the "heavyweight champion of the world" competition to avoid being drafted into the army, which would mean going against his belief that he should not kill people he had no argument with.

• Mickey Mantle, speaking from his hospital room just a few weeks before his death, admitted how ashamed he was of his mistakes and encouraged people to use him as a role model of what not to do.

• NASCAR champion Jeff Gordon shining the spotlight for his first world championship onto the needs of others.

These athletes cared about the effects they had on other people, and it certainly did not do any harm to their careers.

The greatest players, the ones who are the most loved and respected by the fans, are the ones who always give their very best effort, who play "to win - fairly, squarely, decently, by the rules - but to win."

These athletes demonstrate what former U.S. President Theodore Roosevelt meant when he said:

"It is not the critic who counts. The credit belongs to the one who is actually in the arena; whose face is marred by dust and sweat and blood; who strives valiantly; who, at the best, knows the triumph of high achievement; and who, at the worst, if he fails, at least fails while daring greatly, so that his place shall never be with those cold and timid souls who knew neither victory nor defeat."

Now let's close with some thoughts from Jose Silva.

Make the world a better place to live

Throughout this book, you have learned how to use the alpha level to help yourself. That's only the beginning of what you can achieve with the Silva techniques.

These techniques would not be available to you if it were not for the efforts of many people who helped to develop them and found ways to use them in fitness and sports.

Once you have benefited from the techniques, you have an obligation to use them to help other people.

The noblest thing you can do is help people who are not in a position to repay you in any way.

Use your visualization techniques to program for other people who need help.

When you hear of someone with a problem, take a few

moments during your next programming session to program for them. Wish them well, even if there does not appear to be anything in it for you.

We are all involved together - you, your competitors, the fans. Whenever we help one another, we help ourselves, as well. The more we give, the more we receive.

Now here is your very last set of instructions for your Silva conditioning. We have saved them for last, because they are the most important:

- You will continue to strive to take part in constructive and creative activities to make this world a better place to live, so that when we move on, we shall have left behind a better world for those who follow.

- You will consider the whole of humanity, depending on their ages, as fathers or mothers, brothers or sisters, sons or daughters.

- You are a superior human being; you have greater understanding, compassion and patience with others.

Chapter 23

A note to parents and coaches

A husky young man walking down a Miami street in late January stopped to ask a hippie for directions to the big game. "Excuse me," he said. "Can you tell me how to get to the Super Bowl?"

"Sure," the hippie answered. "Practice, man, practice!"

Helping young athletes achieve greatness

Here is what Western author Zane Gray had to say about greatness:

- To bear up under loss;
- To fight the bitterness of defeat and the weakness of grief;
- To be victor over anger;
- To smile when tears are close;
- To resist disease and evil men and base instincts;
- To hate hate and to love love;
- To go on when it would seem good to die;
- To look up with unquenchable faith in something ever more about to be.
- That is what anyone can do, and be great.

Studies have shown that many young people are not as physically fit as they should be to ensure good health. This reason alone is enough to encourage them to participate in fitness or sports programs.

But there are many more benefits than just physical fitness.

Athletics can teach young people such important things as:

- Setting goals and striving to reach them.
- Working cooperatively with others to achieve a goal.
- Conflict resolution skills.
- The value of persistence.
- How to think clearly under pressure.
- Confidence in their ability to solve problems.
- How hard work and practice pay direct dividends.
- People aren't interested in excuses or reasons for failure.
- Respect for fair play.
- Rewards for success.

Many physical, mental, character-building, social, emotional and spiritual attributes are experienced through participation in athletics. Athletic experience can help people build skills and character traits that will help them in their careers, marriages, friendships and every other aspect of life.

On the other hand, being totally obsessed with sports and winning can have detrimental effects that can outweigh the benefits.

A sense of self-worth

Diving champion Greg Louganis said on national television that if he had been better adjusted as a child, he wouldn't have won four gold medals at the Olympics.

Louganis, who was adopted, said that growing up, he felt that the only value he had was his ability to win at sports. Without sports, he felt worthless.

But participation in sports should be a means to an end. It is a way to build character and to learn skills that will benefit a person for a lifetime.

Sports is not just about winning, either, just as life is not about accumulating everything that you possibly can for yourself. As they say, you can't take it with you.

Hall of fame football running back Gale Sayers says, "The Lord is first, my friends are second and I am third." He believes in that so strongly that he titled his book *I Am Third*.

How children mature

As we discussed in detail in Chapter 19, people seem to go through seven-year cycles.

During the first seven years of life, up to the age when the child loses its baby teeth and gets its permanent teeth, the overall average brain frequency is in the delta and theta ranges. Children simply take in information, without analyzing it.

The development of permanent teeth seems to signal a change of life. The child is now going to school. The alpha part of the brain matures and becomes prominent.

From then until the age of puberty, the overall dominant brain frequency is in the alpha range. This 7-14 cps functioning corresponds to the child's age, which is approximately 7-14 years old. During this second life cycle, the child is very creative and imaginative characteristics of the alpha level.

Puberty signals a third life cycle.

The child matures and so does the brain. Now the beta frequencies - 14-21 cps - become prominent.

Then, in nine out of 10 people, logic takes over, and imagination, creativity and intuition are mostly left behind.

A source of valuable skills for young athletes

Sports and fitness programs can be very valuable teaching tools for young people, helping them to hold onto that imagination, creativity and intuition. A teenage athlete can learn both left- and right-brain skills while participating in sports.

Children are great imitators. They will follow your lead.

All champions, superstars and leaders in every field have found ways to relax, clear their minds and concentrate their full attention on their goals. When they do this, they lower their brain frequency to alpha, where they can use the full power of both brain hemispheres to help them achieve their goals.

Teach your young athletes how to enter their level. Go to level with them. Program with them and for them.

The inner game was once the most difficult to master because a reliable way to teach people to enter the alpha dimension did not exist.

Jose Silva changed that.

Now any athlete can attend the Silva UltraMind ESP System and learn the secrets of the superstars.

Or they can get the fundamentals from Silva UltraMind ESP System Complete Home Seminar.

Or they can learn from the book that you are now holding in your hands.

Give positive reinforcement

Remember that words can hurt people, causing injuries that sometimes last much longer than those caused by "sticks and stones."

According to the July 1995 issue of *Incentive* magazine, OPTUM, a phone service that answers consumer questions about health issues, polled 1,000 people in 1995 and found that:

- 28 percent of people with disrespectful bosses reported such physical problems as sleep trouble, headaches and upset stomachs, compared to just 5 percent of those with respectful bosses.

- Half the workers with nasty supervisors said they felt anxious on the job, versus 11 percent of those with nice supervisors.

- 25 percent of the survey respondents said they had left a job because of a supervisor who was disrespectful to them.

It's easy to point out someone's faults and to do so forcefully.

It's also easy to create a strong, long-lasting impression on a young person's brain.

Suppose you shout angrily at a child who has just made a mistake, "You are so stupid! You can't do anything right!" Imagine the impression this makes in the child's brain. The child might carry that message - "I am stupid, and I can't do anything right" - throughout his or her life.

It is all right - important, even - to identify problems and make sure children are aware of them. But keep them in perspective.

Children don't want "constructive criticism"; they want "constructive compliments." Ralph Waldo Emerson said, "The glory of friendship is not the outstretched hand, nor the kindly smile, nor the joy of companionship; it is the spiritual inspiration that comes to one when he discovers that someone else believes in him and is willing to trust him."

Review Chapter 2 on Mental Housecleaning and positive thinking, and program yourself to give positive reinforcement to the children and athletes in your care.

Advice for parents and coaches

Giuseppina Del Vicario ("Vidheya") recommends teaching young people how to relax and visualize to correct their mistakes.

"First, teach them to relax themselves, to make the mind free," she said.

"Then have them do the movement mentally, and observe the mistake.

"Then have them correct the mistake and do the movement correctly, in their mind.

"Then they can get up and do it physically, correctly.

"This is much better than asking them to remember instructions that you give to them.

"It is much easier for them to remember what they see and to remember what they visualize.

"Discipline of the mind is the best discipline you can have," she added.

She encourages people to get totally involved in their mental training.

"While programming, feel like your body is moving," she says. "Sometimes the body actually moves. It is so precise that you can actually feel it. If I don't picture it mentally and feel it, it doesn't work."

Deep breathing can help control nervousness, Vidheya pointed out.

"Have them take several deep breaths. We are programmed for this naturally. When we are excited, we breath rapidly. So take a few deep breaths, and relax as you exhale. Breath control is an activity that connects the mind and the body."

Advice from a record-breaking athlete

Bruce Schneider of East Brunswick, N.J., used a lot of positive thinking and visualization to go from being an average player to batting "cleanup" on the fourth-ranked team in the world.

Along the way, Schneider set a new single-season home run record. (A "cleanup" batter is usually the strongest hitter, selected to bat fourth in order to score any of the first three batters who may be on base.)

"It has only been in recent years that athletes and coaches started to understand the powerful resource that is available to all of us: the mind," Schneider said. "Realizing this and learning to use this knowledge - and new mental skills - to its advantage can and will help every single athlete become better. Your mental abilities, once increased, can help you in every aspect of your life. I know, because I've done it myself."

Schneider observed, "The biggest mistake coaches make is placing too much emphasis on mistakes. It is important to give positive images, positive reinforcement.

"Teammates can help others by keeping all comments and suggestions positive. When an athlete is performing, do not use words, or let anyone else use words, like don't' - or any other negative word or expression."

Schneider continued, "Motivate your children and your athletes by finding out what they want, not what you want. Find out what they desire, and paint mental pictures of it for them. Help them increase their desire, their belief in their ability and their expectation of success.

"Never let them use drugs to get ahead," Bruce cautioned. "I know people on dialysis, people who have died, because they used steroids to help them improve their physical performance.

"You have to be very, very motivated to take steroids because they will ruin your life! Take that same motivation and use it to train harder, to concentrate better, to give that something extra' that helps people win.

"Show your children and your athletes how to use the alpha level to increase motivation, to improve physical skills and to achieve whatever they desire."

Programming produces positive results

You can use the visualization technique to program for your children to be successful. You can use the Silva Mental Rehearsal Technique to program yourself to think the right thoughts, say the right words and take the right actions to help your children.

You can teach your children how to use visualization and imagination to help them achieve their goals.

If your children are between 7 and 14 years old, have them close their eyes and use visualization and imagination. They will probably be at alpha while doing so.

You can use your Three Fingers Technique when working with your children to program yourself to do what's best for them. (For further guidance, we have additional materials listed in the Resources section in the back of this book.)

You can even project to them mentally while they are sleeping and change their behavior for the better. (This works best when a mother programs her child, because of the special mother-child bond that exists.)

How can you do this?

After the child has been asleep for at least one hour, enter your level. Once at your level, imagine that the child is there with you. Now imagine the child changing the behavior that needs to be changed and corrected.

For instance, if the child has a habit of breaking the rules by tripping other children, and the team is penalized for this, imagine the child learning to play without tripping and the child's team doing well and scoring as a result.

You can imagine that you are talking with the child about this. But remember that the primary means of communication is visual, so while you imagine talking with the child, create mental pictures of the child doing what you are asking.

You can even learn to help other people's children. It takes practice and a strong desire to help people. One school teacher, as described below, helped turn around some troublemakers and surprised other teachers and counselors.

Troublemakers see the fun in being good

Shortly after completing the Silva course, Marie Buckingham (now Burleson) found herself faced with a challenge in a junior high school classroom.

There were four troublemakers in the room four girls who seemed to have no interest in getting an education. Instead, they wanted to attract attention to themselves and disrupt the class so nobody else could participate. Their behavior was not limited to this one classroom. The same four girls had a reputation among the faculty and counselors at the school for causing similar trouble in all their classes.

For one week, Marie programmed herself to wake up a little earlier than usual so that she could project to these four girls while they were still sleeping.

"I would get up, maybe 15 minutes early," she recalled, "and project each one on my mental screen, sometimes all of them together, and spend maybe five minutes, maybe less, with each one. I'd just remind her that I thought she was a wonderful person.

"And they were all nice little girls. They were rebellious. They didn't know what they were rebelling against, but they were rebelling against the system of boredom and all that, because they were very intelligent.

"And I told them that I did love them, and I hoped that they would cooperate in the class so that they and their classmates and I could all enjoy the class, and that I looked forward to having them do this, and I'd appreciate it. And I thanked them."

After the next class session, Marie asked the four girls to stay for one minute. "I told them verbally that they were creating problems in the class, and that I knew they could enjoy the class and help the other students enjoy it. Then I told them, I know what kind of people you are.'

"One little girl looked alarmed. Then I said, I don't know what you're doing that for, because I happen to know you're a nice person, but you don't seem to think so.'

"And I told them that we were just not going to have that kind of behavior in class, and I wanted them to know it."

Class met only twice a week. When they came the next week, Marie reported, the ringleader refused to let herself become involved with the antics of the other three. She sat apart from them, and while she did not actually become involved in the activity of the class, she did not cause any trouble.

The next class, one week after Marie had projected to them for the first time, the ringleader asked a question in class.

"The others looked at her like they didn't believe it," Marie said. "We answered the question. Pretty soon, she came up with some ideas. And by the end of class, they were all participating, coming up with ideas, asking and answering questions.

"As they left the room at the end of class, the ringleader looked at me and smiled and said, You know, Mrs. Buckingham, I think it's more fun being good than being bad.' And I just reached across and hugged her shoulder and assured her that I think so, too."

The ringleader and the other girls smiled as they left.

"I saw the school counselor later," Marie added. "I asked her to guess what the girl, the ringleader, had done. She said, 'No telling.' I told her that she had been asking and answering questions and had looked up at me and smiled, and she said she thinks it is more fun being good. And the counselor exclaimed, 'That girl said that?!' She couldn't seem to believe it.

"I never had any more problems with them," Marie said. "That doesn't mean they never did anything out of place, but they were really quite good."

How a coach turned losers into winners

Another educator, basketball coach Hector Chacon, turned a whole season around with a simple change in attitude. Here's the story in his own words:

"Sometimes the drive to win becomes so intense that we start doing things that cancel out the very traits and characteristics that made us winners in the first place. That's right: An intense desire to eliminate mistakes can lead to defeat your defeat. I should know, because it almost happened to me.

"As we gain more skill and experience, we begin to concentrate more and more on playing that perfect game, eliminating every mistake. And that can be a dangerous attitude.

"You see, the mind moves in the direction of the most dominant thought.

"If that thought is of making the winning score, or of making the great defensive play, achieving your desired end result, then you are likely to do just that. But if you are thinking about mistakes, you will be attracted to the mistakes.

"When the professional golfer looks down the fairway, he or she sees the pin on the green and shoots for it.

"The duffer looks at the sand traps on both sides of the green, and guess where the ball goes?

"The high school basketball team that I coach had some excellent players during the 1987 season. They had the skill and, more importantly, the desire to go to the state championships. But the last state championship basketball team we had was in 1956 when I was a player on the team.

"I could sense that this team had the chance to go all the way. And I wanted that for them very badly. I had just as much desire for it as they had.

"I started looking to see what mistakes they were making so that we could correct them. I was showing them how to play the game right and pushing them to play to their full potential.

"Then a funny thing happened. We'd build up a big lead in the first half, and then blow it in the second half.

"We lost four games by a total of six points! Just three baskets at the right time, and we would have had a 5-0 conference record. Instead we had a 1-4 record.

"While talking with Ed Bernd Jr. of the Silva Star Athlete Program, I realized what the problem was: I needed to give the players positive images of success.

Ed suggested three things for me to do during halftime:

"He suggested that I point out the mistakes I wanted to correct at the beginning of halftime and not mention them again.

"He said that after I pointed out their mistakes, I should tell them exactly what I wanted them to do.

"Then he suggested that I take it one step farther: that I remind the players of a successful play they had made and then tell them to do it like that again.

"I put those three suggestions to work immediately. After all, it was that kind of thinking that had gotten us to the state championship when I was a player.

"During the first half of that night's game, I encouraged them, I praised all the good plays they made and I made sure that they always went onto the court with positive images of what I wanted them to do.

"At halftime, my assistant coach went to the blackboard and started to write down the mistakes that we needed to correct.

"I stopped him and erased what was on the board. Instead, I talked to the players about what had happened in the game so far, and I told them what I wanted them to do in the second half: 'Juan, remember to get under the basket so you can get the rebounds.' 'Tony, guard that big guy a little bit closer, and he will miss his passes.'

"Then as we were ready to leave the locker room and go out for the second half, I spoke to each player, praising them for something good they had done in the first half: 'Robert, you made some great passes that helped us to score those points.' 'Jerry, that was great the way you stole the ball and drove it down the court.'

"Then we went back out on the court, armed with our new positive mental attitude.

"Did it work?

"One of our players was hesitating to take a shot because he was so far out. I kept calling to him, 'Shoot it, you can make it.' But he passed to a teammate.

"The teammate passed it right back to him. 'Shoot it, you can make it,' I called out again. Finally he turned and shot.

"The shot went in. We got two points. And he turned to look at me with an expression of amazement.

"We could do no wrong that night. We did everything right. We amazed the other team, and especially their coach. We were playing a team that had beaten us just two weeks before.

"The final score was 80 to 47 in our favor.

"My favorite quote came from the coach of the other team. He told a reporter, 'This was a much improved team.' He said it was the most improvement he had ever seen in such a short time, only two weeks.

"If only he had known that all of the improvement had come since 3 o'clock that afternoon when I talked with Ed Bernd!

"The coach even came and asked me what we had done differently. I told him that we had changed our way of thinking, that we wanted to win. He found that hard to believe.

"But it was true. We had not changed the way we practiced. We still had the same players on the team. We still had the same plays and the same strategy. The only thing that was different was a new attitude.

"Our players beat a team that had beaten us earlier in the season. That's the mark of true champions. When a team can come back that strong after being beaten, then they have the right stuff to go all the way. They are stars in my mind superstars in fact. And I let them know it.

"How did we do the remainder of the season?

"The first five games we were one win and four loses. After that shift in attitude, we finished the season by winning eight of our last nine games, giving us a season district record of nine wins and five loses. We lost our final game 77-74. In the final three minutes, we scored 12 unanswered points. As somebody once said, we were winning, but time ran out on us.

"Ed continued to work with us the rest of the school year. The following year, we won the bi-district championship for the first time in 25 years. And we had the best record of any Martin High School basketball team in history, with a 30-4 overall win-loss record."

Tips for Teaching Young People

Jose Silva is the father of 10 children, 27 grandchildren and six great grandchildren. Knowing that, wouldn't you like to read the following tips he has for working with young people?

1. Teach young people to focus on the task they are working on to concentrate on it and not be distracted by other things.

2. Give them positive reinforcement. Talk to them about what you want them to accomplish. Avoid dwelling on mistakes and calling their attention to the things that you do not want them to do. Keep focusing on what you want them to do.

3. Always remember that you are responsible for preparing your children for the future. They should have long, healthy, productive and happy lives. Everything that you teach them, all of the things that they do, are part of the educational process to help them gain knowledge and experience and develop skills that they can use to solve problems and be productive adults.

4. Try not to subject them to situations that can cause serious injury, either physically, mentally or emotionally. When injuries do occur, as they sometimes do, help them to recover quickly and get back on track.

5. Enter your level and sense their needs. If they make a mistake that causes the team to lose, enter your level and sense the best way to handle the situation. Maybe they need to feel bad about it for awhile. They have a right to feel bad. But there comes a time when they need to get over it and move on to the next challenge.

6. Young people are very resilient. They bounce back well. Once they understand their mistake and know what to do next

time to avoid making the same mistake again, help them focus on their goals. Help them concentrate on what they are doing, and show them how to do it well.

7. We all make mistakes. In order to be successful in life, we must move past our mistakes and concentrate on solving problems and reaching our goals. You can use all of your Silva Method techniques to help you with that.

8. Review this book from time to time. If you have an opportunity to attend the Silva UltraMind ESP System, you will learn even more techniques you can use for yourself and your loved ones.

9. Finally, remember to be a good role model for your children. They learn by example. Children are great observers and imitators. Concentrate on using the alpha level and your mental techniques to help you improve the quality of your life, achieve greater success and enjoy life more and your children will do the same.

Chapter 24

Persistence

Great works are performed not by strength but by perseverance. - Samuel Johnson

Perseverance is a great element of success. If you only knock long enough and loud enough at the gate, you are sure to wake up somebody. -Henry Wadsworth Longfellow

In this final chapter of our book, here are our personal thoughts on achieving and enjoying success.

Develop superstar qualities to bring you more success in life
by Jose Silva

What makes a champion? What are some of the star qualities you see in highly successful people? What goes through the mind of a superstar during training? While practicing? In competition when success or failure hangs in the balance?

There are several characteristics that are common to the stars in athletics, as well as those in business, industry, science, art and other endeavors. Champions are persistent and dedicated. They are able to control and direct their physical and their mental energies. And when they make decisions, they are more often right than wrong.

The most important quality

The most important quality I've observed is persistence.

You can achieve any kind of goal you set for yourself if you make it the most important thing in your life and sacrifice everything else for it. There are people who do that. But that is not necessarily what I'd call success. Achieving a single limited goal at the expense of everything else is usually not worthy of a person's whole life. To achieve success in life takes as much persistence as reaching a single goal. Perhaps more.

To reach your goals, you must make them more important than anything else. Any time something else comes up that seems important, you should analyze it at your level and put it in its proper perspective: second to your primary goal.

Sometimes things distract you from your primary goal. At that time it is important to relax, enter the alpha level and analyze it. If you want to be a champion, you have to stick to your major goal, whatever it is. All else must be secondary, regardless how attractive it may be at the time.

Achieving success

How can you use this quality of persistence to become successful in all aspects of life? Let's say you are a busy executive with many important tasks. This is an appropriate example because the ability to manage your time is important if you want to become a star athlete and also because you will need to manage the business of your life when you are no longer a competitive athlete.

If, as an executive, you value your health as an important part of reaching your primary goal, you must program to do the things necessary to maintain good health, vitality and energy to get what you want out of life.

To put this idea into practice, you must first determine what you need to do: How many hours per week must you exercise if you are to reach your goal? How much time do you need to devote to fitness? To strength training? To practicing the skills specific to your sport?

Then set up a schedule, and do not let anything interfere with that schedule. The time that you set aside for exercise is just as important as your performance on the playing field, maybe more so. If you sacrifice one exercise session to deal with some other problem associated with your primary goal, you are not helping yourself, for your health and fitness will suffer.

Use a holistic approach: Determine your primary goal, then determine the ingredients necessary to help you reach that goal. In addition, analyze why you want to reach that goal. When you do this, you may find goals that are really important to you, goals that will spell success in life for you.

If you cannot demonstrate discipline for the various ingredients that go into reaching your primary goal, you are not likely to have the discipline necessary for the big things when they come along.

How to proceed

You must be healthy both mentally and physically. The best way to decide what to do is to spend some time in quiet contemplation and meditation. To achieve your goals, program yourself at your level. Whenever you deviate, reprogram yourself at alpha and correct your ways. Make the correction as soon as you notice a tendency to deviate. Avoid developing bad habits. Use the Silva Method Habit Control Techniques in Chapter 14 to eliminate bad habits and initiate good ones.

Meditation brings mental health. Physical exercise promotes physical health. The two together will thrust you towards your goal.

Set your goals. Take time to learn and use the alpha level to help you make correct decisions and to program yourself to achieve your goals. And persist. Do this, and you will succeed.

Take the best road to success

Many people have sacrificed everything to reach their goals, only to find that the rewards were not worth the price.

An all-pro football player, who blamed steroids for causing the cancer that took his life, once said the prize was not worth the price.

I'm not saying that you should not do everything that you reasonably can to achieve your goal. But sometimes the price is just too high.

If you use your alpha level, and a little bit of common sense, you can achieve greatness without paying too high a price.

Here is my formula for accomplishing this:

Set your goal, using your alpha level, and give it everything you've got. If you are repeatedly blocked from reaching your goal, then step back and analyze the situation, at your level. If things keep getting more and more difficult for you, perhaps you are on the wrong path.

I like to put it this way:

If you are trying to open a door that leads to your destination, and the door won't open even after repeated attempts, then step back and look around. Is there another door that could be going to the same destination? Then try that door. Maybe it will open for you.

When I'm working on a project and I encounter an obstacle, I do whatever is necessary to get past that obstacle. That takes a certain amount of time and effort.

When I encounter another obstacle, I do whatever is necessary to get past the second obstacle. That takes a certain amount of time and effort. I notice whether it took twice as much time and effort as it took to get past the first obstacle, or half as much time and effort.

Then I proceed toward my goal.

When I reach the third obstacle, I again do whatever is necessary to get past this third obstacle. If it takes twice as much time and effort to get past this third obstacle as it did to get past the second one, and the second one took twice as much time as effort as the first one, then I figure that maybe I am going in the wrong direction.

If that is the case, then I enter my level and analyze the situation. I check to see if some other way for me to proceed exists. If I notice another way to proceed toward my goal, I try it.

Then, when I encounter an obstacle, I again do whatever it takes to get past it. If the next obstacle requires only half as much time and effort to overcome, I feel that I am on the correct path. And when I am on the correct path, the obstacles become progressively less difficult to overcome, until soon it is smooth sailing.

This approach works when you spend enough time at your level. At your level, it is easier for "higher intelligence" to help you and guide you. We believe that this is the way that higher intelligence guides us. It nudges us in the correct direction by placing obstacles along the wrong path and clearing the way on the correct path.

Persist - but remember that we do not batter down doors. If a door won't open, look for another door. There might be a better way for you to get into that room. Perhaps you have always wanted to be a star tennis player, but you are only average at tennis and are a superior golfer. Then become a golf champion!

Persist, and be practical. Set your goals, and accept guidance from higher intelligence. Do these things, and you will succeed.

Never give up, and you will break through into glory
by Ed Bernd Jr.

We all need a support system - people who will be there to help us and encourage us when we need it. And we, in turn, can help and encourage them.

Nothing in the world is more valuable than this, because nothing in the world is more important than people.

Not winning.

Not fame.

Not fortune.

Nothing is more important than people.

You never can tell, when you say or do something, how much of an impact you will have on another person's life.

I've benefited from the kindness and encouragement of many people, too many to mention now. So I'll let one friend represent them all.

A few kind words from this person, an athlete I knew briefly while in high school almost 40 years ago, probably saved my life.

When you need a friend

Freddie Whittemore lettered in five sports at his high school in Washington, GA. He was an all-state football player - a big, tough lineman.

Our friendship must have seemed strange to other people, for it would have been difficult to imagine two people more different than we were.

I was the classic 97-pound weakling. I'd had polio when I was five, and even though I had been exercising ever since, I still could not run fast and had never been allowed to play sports.

On the other hand, I had become an excellent sports photographer. That was as close as I could get to being on the team.

It wasn't until after I had completed the Silva Mind Control course, at the age of 35, that I had the opportunity to compete in my first organized athletic event. I won a third-place trophy in a novice AAU (Amateur Athletic Union) Olympic Weightlifting Meet in Vero Beach, FL.

But back to Freddie. He was very popular in Washington. When we moved there, it was my third high school in three years. I wasn't optimistic about trying to fit in and make friends.

Freddie changed all that.

He spotted me when I cautiously stuck my head into the doorway of our homeroom, and he rushed over to meet me.

The sight of this huge athlete, twice my size, charging towards me with a big grin on his face was rather terrifying.

He stuck his hand out and said, "You must be the new kid. Welcome to Washington. Let me introduce you to everybody."

Freddie and I became such close friends that the teachers had to seat us in opposite corners of the room to keep us from talking to each other constantly.

We all face challenges

Three months later, as our junior year came to an end, things had changed. I was having the best time of my entire life, living among the nicest people I'd ever known.

But Freddie was getting ready to move. His father had been transferred. Freddie would miss his senior year at Washington-

Wilkes High School. He had to leave all his friends behind.

His future didn't look bright. He had injured his knee, and despite his all-state credentials, no college wanted to risk giving him a scholarship. He had no idea what he might do in the future if he couldn't play ball.

Freddie was devastated, seemed deeply depressed. Yet as we took turns signing each other's high school yearbooks on the final day of school, he was able to write some words of encouragement to me, words that changed my life.

By the end of the summer, my family was moving, too - moving away from the only place I'd ever fit in and been accepted. We moved to Atlanta, where I started my senior year in my fourth high school in four years.

For the next dozen years, I struggled through many challenges and many bouts of depression. I drank heavily. I was not happy.

Sometimes, when things got so bad that I began to think that there was no point in going on, I'd get out that high school yearbook and read the words that Freddie wrote to me when he was going through hard times.

And I always thought to myself, "If Fred Whittemore could write such optimistic words when things were so bad for him, I have to believe him."

True champions find a way to succeed

Before I tell you what he wrote, let me tell you what eventually became of Freddie.

We lost track of each other for more than 35 years, but while working on this book, I decided to track him down. The story he told me inspired me all over again.

In Forsyth, GA, where he had moved, everybody wanted to

take him down. They wanted to prove that they were better than this small-town superstar who had moved into their school.

"It was the worst time of my life," Freddie told me.

"I went back to my old coach in Washington," Freddie said, "and he told me that they would all challenge me and give me a hard time, but to just hang in there and do my best, and show them what I could do. So I decided to do that. I decided that I was going to beat them at everything, even if it was just spitting, I was going to do it better than they did."

After high school, he had his knee operated on and played football at a junior college.

The knee held up, and Baylor University gave him a football scholarship.

Then, just before the season started, he injured his shoulder. He never did get to play in a college game. But Freddie graduated from college and had a successful career in sales.

A successful athlete with his optimistic outlook and his kindness towards people could succeed at just about anything. Today he has a wonderful family, including a son who won a golf scholarship to Southern Methodist University.

And Freddie, who had trouble selecting the words that could express his feelings to me on our last day at Washington-Wilkes High School, has now written a children's book.

Fred did not know, until I called him, how his friendship and inspiration had kept me in the game when things got tough. It came as a surprise to him.

You never know who you might be helping

He surprised me, too, when he wrote to me afterwards and said that I had helped him get through some tough times.

In all those years, I had never imagined that I could have inspired Fred Whittemore in any way.

"I did not realize how our friendship, even for that short period of time, prepared me for my future," he wrote to me.

"Had you not come along and showed me that moving into a new town could be done by a teenager and could have positive results, I don't know if I would have had the determination to stick with it when it got tough.

"I'm sitting here now thinking, 'How ironic that two 17-year-olds would become friends so quickly and how that friendship formed their character.' Somebody up there liked us, and looked after us."

Somebody certainly looked after me, because I know I didn't do it on my own.

Fred Whittemore inspired me to stay in the game. He is still an inspiration to me today.

Jose Silva's system gave me what I needed to become a winner.

I owe them both more than I can ever repay. All I can do is pay it forward and share with others what I have learned.

You now hold in your hands the techniques that Jose Silva developed - techniques that can make you a winner and help you achieve all that you are capable of achieving.

And now - for whatever help it may be to you - here's the message that Fred Whittemore gave to me:

Break through into glory

In the battle that goes on through life you are going to find many immovable objects in appearance. But don't quit and you will eventually break through into glory. Don't ever quit and you will go far. God bless you in all that you do. -Fred Whittemore, 1957

Resources

For information on genuine authentic Jose Silva courses and products, please visit www.SilvaCourses.com. You will find:

The *Silva Star Athlete Superstars Fitness Secrets* audio-video home workshop

The *Silva UltraMind ESP System Complete Home Seminar*

Jose Silva's Holistic Faith Healing System home study course

The *Silva Choose Success* program

Learn how to raise a genius at www.SilvaParentingCenter.com

The *SilvaMind Method Sales Power home workshop*

Silva books and audio recordings and other products to help you in ever area of life.

For a list of *Silva Instructors and Seminars* worldwide please visit www.SilvaInstructors.com

For the *Silva Trainer 1 biofeedback instrument* please visit Jose Silva Jr.'s web site: www.SilvaJoseJr.com

Thank you for taking this journey with us, and please feel free to contact us any time we can be of service.

Avlis Productions Inc.
P.O. Box 691809
Houston, TX 77269

help@avlispub.com

Phone: 903-948-2312

www.SilvaCourses.com

www.SilvaStarAthlete.com

www.SilvaInstructors.com

Made in the USA
Lexington, KY
09 May 2015